Lasallian Ruminations

Essays on Various Topics

George Van Grieken FSC

For information contact: Lasallian Resource Center
4403 Redwood Road
Napa, CA 94558

Book Layout and Cover design : George Van Grieken, FSC

ISBN: 9781658229531

First Published Edition: 2020
(Version 2020.04.15)

TABLE OF CONTENTS

INTRODUCTION

This collection of essays and papers is an eclectic mix. They represent a 30-year range of rumination on a host of topics. Almost all of these were intentionally written in a style that I would have appreciated reading myself. In others words, as I was trying to understand the material myself. It was also my intention to reflect on the topic in such a way that in later years I might be able to once again gain from the insights gained from the insights of other writers, from various group discussions, and from spending hours researching and thinking about the materials addressed. As such they may not be as interesting or relevant to others, but since I found it beneficial to look at them once again – and with some benefit – this may also be the case for a few others. It is for this reason that they have been made available in this format.

FOUNDATIONAL AREAS FOR THE CONSIDERATION OF RELIGIOUS EDUCATION

The first set of six short papers are a compilation of the topics covered during my comprehensive exams at Boston College in the early 1990's. All of them were related to my dissertation on the pedagogical spirituality of St. John Baptist de La Salle, the Patron Saint of All Teachers of Youth, and the Founder of the Brothers of the Christian Schools (De La Salle Christian Brothers). Given when they were written, you may sometimes wonder, "Why didn't he include what author X said about this?" Yes, I could have sought out modern authors on the same topic. But it would have taken a significant amount of time to do so adequately, given the broad scope of the areas covered. However, these overviews may provide an accessible ramp for readers interested in one of the topics; i.e., to take the plunge into how these areas might be thought about within a more contemporary context.

A SHORT INTRODUCTION TO DEVELOPMENTAL THEORIES

One of the more engaging courses from Boston College was in the area of theories of human development. Sr. Margaret Gorman was the instructor, and she was both kind, smart, and feisty. At the time, I thought to put together a summary of the theories for the benefit of those who didn't have time to delve into all of the specifics of each developmental area. This was the result of those labors.

SOUL FOR SOUL
THE VOCATION OF THE CHILD IN LASALLIAN PEDAGOGY

This article was for a chapter in the book *The Vocation of the Child*, published through Emory University (by Eerdmans Pub. Co.) and containing a host of wonderful insights into the topic. I was invited in 2005 to contribute to the book because its editor had been an 8th Grade student of mine – certainly one of the smartest kids I've taught – and wanted to make sure to include something from the educational tradition that had been so pivotal in his own life. The book's production included a symposium at Emory where all the authors delivered a paper on their topic, followed by mutual insights and suggestions. The process became an opportunity to look at John Baptist de La Salle's convictions about the children "confided to our care," and to see just what it was that set him and his Brothers apart, based on his writings and on the features of the educational tradition that came to bear his name.

THE FIVE CORE PRINCIPLES: THEIR ORIGINS, INTEGRATION WITH CATHOLIC IDENTITY, AND RESONANCE TODAY

This is a more recent paper that addresses the background and contemporary relevance of what have come to be called the "Five Core Principles" of the Lasallian heritage, as experienced in the United States. Originating on the West coast in the late 1990's, students have found them to be helpful in articulating and living out those elements of the Lasallian educational experience that they can identify with and in language that is relevant to them. They have emerged from the ground up, instead of from the top down, and they continue to be popular among schools today.

TECHNOLOGY AND LASALLIAN EDUCATION
SOME ESSENTIAL PERSPECTIVES

In 2017, I was asked to prepare a presentation for a symposium at our Motherhouse in Rome. The focus centered around the guide for formation that was in preparation at that time. The paper was given in Rome, among other presenters covering different topics, and subsequently became a workshop for various conferences of Lasallian leaders. It is also published in the AXIS Journal.

OUR LASALLIAN VOCATION & THE THEOLOGY OF VOCATION

The theme of vocations was the focus of Huether 2018, the annual gathering of Lasallian educators from around the Region of North America. I was asked to do a workshop on the topic *Called to Live Lasallian: Our Lasallian Vocation, a Sign of Hope for the Church and World*, with a concentration on the theology of vocation. This paper was the result, and it has proven to be helpful to others in understanding how our Lasallian vocation integrates into the Church's theology about the nature of vocation and its specific application in the lives of individuals.

TRANSFORMATIVE LASALLIAN OPERATIONAL DIMENSIONS

This talk was delivered in Melbourne, Australia, in 2019, at the Asia Pacific Lasallian Educators Conference. This gathering of Lasallian educators in the Asia Pacific region (PARC) included a wide variety of presentations, workshops, and experiences that would contribute to a better understanding of the Lasallian educational charism and how it is lived out today.

VARIOUS LASALLIAN REFLECTIONS

In September of 2018, I began to write short monthly Lasallian reflections on a variety of topics. The goal of the reflections was to provide something that might be used by individuals, boards, faculties and staff groups, and other Lasallians interested in engaging in conversations about such topics. They are meant to be thoughtful and slight provocative, catalysts for dialogue and shared reflection.

The wide variety of topics throughout this volume will hopefully captivate you as much as they captivated me when I first began investigating them for these papers and presentations.

I pray that you will be inspired to pursue them further on your own, because that's the only and best way that true learning takes place.

George Van Grieken, FSC
January 20

FOUNDATIONAL AREAS FOR THE CONSIDERATION OF RELIGIOUS EDUCATION

NOTE: This series of reflections were written in preparation for the eventual PhD dissertation at Boston College in the 1990s. They were not originally meant to be published as scholarly papers, and therefore they do not have detailed footnote citations from the works mentioned. In this case, it was the processing and thinking that were uppermost. For that reason, the footnote citations are incomplete. The works read and cited are provided at the end of each essay.

Jesus' Use of Parables as a Teaching Medium in the Synoptic Gospels

The parables attributed to Jesus in the New Testament represent the record of a distinctive teaching medium, one that those who would be authentic disciples might well emulate. In order to come to some understanding of the "teaching" qualities of these literary forms, something will have to said about what they are, how they are situated in the Synoptics, and how they compare to "teaching" as it was viewed in New Testament times.

Among Jesus' teaching discourses, parables take up one-third of all his instruction. According to many, they best embody Jesus' own speech. While there is disagreement as to what might legitimately be called a parable, there are generally [42] places in the synoptic gospels that are commonly recognized as "parables." Six occur in Mark, twenty-two in Matthew, and thirty-one in Luke. Twenty-nine parables are found in only one of the three; two in Mark, nine in Matthew, and eighteen in Luke. Only four parables occur in all three of the gospels: The Sower, The Mustard Seed, The Wicked Tenants, and The Budding Fig Tree. Already it is evident that Luke and Matthew convey the bulk of the parables, with Luke including by far the largest number of independently recorded parables.

Brad Young maintains that Jesus regularly spoke Hebrew and that the gospels came from a Hebrew source that was later translated, and edited, into Greek. (Aramaic and Hebrew were both spoken at the time; written Aramaic sources cite parables in Hebrew.) Parables seem to have been part of the Jewish *agadah*, the implicit story-telling teaching tradition. They appear frequently in midrashic texts representative of early Jewish homiletical instruction. Parables here often functioned to illustrate the meaning of a verse. They took shape as artistic creations in what was essentially oral teachings. Young concludes after an exhaustive study of early Jewish sources that "the story parable as it appears in the gospels and rabbinic literature, though somewhat similar to a few select biblical passages and fables, is not fully paralleled elsewhere and seems to be an inner Jewish accomplishment from the Second Temple period."

Did Jesus invent the story parable, or is it more likely that he employed a didactic device already in use and reflected in the biblical text? (e.g., Nathan's parable to David). While parabolic teaching 1) became popular and effective in rabbinic teaching, 2) is unknown outside of rabbinic literature and the Synoptics, and 3) represents a unique literary type (mini-drama with attractive plot, colorful characters, concentrated action, specific message, geared towards eliciting a response), the fact that all the written rabbinic sources supporting Young's argument come mainly from the time after the Synoptics were written leads me to believe that Jesus, in fact, did bring about a distinctive literary form that subsequently came to be utilized by general rabbinical teaching.[1] It emerged from his Jewish roots, where allegorical exegesis may have been part of the oral tradition, and it may have been influenced by popular fables or actual happening that were adapted to illustrate a theme, or even wisdom sayings that were developed into a story. But the distinctive character that the parables illustrate appears to be something that sprang out of Jesus' personal synthesis, an expression of himself.[2]

"Parable," from *para* (alongside of) and *ballein* (cast, place, or throw), comes from the Hebrew masal, a word used to describe a wide

---

[1] While Young doesn't come to this conclusion, I find it more likely that the kind of allegorical interpretation evident in Jewish homiletical teaching is a development that parallels similar interpretation by the desert Fathers. Joachim Jeremias has pointed out that Hellenistic Judaism's practice of allegorical exegesis had an influence on the early church's allegorizing of parables, as did the intent to conceal the mystery of the Kingdom of God from outsiders. (Cf. Mk 4:10) Also, all Jewish use of allegory deals with Scriptural interpretation and utilizes many scriptural quotes, while Jesus never includes scriptural quotes.

[2] As Donahue points out," Jesus' language is powerful, not because of its aesthetic brilliance or paradoxical quality, but because of the experience of God it mediates and the kind of life Jesus himself lived."

variety of literary forms (proverb, wisdom saying, allegory, narrative, etc.).[3] Most generally, parables lie in the realm of figurative language where "communication takes place through images and the suggestive power of language rather than through literal and precise speech." (Donahue) Each of the authors I read had his/her own breakdown of literary forms that fell under the rubric of parables. Generally, however, it will be sufficient to point out that parabolic language, following C.H. Dodd's definition[4], have 1) a poetic and metaphoric quality, 2) a realism, 3) a paradoxical and engaging quality, and 4) an open-ended nature. There is a distinction between a metaphor (an implied comparison that is not obvious; "You are the light of the world."), a simile (an illustrative comparison; "The Kingdom of God is like . . . "), and an allegory (a developed metaphor where the link is provided and spun out; "The seed sown on the path is . . . "). But even these tend to break down once they are applied to particular parables.[5] Perhaps it's best to call the parables "metaphoric," since it is the dynamics of metaphor rather than particular literary forms that empowers them. Metaphorical language can't be translated into discursive language, it must be experienced. Jesus took people's immediate experience and called them to see it as a carrier of transcendence. Metaphoric language is especially well-suited to express this dimension of religious experience.

Parables originated in oral tradition, were written down as story units removed from their original context, were rearranged, and were made the subject of redaction and abridgment according to an author's use of earlier written sources.[6] It's likely that parables were

---

[3] Etymologically, parable carries more the sense of juxtaposition and comparison, while *masal* suggests that one thing is like or similar to another

[4] Many find C.H. Dodd's definition of parables most comprehensive and adequate: "At its simplest the parable is a metaphor or simile drawn from nature or common life, arresting the hearer by its vividness or strangeness, and leaving the mind in sufficient doubt about its precise application to tease it into active thought."

[5] Joachim Jeremias: "...it is certain that the sharply defined distinction between parable, metaphor, and allegory is not Palestinian, and in particular the transition from metaphor to allegory is easily made."

[6] Whether or not the two-source theory for the Synoptics is adopted (Mark and Q as being original), or whether credence is given to arguments that each used a

originally much more transparent than the synoptic authors make them seem.[7] Certainly, the situation of the primitive church influenced their use in the gospels, and the ethos of Jewish life in the time of Jesus, or Jesus' original intent behind each parable, cannot be adequately recovered. Nevertheless, for both the original disciples and ourselves, "understanding" of the parables is predicated on faith. In order to see the kingdom one must first believe it. "In the end it might be said that even the close disciples do not really understand Jesus' life or teaching, and the reader is left as one of the outsiders trying to puzzle out the riddle-like parables that finally lead only to silence." (Borsch) It is to that evocative power of parables where one must look for its teaching strength.

Each of the three synoptic authors shows evidence of particular concerns and perspectives regarding the identity of Jesus and the nature of his teaching.[8]

Mark is writing for a primarily Hellenistic audience. Jesus acts more than he teaches. He is a surprising, unpredictable, cryptic figure (Cf. the frequent use of "they were afraid . . . ") who is known to be of God and who is shown to have strong emotion and compassion. People's preconceptions are challenged as Jesus himself must be engaged. Parables blind those who do not believe and reveal mysteries to those who do (4:10 ff.). The world of Mark's few parables is the world of the village, with its images taken from farming and nature's processes. They convey a message of being watchful and ready for God's coming (Wicked Tenants: 12:1-11; Growing Seed; 4:26-29, Doorkeeper: 13:34-36). According to some, this gospel itself might best be called an extended narrative, a parable. It begins and ends abruptly (no Markan infancy or resurrection narrative), is open-ended (calling for personal appropriation / interpretation), and is couched in concrete and particular language. His use of

---

separate "parables" source, our concern in this essay is the way that the parables we do have illustrate Jesus as teacher.

[7] Luke's simplicity of parable narration might be more faithful to the original spoken versions, although his non-Jewish audience of Christians would also not have taken to many complexities of meaning.

[8] The brief citations to particular parables are from material unique to each writer, except for the Wicked Tenants story which supports Mark's concern with being watchful but is used by both Matthew and Luke.

"immediately" shows a sense of urgency for the reader's response. As with parables themselves, one is challenged "now" by the person of Jesus.

Matthew is writing primarily for Jewish Christians. His well-organized collection of sayings and deeds show a marked concern for the living and teaching church. It's the most Jewish and anti-Jewish of the three. His heavy use of allegory (Hidden Treasure & Pearl; 13:44-46, Working in the Vineyard; 20:1-16, Wise and Foolish Virgins; 25:1-13), stark contrasts / reversals (Unforgiving Servant; 18:23-35, etc.), and apocalyptic language (Weeds and Wheat; 13:24-30, Last Judgment; 25:31-46, etc.) emphasize the importance of making a decision to become a follower of Jesus. His parables are ornate, dramatic stories, concerned with people who determine their fate in response to surprising opportunities. Jesus is the Son of Man and judge of all, the great teacher who founds the church and sends us on a mission.[9] The structure of the gospel, with its 5 principle discourses (one of which is a collection of parables), emphasizes Jesus' teaching. Miracle details are left out in favor of the person of Jesus and his words. Dialogue details emphasize the importance of personal encounter. Disciples are those who learn in response to the God's love and mercy made present in the life and teaching of Jesus. Dramatic interaction, imaginative language, and religious awe, in the context of a continuous community, shape Matthew's world.

Luke is writing primarily for Gentile Christians. While Matthew allegorizes, Luke moralizes. Jesus here is the most outgoing to strangers, from the Centurion to the criminal on the cross. He is the spirit-filled man of compassion and prayer who takes the initiative and offers models of discipleship in both his life (persecution, death, resurrection) and his parables. Luke's most extensive collection of gospel parables includes the "classics"(Good Samaritan, Prodigal Son, Lazarus, etc.). He lets us into the mind of the characters (Persistent Friend; 11:5-8, Rich Fool; 12:16-21, Places of Honor; 14:8-11, Planning a War; 14:31-32, etc.), letting parables

---

[9] "Teaching" occurs only after the resurrection in Matthew. Christ is the true teacher, the founder of this "school," who through personal authority and contact evokes a personal response that makes a difference.

speak in their simplicity and directness (Lost Coin; 15:8-10, Pharisee and Publican; 18:9-14, etc.), and letting the drama unfold not from the mystery of nature (Mark), or the threat of judgment (Matthew), but from the mystery of human interaction (Two Debtors; 7:41-43, Unjust Steward; 16:1-8, etc..). Instead of the eschaton, the everyday life of Christian is the primary focus. Jesus summons us to conversion towards a new way of life and a new view of the world wherein each encounter is filled with the possibility of God's saving presence.

Parables have been seen as descriptions in story form of Jesus' own life-style and approach, giving shape, direction, and meaning to the gospels where they are found. Early church efforts towards allegorical interpretation moved the parables back into well-known literary vehicles that were derived from carefully constructed rabbinic pedagogy. Jesus' use of parables to announce the Kingdom of God led the early church towards a parabolic vision of Jesus' life, death, and resurrection. Parables were now free to become examples and allegories. Jesus became the message that he proclaimed. In John Dominic Crossan's cryptic words, "Jesus died as parabler and rose as Parable."

To read the New Testament, one would think that Christian "teaching" (*didaskein* - used 50 times) is done mainly within a traveling commune. In Jesus' time, teaching was done by philosophers, sages, teachers of the law, and prophets / visionaries. Each had their own style and ideals. Jesus neither established a philosophy nor a special method of interpreting the Law. The disciples learned by observing what he said and did in different situations. He conveyed his message through personal appeal, without the expected status or authority from some "school" or historical chain of teachers. His teaching style was inclusive of women and children. "Discipleship" meant constant companionship. Reversing custom, Jesus chose his disciples, and they were expected to share in his mission. He taught by providing concrete opportunities of imitating his example (Cf. the frequency of "Follow me" and "Come after me"), never asking his followers anything he had not already done himself. He made his way known by the visible example of his actions, and his speech was fresh and creative; no mere repetition of rabbinic teaching, but live communication in concrete situations.[10]

Jesus' parabolic teaching captured the imagination and heart of the people, conveying religious complexities in remarkable simplicity, without moralizing or providing platitudes.[11] Readily understood metaphors and a plausible realistic surprise in an unusual, attractive narrative forced hearers to become part of the story, to make the connections between its various images, and to place themselves within its context. Parables shook people out of old patterns to look at life in a new way, prompting a decision to take on the life-style that the parable proposes. Many of the parables are concerned with engendering a new sense of community characterized by inclusion. When Jesus responds to important questions with stories, living experience becomes the arena in which life's meanings are to be discovered. In order to realize the Kingdom of God, one must participate in its particular manifestation in experienced life. Parables invite hearers to enter in and to participate, initiating a process in which the entire person becomes involved.

With the importance that familial relationship and social structure had in Jewish life, Jesus' call for a shared discipleship was a radical move. The Jewish family was the first and most important setting for religious education, and education was accomplished by imitating religious behavior (Cf. Proverbs). One learned through religious acts (the schema, Sabbath, halachah, etc.) and holidays such as Passover and Tabernacles were times of "live teaching" when one remembered what God had done by word and action. Jesus' call for switching the locus for one's religious identity and formation away from the family and traditional social structures towards the new community of the Kingdom of God was as new as his injection of realistic life experiences into the traditional stylized debates of

---

[10] I wonder if there isn't a key to Jesus' teaching here. It's likely that he was literate, yet the lack of any written record by him highlights the sense of immediacy and concreteness behind his teaching. In a sense, one can say that the written form of the parables, while rich, don't do justice either to Jesus himself or to his teaching. But it's the best contact we have with his spoken words.

[11] "Through its concreteness the language of Jesus captures our attention, through its rhythmic cadences it resonates in our memories, and through its puzzles and enigmas it engages our quest for understanding." (Donahue)

rabbinical teaching. While being an example of what he taught wasn't new, the nature of what he taught certainly was, as was the way that he taught; i.e., in parables.

The style of teaching that is implied by that of Jesus is one characterized by

1) a respect and use of poetic and metaphoric language. Christian teachers have a deep respect for language and its use, especially language's power to evoke images that may stretch, challenge, and shape pattern of thinking and acting.

2) a commitment to engage the real experiences and images of students. As Jesus found his primary images "on the road," so should Christian teachers.

3) a perspective that points out paradoxes in nature and human life. Things are not as they seem, Christian teachers would maintain. There's more here than is obvious. Such habits of looking more deeply form the capacity of finding God's presence in our midst.

4) an open-ended attitude to knowledge and experience. Christian teachers allow God to work through others as they see God working through them. True stories have no final ending. They always call for something more, something personal.[12]

5) a view of learning that runs counter to general perception. Christian teachers view learning as a way of opening up the deeper, more important and personal realities of individual lives, finding God in unexpected places when ordinary experiences are challenged by faith's perspective.

---

[12] John Dominic Crossan: "Parables give God room. The parables of Jesus are not historical allegories telling us how God acts with mankind; neither are they moral example-stories telling us how to act before God and towards each other. They are stories which shatter the deep structure of our accepted world and thereby render clear and evident to us the relativity of story itself. They remove our defences and make us vulnerable to God. It is only in such experiences that God can touch us, and only in such moments does the kingdom of God arrive. My own term for this relationship is transcendence."

In religious education, *per sé*, the following additional dimensions are found:

1) Formation in Christian life comes from a teacher through association, participation, and shared involvement in action.

2) Common life and community are the best teaching environment. Learners must know each other on more than a casual basis in order to reach the vital dimension where parabolic teaching can take place.

3) The content of religious education consists of A) working towards the Kingdom of God (peace, justice, etc.) through concrete action, practically and effectively initiated, B) experiencing the Scriptures as the living words of Christ addressing us here and now, C) perceiving the world around us and the response that's called for, juxtaposing its paradoxes with those of the gospel, D) aligning our personal stories with those told by Jesus and about him, allowing us to engage our stories from a new perspective

4) In a very real way, the Christian teacher has to get out of the way, or as Joseph Grassi puts it, "The role of teacher is indispensable, yet they become true teachers only when they make themselves dispensable. ..What is certain is that no human teacher can possibly take the place of the Spirit and that all such teachers are real teachers to the extent that they are willing to let themselves and their influence over others 'die' so that they may live with a deep freedom and trust in the inner guidance of the Spirit."

As a parable is "performative," aiming to bring about existential change, so Christian teaching strives to bring about personal renewal by using words and images that evoke a personal response. Stories, whether "secular" (from fairy tales to science theories) or "sacred" (from Scripture stories to dogmatic theology), are focused events. When teachers tell a story, they become personally engaged; they become involved with the learner in an implicit, authentic, and complete way. "It is clear that parable is really a story event and not just a story. One can tell oneself stories but not parables. One cannot really do so just as one cannot really beat oneself at chess or fool oneself completely with a riddle one has just invented. It takes two to parable." (Crossan) Any subject matter benefits from participating in the dynamics of parables, but religious education is especially conducive to this style of teaching, concentrating as it does on that which gives parabolic teaching its dynamic character; i.e., God's active presence among us.

The kind of teaching that parables call for is a kind of teaching that brings others into engaging God's presence among the most ordinary parts of life. Doing so attentively will fulfill the Christian teacher's vocation as authentically as it fulfilled Jesus' teaching vocation.

WORKS READ & CITED

<u>Books</u>:

Borsch, Frederick Houk. *Many Things in Parables: Extravagant Stories of New Community.*   Philadelphia, PA: Fortress Press, 1988.

Crossan, John Dominic. *The Dark Internal: Towards a Theology of Story.*   Sonoma, CA: Polebridge Press, 1988.

Donahue, John R. *The Gospel in Parable.*   Philadelphia, PA: Fortress Press, 1988.

Grassi, Joseph A. *Teaching the Way: Jesus, the Early Church and Today.*   Washington, DC: University Press of America, 1982.

Jeremias, Joachim. *The Parables of Jesus.*   London: S.C.M. Press, 1972.

Lambrecht, Jan. *Once More Astonished: The Parables of Jesus.*   New York, NY: Crossroad, 1981.

Perkins, Pheme. *Jesus as Teacher.*   Cambridge: Cambridge University Press, 1990.

Young, Brad H. *Jesus and His Jewish Parables: Rediscovering the Roots of Jesus' Teaching.*   New York, NY: Paulist Press, 1989.

Education for Christian Character and the Character of the Teacher

"In modern times there are opposing views about the practice of education. There is not general agreement about what the young should learn either in relation to virtue or in relation to the best in life: nor is it clear whether their education ought to be directed more towards the intellect than towards the character of the soul. The problem has been complicated by what we see happening before our eyes, and it is not certain whether training should be directed at things useful in life, or at those conducive to virtue, or at nonessentials. All these answers have been given. And there is no agreement as to what, in fact, does tend toward virtue. Men do not all prize most highly the same virtue, so naturally they differ also about the proper training for it."

This quotation illustrates how the question of character is inextricably bound up with the role of virtue in the moral life. Education for character is an education for virtue in terms of the perspective of the person. Not only is the notion of virtue one that has many definitions, but its "education" is also spoken of in a variety of forms. The one thing that does seem clear, at least if we look at our experience, is that learning, for virtues, is qualitatively different from learning other things.

Aquinas understood virtues not as acts of reason but as strategies of love by which we form ourselves through habits. These formative habits, in turn, by the Spirit's gifts are brought to fulfillment within God's goodness. The measure of virtue's growth is limitless because it is not identified in the possessor but in the goodness that it seeks. Virtue manifests itself through the conscience, arising out of an innate disposition towards what is good and acting out of prudence.[13] "The Thomistic school distinguished conscience, the

---

[13] Discussions about virtue tend to end up describing ways in which particular virtues interact and depend on one another. "If something is virtuous, it is prudent inasmuch as it is right judgment about what needs to be done; it is just insofar as it does what needs to be done in the way it needs to be done; it is

judgment of the practical reason about a particular act, from synteresis, the quasi-innate habit of the first principles of the moral order." (Charles Curran)

Homer saw virtue as a quality enabling individuals to discharge their social roles; Aristotle (& the NT, Aquinas, etc.) as a quality enabling individuals to achieve the specifically human telos (end), natural or supernatural; and Franklin (among others) saw virtue as a quality enabling individuals to achieve success. The crucial ethical question today is whether the Aristotelian tradition can be maintained even while alternative secular accounts of morality are proposed and discredited.[14] How might the autonomy of the moral agent be consistently combined with a view of moral norms as having an independent and objective authority?[15] In terms of this essay's concern, the question is of what the nature of Christian character consists, and what kind of the teacher educates towards such character. In order to make a sensible reply, we will first have to look at the nature of character and its "education," and then to the nature of Christian character and its formation.

The definition of character I will use comes from Thomas Lickona: "Character consists of operative values, values in action. We progress in our character as a value becomes a virtue, a reliable inner disposition to respond in situations in a morally good way." Such character involves three interrelated parts: moral knowing, moral feeling, and moral behavior. I would add that character is not a static "something," but is rather an active dynamic that operates

---

temperate because it displays the right amount of passion or energy in the doing of good - the act flows from a well-ordered affection; and it is courageous because it is not deterred by fear or hardship." (Paul Waddel on Aq.)

[14] Discussions about virtue tend to end up describing ways in which particular virtues interact and depend on one another. "If something is virtuous, it is prudent inasmuch as it is right judgment about what needs to be done; it is just insofar as it does what needs to be done in the way it needs to be done; it is temperate because it displays the right amount of passion or energy in the doing of good - the act flows from a well-ordered affection; and it is courageous because it is not deterred by fear or hardship." (Paul Waddel on Aq.)

[15] My answer would agree with those who hold that notions like intention, purpose, and reasons for action have to be reattached to the notion of what is good. In other words, the notion of character's unitive role should reshape what the penchant for analysis has fragmented.

between who I am and what I do, binding together my life's episodes and commitments. Character has to do with the unity of an individual life and the narrative that is embodied in that life. It's original meaning, a printer's physical impression upon a woodblock, highlights that it connotes something that is distinctive or individual in a human being. At a deeper level it refers to the deliberate intentionality that shapes us, what Hauerwas has called "the qualification of our self-agency." Buber has pointed out that character (the link between what this individual is and the sequence of his/her actions and attitudes) is different from personality (a unique spiritual-physical form with all the forces dormant within): "One may cultivate and enhance personality, but in education one can and one must aim at character." Character is the locus for responsibility; not just a mix of virtues but a name we give to the unitive aspect of life.

Educating for character had its heyday in the 1920's, when many spoke and wrote on the subject. (The phrase "character education" was first used at the 1918 NEA convention.) The focus of concern at that time was the independent moral personality, social integration, and explicit religious goals without specific roots in any tradition. Their disciplinary basis was strongly centered on the social sciences, psychological development of adaptive mechanisms, and socialization for specific values through social institutions. Educational strategies included classroom instruction, initiation into new social groupings, psychological conditioning/therapy, and creative experiences leading towards the discovery of values and putting them to work in reconstructing experience. It became evident that the major concern was the legitimacy and role of instruction in the character education process.

The pivotal Hartshorne and May study (1928 ff.) dashed much of the movement when it was found that the honest/dishonest behavior of individuals was highly variable and determined by the specific situation, not some consistent internal state.[16] Later studies

---

[16] In summary, Hartshorne and May found that 1) when dishonesty is rewarded, it's practiced, 2) verbal promises or formulations of the ideal of honesty don't produce general honest behavior, and 3) school changes that encourage cooperation between students/teacher and the exercise of initiative and self-judgment may tend to eliminate dishonest practices in schoolwork.

generally agreed with their outcome that all-or-none formulations of personal character were to be rejected. Today's neo-conservative public-school movement for educating towards positive changes in values, dispositions, and conduct seems to be resurrecting the issue with renewed vigor.[17] Its current popularity comes from society's stark need for even the most basic moral education and from the evident formative power of the social sciences. Whether or not it will, in fact, succeed will be evident in the movement's future. I suspect that influences such as a school's mission, consistent ethic, and communitarian unity will be found to have greater effect than particular teaching strategies. If that proves to be the case, it further demonstrates that a concern for the "character" of the school, the unitive dimensions of its theory and practice, will shape those within the school.

The nature of Christian character, according to Hauerwas, is diametrically opposed to that of autonomy-focused popular character education. " . . . [T]he kind of life Christians describe as faithful is substantively at odds with any account of morality that makes autonomy the necessary condition and/or goal of moral behavior." Since our character provides us with a history of commitment, Christian character proceeds out of the convictions that shape our

---

[17] Lickona, for example, states that public schools must "find a basis for defining and teaching morality that compels rational assent without requiring religious belief." He then advocates that "a natural moral law" arrived at through reason, consistent with revealed religious principles, and grasped with an independent logic available to children; that such a law dictates values such as respect, responsibility, honesty, fairness, tolerance, prudence, self-discipline, helpfulness, compassion, cooperation, courage, and democratic values (rule of law, equality of opportunity, due process, reasoned argument, etc.). "Respect, responsibility, and their derivatives are the values that schools may legitimately teach. Moral knowing, feeling, and action in their many manifestations are the qualities of character that make moral values a lived reality." Joel Kupperman, in a similar vein, advocates that character education can be accomplished at different school levels according to their different capacities. During primary school, center on dogmatic instruction of central moral norms. During high school, take a closer look at life structures and the "rules." (biographies, novels, etc.) During college, convey a sense that there are multiple perspectives that reasonable people bring to bear on moral questions. As with Lickona, the presumption is that one can educate for character outside of a specific communal narrative. The narrative of American Democracy has problems enough of its own without becoming responsible for supporting such an enterprise.

Christian identity. Christians follow a pattern of thought and behavior that flows from the basic operative commitment of seeing the world as redeemed in Jesus Christ. Moral growth involves the increasing apprehension of, and participation in, this mystery. Christian character, then, is a dimension of Christian life. It includes the making of certain decisions, the practice of a certain intentionality, and the participation in a certain kind of community. It would finally be unfair, and inaccurate, to say that "Christian" is merely an adjective of "character," referring to one particular kind of character among many. This is not to say that speaking of "Christian character" in this way is not valid, only that those who speak from within an authentically Christian character will complain that being a Christian can only be looked at in a certain way as an expression of character, but that finally it's much more than a particular kind of something else.[18]

Christian character, following a schema laid out by John Dykstra, is more like visional ethics than juridical ethics. Juridical ethics views the structures of reason as the only way of organizing moral life. It sees no essential breach between human beings and the world's mystery; rationality makes an adequate bridge. Visional ethics concentrates on a quality of consciousness and character. It doesn't try to provide clear guides to actions based on norms, finding appropriate and responsible actions as a consequence of a truthful seeing that peers into the world's depths with long discipline, patient effort, and continuous shaping of the self by what is real. Juridical ethics is problem-solving while visional ethics is mystery-encountering.[19] "Good" for juridical ethics is a description for evaluating

---

[18] Hauerwas speaks of how "...the language of character and virtue is especially fruitful in providing moral expressions appropriate to Christian conviction" and helps to situate the locus for Christian growth, but that it's not enough to show the required kind, something that comes only from the appropriate negotiation of many narratives. When, as John Dykstra puts it, we no longer put ourselves at the center of the universe, succumbing to the illusion of moral egocentrism, and move out of the center by a transformation of our imaginations, then the very notion of character undergoes a similar transformation and becomes an expression of how the Christian life is made manifest.

[19] John Dykstra's critique of Kohlberg's ethics is based on this schema. He finds that Kohlberg has found stages of social reasoning, but not states of moral development. Kohlberg presumes that the moral landscape consists largely of

                    George Van Grieken, FSC

human acts, while for visional ethics it is a symbol for an outside reality to which we hold acts, persons, and things, something that draws one out like art and true mysteries do. Christian character, following visional ethics, is a unitive quality of life that's drawn to Christ as to the good. Christian character points to a unifying dynamic in Christian life formed, and perhaps transformed, through discipleship to Jesus Christ. Christian character is what the Rich Young Man in the Gospels might have set out towards had he been able to break the character he had become; i.e., had he moved from being autonomous to becoming a person in relationship to the mystery of God made present.

Educating for Christian character must be seen in terms of the values and operative commitments that define and form Christian character. Following John Dykstra, Christian character is an encounter with the mystery of Christ made present through revelation. Revelation is an experience of the transformation of the imagination, and our character - our fundamental way of seeing and living - changes when this transformation takes place. The imagination is the foundation for perception, understanding, interpretation, cognition, and is an integrating process that links body, mind, and emotions. Its transformation leads to a new patterning of the imagination that allows for new ways of living in relation to some conflict that initiated the process. Christian images, we believe, are images that bring us closer to reality and draw us further into the mystery of God's presence.

That's all very nice, but how is it done. One operative commitment of Christians concerns faith's context. Christian habits are informed by faith that comes out of sharing an historical, tradition-bearing community of faith. As Hauerwas puts it, " . . . only those who are

---

problematic circumstances, and that the moral person is a problem-solving agent. Kohlberg is seen to hold that "Virtue is knowledge, the psychological structure of morality is cognitive, and the testing technique involves eliciting and analyzing people's cognitive judgments and patterns of reasoning." Dykstra argues that all three of these assumptions are false, and that "By defining morality the way he does, and by studying moral development in the manner that he does, Kohlberg blinds himself to what relation between religion and morality there might actually be." Dykstra thinks Kohlberg's work is helpful for moral philosophy or Christian ethics, but it's finally inadequate for forming a moral education in a religious context.

willing to be the story are capable of following it." Participating in a community of faith help Christians face ambiguities and conflicts while forming Christian character and virtue. Knowledge about religion is one thing, but Christian character can only be expanded in faith, acted in faith, lived in faith. Christian character is formed out of the life of faith.

Since Christian character is an expression of discipleship, it is formed by becoming ever more deliberate disciples.[20] We learn to apply faith to life in the context of our decision-making. For the Christian, discipleship and character is formed by repentance (reorienting the whole self to reality as mystery and to our utter dependence on God; allowing God to transform us), prayer (listening attentively to what absorbs our attention), and service (being present in vulnerability, equality, and compassion to all others). Repentance, prayer, and service increasingly transform us by God's grace so that receptivity, attention, and compassion for all reality grows. Our worship becomes central because it is here that we enact the core dynamics of the Christian life, making known and acting out symbolically the paradigm for the rest of our experienced lives. Dykstra explains that these disciplines " . . . are ways in which we intentionally put ourselves in particular fundamental situations of conflict, engage them, and then wait in order to allow something to happen to us." This is not passive non-involvement, but rather active involvement that follow the dynamics of our imaginal transformation through revelation. The Christian character is "educated" when "whatever capacities we have are activated in repentance, prayer, and service."[21]

---

[20] John Dykstra puts it well: "If we believe that reality is revealed to us through the eyes of Christ and that our lives are transformed by being with him, then the way to grow morally is to undertake the discipline of becoming disciples."

[21] Dykstra describes how, as one grows older, our capacities and types of moral or character growth become more complex. Intentionality and responsibility increase as our capacities take on the character of the disciplines of repentance, prayer, and service. This dynamic is similar to Paul Waddell's description of the way in which Aquinas describes the virtues as essentially invitations for the Gifts of the Spirit that will complete them. The Gifts are what the virtues born from charity finally become. "...God's love is no longer something to which we tend, but the power by which we move."

It is important to see that this "education" is an outgrowth of a particular kind of community. As Hauerwas puts it, "The truthfulness of Jesus creates and is known by the kind of community his story should form." He is known by the kind of life he demanded from his disciples and, by extension, that he demands from those participating in the formation of Christian character. The person of Jesus is key and unique in Christianity. Still, "the Gospels are not just the depiction of a man, but they are manuals for the training necessary to be part of the new community."[22] Along with habits informed by faith, our Christian character is shaped by Christian communities.[23] "A community shapes our perceptions, values, and identities by the many subtle ways it uses language, sets norms, makes decisions, and carries out actions. . . . In the church we are impelled by the very dynamics of what it means to be the church to meet the enemies and strangers of our lives." (Dykstra) The growth of character, then, is a correlative of our being initiated into a determinative story as that story is lived in the unique kind of community that defines itself outwards, towards the meeting of the strangers and enemies of our lives. (Cf. Mt. 28)

"Teaching" in such a context entails at once an investigative, critical, hermeneutical, and caring process that leads exploration, challenges

---

[22] Gifts of the Spirit that will complete them. The Gifts are what the virtues born from charity finally become. "...God's love is no longer something to which we tend, but the power by which we move." John Westerhoff makes a convincing argument for engaging in a new teaching paradigm consistent with the life of such a community. He argues against the schooling-instructional paradigm that looks to technology, psychology, and group dynamics, and instead argues for looking at new ways of being together, the meaning of relationships, and the nature of community. He develops a community of faith-enculturation paradigm based on liberation theology, finding it more focused on the character and quality of life lived together in a community of faith (vs. behavioral objectives, etc.). While it's difficult to see exactly what such a paradigm would look like on a practical basis, it does seem to respect those elements of Christianity which are distinctive to its character (the activity of God in history, the biblical promise of liberation, our created and corporate selfhood in essential relationship with others, the Church's identity as a radical community biased towards the marginal, etc.)

[23] Dykstra defines communities succinctly, and accurately I believe, as "organic bodies of people who are intersubjectively related to one another as mysteries, and who hold convictions, stories, and visions in common."

limited experience, aids and defines the interpretation of reality, and facilitates engagement in the world in ways consistent with the convictions and practice of Christianity.

The character of the Christian teacher is important because the teacher is a focused incarnation of the living community, intentionally responsible for involving learners in the experience of Christian life (repenting, prayer, and serving - according to Dykstra) in such a way that its various aspects might be explored, shared, understood, and engaged.

Such teachers will need to have the following characteristics:

1) They have worked on their own character as a matter of consistent practice, shaping their own being according to the dynamics of Christian character previously outlined.

2) They actively participate in a Christian community, involved in all of its aspects: worship, service, education, etc. Such participation will both form their own character, highlight relationships and perspectives unique to a particular Christian community, and provide learners with an avenue for understanding and participating in a specific community of faith.

3) They pay attention to the relationships that learners have with themselves, other teachers, and each other, since morality and Christian character deals in large part with the nature of one's relationships.

4) They recognize their role as models and mentors whose greatest effect on learners comes about through their implicit presence and actions. The way they treat those in the classroom constitutes the most basic form of moral/character education.

5) They are receptive, attentive, and present to their learners, recognizing them as part of the community of faith, with individually distinctive strengths and weaknesses. They let the students be themselves, and they respect them as such. Students are not there to fulfill the teacher's needs.

6) They determine at the outset who are the learners' loved ones, neighbors, enemies, and strangers; what are the learners' struggles and conflicts. They provide resources that help learners explore new dimensions of those struggles, and time and space to move through them. They stimulate actual encounters between persons of conflict so that interaction for Christian growth may become possible.

7) They find teaching in the context of Christian character to be an essential, vibrant, and personally rewarding activity, bringing into practice their discipleship and furthering their own Christian character in adventurous ways.

The mystery towards which Christian character is directed is not subject to domestication. "The revelation of the mystery of a particular reality is not the teacher's to give." (Dykstra) Yet through authentic participation within a community of faith, the operative commitments that shape Christian character may become discerned and practiced more fully. It is that discernment and practice which remains the focus for the Christian educator and that discernment and practice which remains key to the teacher's character.

WORKS READ & CITED

Books:

Chapman, William E. *Roots of Character Education.* New York, NY: Character Research Press, 1977.

Dykstra, Craig. *Vision and Character: A Christian Educator's Alternative to Kohlberg.* New York, NY: Paulist Press, 1981.

Hauerwas, Stanley. *A Community of Character: Toward a Constructive Christian Social Ethic.* Notre Dame, IN: University of Notre Dame Press, 1981.

Kupperman, Joel. *Character.* New York, NY: Oxford University Press, 1991.

Lickona, Thomas. *Educating for Character: How Our Schools Can Teach Respect and Responsibility.* New York, NY: Bantam, 1991.

MacIntyre, Alasdair. *After Virtue.* Notre Dame, IN: University of Notre Dame Press, 1981.

Wadell, Paul. *The Primacy of Love*. New York, NY: Paulist Press, 1992. (Ch. 7 - The Virtues: Actions That Guide Us to Fullness of Life; Ch. 8 - The Virtues: Finding Our Perfection in a Gift.)

Westerhoff, John H. *Will Our Children Have Faith?* New York, NY: Seabury Press, 1976.

Wynne, Edward, and Kevin Ryan. *Reclaiming Our Schools: A Handbook on Teaching Character, Academics, and Discipline.* New York, NY: Merrill, 1993.

Essays:

Hauerwas, Stanley. "Towards an Ethics of Character." *Introduction to Christian Ethics.* Ed. Ronald P. Hamel and Kenneth R. Himes. New York, NY: Paulist Press, 1989.

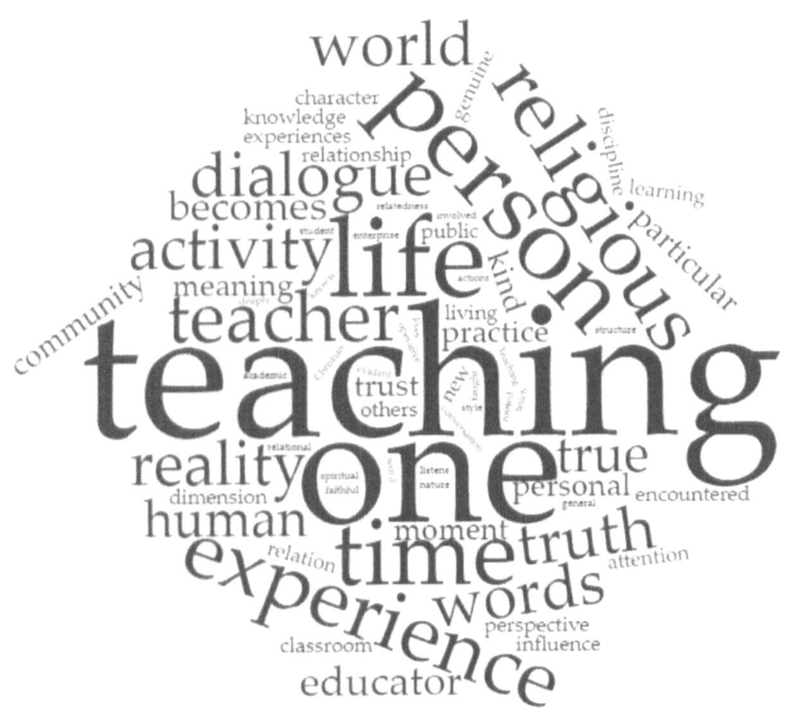

Spirituality and the Activity of Teaching

To speak of "spirituality" is to immediately jump into a world-wide conversation that is more vocal than it is clear. Everyone seems to have some kind of "spirituality" that they are willing to claim. The word refers both to a fundamental dimension of being human, to the lived experiences in which that dimension becomes actual, and to the academic discipline that studies that experience. General conversation about spirituality is marked by references to the things that one holds as important, along with the ways that one reflects such importance in the way one lives. For most people, spirituality is something that one lives rather than something that one studies. As an academic discipline, its emergence is yet in its infancy.

From the time Paul coined the adjectival form to describe any reality (hymns, charisms, etc.) under the influence of the Holy Spirit (1 Cor 2:14-15), the "spiritual" has undergone wide swings in its meaning. Paul's reference distinguished the person under the Spirit of God's influence with the simply natural human being. It was an added dimension of a person. This meaning lasted through the church's history until the 12th century, when the philosophical meaning developed which contrasted the spiritual from the material or corporeal. Through the 17th century, when "spirituality" took on a pejorative character vis-a-vis movements of questionable enthusiasm (in contrast to proper "devotion"), and into the 18th and 19th centuries, when it came to refer to the "interior life" of those elite who are "striving for perfection," the word was used in various contexts, finally being used almost exclusively by Roman Catholics before Vatican II as referring to the interior life of anyone who was trying to deepen their Christian life. Today the term refers to an all-encompassing integrity within a person, being used by both specific religious traditions and analogously by nonreligious or even antireligious movements such as feminism and Marxism.

Helpfully, Sandra Schneiders discerns two basic approaches to the word today: 1) a definition "from above" that derives from Christian dogmatic theology and the life of grace, where other kinds of "spirituality" share definition through extension or comparison, and 2) a definition "from below" that sees spirituality as an activity of human life located in the structure and dynamics of the human person, thereby in principle equally available to all. She makes an argument for adopting the latter kind since, in fact, more and more people are using it in that way, and such a definition is helpful for interfaith and inter-denominational dialogue. She defines experienced spirituality (vs. the academic discipline) as "the experience of consciously striving to integrate one's life in terms not of isolation and self-absorption but of self-transcendence toward the ultimate values one perceives."

The definition used in this essay follows in this same vein. I will call spirituality the experience of that personal dimension which shapes praxis by the integration of deepest convictions with basic operative commitments. Spirituality here refers to acknowledging a "deep structure" lying beneath personal experience, one that defines the way that experience is appropriated. Its key elements are a "that from which" and a "that to which." Spirituality arises out of deeply rooted convictions and is expressed through certain words and actions. Spirituality, *per sé*, refers to the kind of continuity that lies between those two poles.[24]

The spirituality of teaching, then, is that which integrates convictions/commitments within the praxis of teaching. Such "spirituality" looks to a deep structure that defines the way teaching is appropriated by those involved. As such, it asks what the basic operative commitments and deeply rooted convictions of a particular style of teaching are. To define a particular spirituality of teaching will involve describing how particular individuals view and encounter A) the activity of teaching itself, B) those most immediately involved in its exercise, and C) those factors that influence and encourage its successful practice.

---

[24] Comparisons with geometric "fractals" would not be out of place. Fractals refer to geometric forms which, when developed onto a larger scale, retain all the properties that were part of its original identity. The simplest example of its occurrence in nature is the fact that a mountain range has the same shape, etc. as the smallest rock taken from that range. In the present context, a "fractaline" aspect of spirituality would refer to the fact that the shape of one's smallest convictions (or actions) are continuous in a real and intimate way with the shape of one's most comprehensive convictions (or the shape of one's whole life).

Martin Buber and Parker Palmer are two eminent educators who have contributed to an understanding of the spirituality of teaching. Their convictions and operative commitments regarding teaching will illustrate a particular spirituality of teaching.[25]

Martin Buber looked to the existential reality of the teaching encounter when developing his philosophy of education. Truth arises through relational criteria and "education means to let a selection of the world affect a person through the medium of another person." In his 60 years as an educator, he came to see education as essentially a dialogue between teacher and learner; one that nurtures hope and meaning. Reading him, it seems as if he spent much of his time undercutting reductionist views of education (the authoritarian "old" style and the progressive "new" style, the gardener / sculptor or the funnel / pump models, etc.) and urging the conversation to delve more deeply into the nature of the teaching encounter itself. His major educational convictions illustrate where he located teaching's "spirituality."

A principle of education "can only be a basic relation which is fulfilled in education", and "the relation in education is one of pure dialogue." Genuine dialogue is more than just words. It's an encounter "where each of the participants really has in mind the other or others in their present and particular being and turns to them with the intention of establishing a living mutual relation between himself [herself] and them." Such mutuality is fostered by the development of genuine trust and confidence between the teacher and the student. "Trust, trust in the world, because this human being exists - that is the most inward achievement of the relation in education."

Dialogue is defined by the act of inclusion, whereby one truly experiences the other's reality. This is done while maintaining one's own actuality - it's not wholesale empathy whereby one is subsumed into the other - and insures that the teaching doesn't degenerate into an arbitrary exercise of the teacher's will. The act of inclusion, experiencing the other side, defines dialogue, makes possible knowing of the other in his/her concrete uniqueness as opposed to knowing

---

[25] In a few pages, it's only possible to give an indication of their views regarding A) the activity of teaching. Their views concerning B) its participants and C) influential factors would emerge from A).

the other as a content of my experience. The sphere of the "be-tween," where the really real is met, is found when one really listens, becoming personally aware of the "signs of address," the accessible opportunities for genuine dialogue. To Buber, "All real living is meeting."

Daniel Murphy, in a book on Buber's philosophy of education, suc-cinctly describes Buber as viewing the human person "as intrinsi-cally a relating, loving, reciprocating, rather than self-fulfilling, indi-vidually creative, or merely socially oriented being." The "nurturing of relational capacities [then] becomes . . . the main function of ed-ucation."

In the teaching encounter, that which needs to be taught to the stu-dent becomes evident as the student is encountered as a Thou, a genuine other of immeasurable worth. The teacher embodies in him or herself the living selection of the effective world that comes, as a person, to meet and encounter the pupil.[26] The educator puts aside any desire to dominate or enjoy the pupil. "He [she] sees them crouching at the desks, indiscriminately flung together, the mis-shapen and the well-proportioned, animal faces, empty faces, and noble faces, in indiscriminate confusion, like the presence of the created universe; the glance of the educator accepts and receives them all." It is that full acceptance which begins the process of trust and confidence, and through that acceptance the teacher is edu-cated into recognizing which forces of the world the child needs in order to grow.

"Education worthy of the name is essentially education of charac-ter", Buber says. True education is the kind that awakens in a person "the courage to shoulder life again." All sorts of influences shape a person's character, dispose and "educate" his/her capacity for hear-ing/responding to unconditioned address; i.e., the latent command of norms inherent in personhood. " . . . [A]mong this infinity of form-giving forces the educator is only one element among innu-merable others, but distinct from them all by his [her]will to take part in the stamping of character and by his [her]consciousness that he [she] represents in the eyes of the growing person a certain

---

[26] "The educator gathers in the constructive forces of the world...the world bound up in community, turned to God. The educator educates himself to be their vehicle."

selection of what is, the selection of what is 'right', of what should be. It is in this will and this consciousness that his [her] vocation as an educator finds its fundamental expression." The master artist/craftsman of old is the evocative model.

Martin Buber, then, roots his educational commitment in dialogue, inclusive mutuality of attention, trust, and genuine involvement in the present teaching moment.

Parker Palmer sees teaching as an activity in which one "creates a space in which obedience to truth is practiced." Obedience here hearkens backs to the Latin *ob-audere*, listening attentively, and truth finds its meaning in its German root of pledging "troth." Teaching, therefore, is an activity whereby one listens attentively, even lovingly, to whatever one has pledged one's attention in a covenant of faithful relationship.

Palmer's convictions about teaching arise out of a decidedly relational view of reality.[27] "Our seeing shapes our being." If we approach teaching as an activity in which we tell others about a reality "out there," then our teaching effectively destroys any possibility of having that reality touch us in any meaningful way. "Instead, we must allow the power of love to transform the very knowledge we teach, the very methods we use to teach and learn it." Taking his cue from the desert Fathers, he develops an educational spirituality based on love's reality in the world. Through the study of texts one maintains contact with tradition. Through prayer, "the practice of relatedness," one learns that one not only knows, but also is known. And through community, one is brought into the discipline of relatedness.

Like Buber, he spends much time speaking about what teaching is not. Perhaps, like Buber, the bulk of effort must be directed against our proclivity for making easy reductions of complex realities. Only by opposing that tendency will the direction of an alternative educational perspective become evident. Palmer rails against

---

[27] "The structure of reality is not exhausted by the principles of empiricism and rationality. Reality's ultimate structure is that of an organic, interrelated, mutually responsive community of being. Relationships - not facts and reasons - are the key to reality; as we enter those relationships, knowledge of reality is unlocked." (Palmer

objectivism, manifested in general educational practice and in religious educational practice. These are the ways in which we manipulate and tell the world what it is, making an object of everything we study. With objectivism, something can only be truly known when all the subjective elements have been eliminated. Palmer maintains that this is not only incommensurate with reality, but it also is a major contributor to the manipulative, de-humanizing actions and perspectives rampant within society today.

If true learning is to happen, then we must be a community of learning. Practicing obedience to the truth in a classroom depends on 1) a teacher with a living relationship with the subject at hand, 2) students that are empowered to identify and articulate their own experience and listen openly to that of others, and 3) an atmosphere of trust wherein the most important concerns in our lives might be addressed. Such classrooms are places where consensus is taught and fostered; a process wherein one doesn't listen for something to oppose or argue against, but listens for something with which one can agree. Here, progress is a communal affair whereby new knowledge has true value and is authentically generated out of the accumulated experience of those present. In such a classroom, new social structures and ways of seeing the world are formed through the doing.

In classrooms, as in church, one practices for "public life," the pre-political interaction and engagement of strangers. Strangers here are both expected and encountered, unlike "private life," but the encounter is governed by a minimum of formal procedures, unlike "political life." This realm of public life is the lifeblood of democracy; it is the locus of general public interaction. Schools can be places where true community without fear, and true learning based on creative exchange of experiences and ideas, will foster that desire in the world at large, thereby contributing to the public life of society.

For Parker Palmer, " . . . [I]f truth is to be taught, then teaching and learning must take the shape of truth itself - a community of faithful relationships . . . . Learning the truth requires that we enter into personal relationship with what the words reveal." Teaching is the practice whereby such truth calls forth a personal relationship with what is known, committing both teacher and learner to becoming involved, even transformed, by that to which we pay loving attention.

Teaching, then, is an activity rooted in commitments to attentive listening, covenantal "troth" with what is encountered, and communal discernment of knowledge. Finally, teaching reaches for relatedness and, as such, is prayerful.[28]

While Buber has been critiqued for being too concerned with the student's capacity for dialogue or the nature of the teaching moment, and Palmer might be criticized for developing a perspective geared more for adult education than education across the life cycle, both of these authors nevertheless highlight the kinds of concerns that must be addressed by anyone considering a "spirituality" of the enterprise of teaching; i.e., the nature of the teaching encounter and the convictions / commitments that shape it.

My understanding of the spirituality of teaching is one that shares Buber's view of the unique teaching moment and Palmer's perspective of love's defining influence.

The teaching encounter is a moment in time when two or more persons pay attention to a common concern and to each other. Some of the convictions and commitments that shape that encounter are as follows:

In all of my experience of teaching, I have never been able to either predict, or fully prepare for, the journey that such an encounter will entail. In some sense, it's always an adventure. Buber and Palmer both speak of the fact that the best teachers teach without conscious effort or technique. They respond and evoke out of their whole personhood. Like an artist, the true teacher is one who encounters each teaching moment as a new and distinct opportunity filled with possibilities. Unlike an artist, the true teacher enables the other, the person who is encountered, to find and articulate his/her voice, his/her unique contribution and experience. The teacher might be likened to a musical improviser such as Oscar Peterson, who once described that he knew what note on the piano he wanted

---

[28] "...when education is not prayerful, when it does not center on transcendence, it fails to create authentic and spontaneous relations between the self and the world." (Palmer)

to reach, but he didn't know exactly how he would get there; that would work itself out as he made his way there (and often he might find himself happily ending up somewhere else).

In a classroom situation, the conviction that students are not empty vessels will allow for an authentic respect for their individual situations, experiences, and beliefs. Classroom time is not a time to primarily in-form or re-form students; students are not clay. Instead, classroom time is a time where primarily words (and implicitly actions) bring knowledge to life. The teacher's words resonate with and/or evoke the students' words, while the students' words respond in kind. (The piano talks back!) As the legitimate authority and degree of involvement of both is respected, the teaching encounter fulfills its commitment to engaging the truth in personal relationships.

What this means for religious education is that the activity of teaching itself already contains dynamics that are often relegated to some outside sphere loosely called "religious." The way in which one engages in the enterprise of religious education teaches as much as its content, if not more so. If the time of religious education is not the time when all that is vibrant and alive about education itself becomes evident, then it is neither faithful to its own task nor representative of the simplest manifestation of education in general. In other words, religious education should be a time when that which students and teachers find captivating about education comes to the fore, is intentionally practiced, is even celebrated. Christian religious education informed by its convictions regarding the Trinity, the human person, prayer, community, proclamation, etc. enriches and broadens those dimensions of education that in most other subject areas remain implicitly religious.

For the religious educator shaped within this perspective, teaching does not become a one-way street; the draining of energy that prefigures "burn-out" should not be a realistic possibility. Instead, that which makes education an appealing, energizing activity becomes a source of strength. "No way leads to any other goal but to that which is like it." (Buber) When the teaching encounter becomes a time and place where the person of Jesus Christ defines what is said and done, then not only will the encounter participate in all that makes teaching a spiritual enterprise, but such an encounter will begin to shape persons who are true disciples.[29]

WORKS READ & CITED

Books:

Buber, Martin. *Between Man and Man.* New York, NY: MacMillan Publishing Co., 1965. (Ch 1 - Dialogue; Ch. 3 - Education; Ch. 4 - The Education of Character)

Murphy, Daniel. *Martin Buber's Philosophy of Education.* Dublin: Irish Academic Press, 1988.

Nouwen, Henri. *Creative Ministry.* New York, NY: Doubleday, 1971.

Palmer, Parker. *To Know As We Are Known.* San Francisco: Harper & Row, 1983.

Palmer, Parker. *Caring for the Commonweal: Education for Religious and Public Life.* Macon, GA: Mercer University Press, 1990. (Pp. 90 - 163)

Whitehead, Alfred North. *The Aims of Education and Other Essays.* New York, NY: The Free Press, 1957.

Essays:

Carfagna, Rosemarie. "A Spirituality of Teaching." *Studies in Formative Spirituality* 9.May (1988): 141-50.

O'Reilley, Mary Rose. "The Centered Classroom: Meditations on Teaching and Learning." *Weavings* 4.5 (1989): 21-31.

Palmer, Parker. "'Learning is the Thing for You': Renewing the Vitality of Religious Education." *Weavings* 4.5 (1989): 6-19.

As Henri Nouwen describes it, "Jesus can be called Teacher in the fullest sense of the word precisely because He did not cling to His prerogatives but became one of the many who have to learn. His life makes it clear to us that we do not need weapons, that we do not need to hide ourselves or play competitive games with each other. Only he who is not afraid to show his weaknesses and who allows himself to be touched by the tender hand of the Teacher will be able to be a real student. For if education is meant to challenge the world, it is Christ Himself who challenges teachers as well as students to give up their defenses and to become available for real growth. In order to come to this conversion, which is the healing of our scotomas, we might be thrown from our horses and be blind for a while, but in the end we will be brought to an entirely new insight, which might well bring about a new man in a new world."

Schneiders, Sandra M. "Spirituality in the Academy." *Theological Studies* 50. December (1989): 676-97.

Sharp, Ann Margaret. "Education: A Philosophical Journey." *Studies in Formative Spirituality* 4. November (1983): 351-68.

Souper, Patrick C. "Spirituality Today." *The Spiritual Dimension of Education.* Ed. Patrick C. Souper. Southampton, Eng.: University of Southampton Department of Education, 1985. 7-26.

The Transcendent Yearning of Humanity
as a Foundation for Religious Education

Hegel once said, "God does not offer himself for observation." This illustrates the difficulty of dealing with the topic of transcendence. In order to say something intelligible about transcendence, I will have to use language that constantly gestures to a reality that fully lies beyond language's reach. The effort of many of the authors I've read has largely been to argue for what transcendence is not, offering ways of looking at our experience that might help us to begin to move towards that which is called transcendence.

Karl Rahner helps one get a foothold on what "the transcendent yearning of humankind" might mean when he speaks of the fact that all of our knowledge and "conscious activity is grounded in a pre-apprehension of 'being' as such, in an unthematic but every-present knowledge of the infinity of reality." This basic element in our ontological constitution as human beings he calls the "super-natural existential." It consists of an orientation towards absolute mystery, a distinctive affinity, capacity, and aptitude for "God" (the term by which transcendence is borne to us). This orientation to-wards and awareness of mystery (the condition of possibility for comprehending anything particular) pervades all the other elements that we perceive as being constitutive of human nature (the existen-tials): freedom, self-presence, self-transcendence, etc. It manifests itself in spiritual knowledge by consisting of the "pure openness for absolutely everything, for being as such." Being itself at once per-meates and transcends the person, and transcendence refers to that which we must posit as permanent in an experience of perpetual mutability and temporality.[30] "God is the one to whom all reality is

---

[30] Karl Lehman nicely summarizes the viewpoint: "Man's power to know and love, assent and consent, grasps particular being against the background of being in general; thus all its particularized knowledge is implicitly based on the unthe-matic awareness it also has of Being simpliciter, which includes an awareness - however inarticulate - of God, spirit, and freedom and thus of the mystery above us and within us. Consequently, the transcendentality of the human spirit is the essential foundation of the person, of responsibility, of religious experience (in-cluding mysticism), and of the possibility of God's self-communication in grace and revelation."

oriented, by a principle which is itself interior in all of reality." (McBrien)[31]

This will to God, or turning toward the ultimate, is not only universal in our time but has been part of the human condition throughout history, although in various forms. The classical world recognized a mysterious center and depth in the nature of humankind which engendered transcendent movement (e.g., Plato's "Good," Aristotle's cosmology). Christianity from the beginning conveyed an absolute quality to the human person, one grounded on, and participating in, a transcendent reality (e.g., Paul's Body of Christ and John's Logos). The patristic era understood transcendence through neo-Platonism (degrees of being in the universe, self-communication of the Good) and biblical historical properties of God that became absolute properties (omnipotence, lordship over history, etc.). But there were also compelling images of "inner" transcendence, such as those of Augustine (God is closer to the soul than the soul itself; people have "a truth already within" that's kindled by "reflection"). The early Middle Ages showed an intensive inward trend and openness to transcendence that appeared in art, prayer, and the general rhythm of medieval life. Aquinas argued for a "natural disposition" that we have, by God's grace, to recognize and appropriate the truth of revelation. God's loving reach towards us (grace) transforms and works through nature and through our built-in connaturality for revelation.[32] Later medieval thought emphasized God's incomprehensible hiddenness, which began the process of isolating faith from its foundation. Transcendence (outside of countercurrents in Pascal, French and Spanish spiritual

---

[31] One can see already that the terms "Transcendence," "Being," and "God" are used in close proximity, each specifying a dimension of this reality not adequately conveyed by the others. The reason for this is that the "essence" of this reality is its incomprehensibility. So in some sense we are most faithful to its nature when we constantly remember that our "comprehension" is always borne by a reality that's finally incomprehensible, like an island floating on the sea of mystery (Rahner's image).

[32] Aquinas also speaks of the "actus essendi", a "positiveness" of being that is the hidden ground of transcendence pervading all immanence, although not simply absorbed there. As Karl Lehman interprets Aquinas, finite actuality, through its being, "soars on principle into the divine uncreated life, which of itself fully eludes us in its own proper essence."

writers, etc.) became so distant with the rise of science, a mechanistic world picture, empiricism, rationalism, and the Enlightenment, that it was essentially impotent. German Idealism banished the Absolute into the immanence of consciousness, and humanity's "yearning" was situated either in humanity's nature (Kant's critique of "reality," Nietsche's will to power, Marxism, etc.) or transcendence became a basically "empty" reality (Feuerbach's "being is sensible being" - materialism).

In modern times, the yearning for transcendence has been called a "metaphysical thirst" (Von Hugel), a yearning for the cosmic connection with a person's inborn Thou (Buber), an "itch for Eden" (O'Malley), etc. Each contribution adds a further dimension for approaching this most elusive, yet most pivotal, of realities undergirding our ability to reach beyond ourselves. In order to give some idea of the nature of transcendence as it is understood today, two major characteristics and a few of its dynamics will be considered.

The predominant characteristics of transcendence in the literature that I read were those of pervasiveness and tacitness. The word "transcendence" recurred within various contexts and multiple conceptual frameworks. Each occurrence was marked by a profound sense of the fact that we are confronted here with a deeply pervasive and tacit reality.

Transcendence is such a pervasive mystery because it deals with a passionate longing, a movement of yearning, an active constituent of our human nature. It's as if one were to ask what it was that made a human being distinctive. The ability to even begin to answer such a question already speaks to the answer.[33] What is distinctive is our capacity to be oriented towards something beyond ourselves, which requires both that orientation and that beyond. We must call it something because that's the only way we can speak about anything. But we also have to acknowledge that that something, in order for it to be the ground for our orientation towards the beyond, has to be truly beyond and always lies beyond any "thing" that we can conceive of. Transcendence is more like a basic operative commitment

---

[33] Michael Polanyi notes that, even in science, to see a problem is to see something hidden, to have an intimation of coherence, to have a tacit knowledge of an answer.

within reality to reality, a vital and vitalizing principle of life within reality.

Michael Polanyi provides an insightful frame of reference for understanding both the nature of transcendence and the reasons why its principles are so difficult to ascertain. He points out that "thought can live only on grounds we adopt in the service of a reality to which we submit." We can know more than we can tell,[34] and that knowledge is finally and basically a tacit, implicit kind of thing. Much of our perception of the external world is often unspecifiable in detail (human physiognomy, diagnosis, performance skills, use of language, etc.). We bring to bear a tacit interpretive framework in our growing awareness, one that involves exercising a personal orientation towards reality more than providing an objective account of it. It is by dwelling within that-which-we-engage that understanding is able to grow. We interiorize that which we engage, shaping and integrating experience according to its nature. This is as true of scientific discovery as it is of the literary insight. Tacitness shapes what Polanyi calls "man's capacity for anticipating the approach of hidden truth."[35] Such a transcendent dimension is constitutive of reality as such, and is defined by that reality, not by us.

Polanyi also seems to offer a way of understanding why the principles of this transcendence are so mysterious and incomprehensible. Extending the insight that we lose sight of a comprehensive entity when we switch attention to its particulars (e.g., you can't type when concentrating on your fingers), Polanyi surmises that the laws over particulars would themselves never account for the organizing principles of a higher entity that they form (e.g., you can't get to the

---

[34] I would add that we can be more than we can know. "To the religious mind the soul is always more than it is; it transcends itself..." (Dúpre) This aspect of humanity is one that brings in both the transcendent dimension, which grounds the profoundly "moreness" nature of who we are and brings in the categorically religious dimension which specifies patterns whereby that moreness might be encountered.

[35] "... [W]hat he pursues is not of his making; his acts stand under the judgment of the hidden reality he seeks to uncover. His vision of the problem, his obsession with it, and his final leap of discovery are all filled from beginning to end with an obligation to an external objective." (Polanyi)

principles of chess from the rules of chess, etc.). Higher principles are always in danger of being reduced and explained away by the laws of a lower reality.[36] Transcendence, similarly, is not a member of the household of all reality (Rahner); God's nature, "organizing principles," and "laws," always lie essentially beyond our us.

What have been some of the dynamics by which transcendence is recognized: how do we become conscious of this disposition for transcendence? Peter Berger recognizes five "signals of transcendence" that are found within the domain of our "natural" reality but that appear to point beyond that reality: our propensity for order (we trust that reality is in order), play activity (alters time structure in an intimation of eternity), our propensity for hope (to refute our experience of death), damnation or outrage (the other side of hope; we trust that justice will prevail), and humor (things are not always what they seem).

__Relational__ Martin Buber focuses on relationality as a participation in transcendence. "Thou" meets me through a grace, through something unattainable by seeking. "Thou" is a direct relation of being to being, a "between" that happens only as fact. Transcendence is found in our capacity for relation. "In the beginning is relation - as category of being, readiness, grasping form, mould for the soul; it is the a priori of relation, the inborn Thou . . . [which is] realised in the lived relations with that which meets it, . . . consummated only in the direct relation with the Thou that by its nature cannot become It." The moment of meeting is not an "experience" but rather something that happens, that is done. "At times it is like a light breath, at times like a wrestling-bout, but always - it happens." And whatever it is that happens, it is always something that is known as received, a Presence.

__Ordinary__ Buber also insists that God is found in the everyday, in the ordinary world where the reality between God and ourselves is manifested in reciprocity. Karl Rahner, without specifying relationality as its exclusive mode, similarly focuses on the ordinary for discovering transcendence: "The very commonness of everyday things

---

[36] "...[E]ach level is subject to dual control; first, by the laws that apply to its elements in themselves and, second, by the laws that control the comprehensive entity formed by them."

harbors the eternal marvel and silent mystery of God and grace." Nicholas Lash likewise interprets human experience as experience of the mystery of God, finding in the doctrine of the Trinity a pattern of speech and action whereby people may live in relation to the mystery of God in all particular and public ordinariness, since the proper metaphor for our relationship with God is our relationship with one another.[37]

Wonder & Respect Louis Dúpre looks to ways in which we might break out of the prison of our autonomous self.[38] In order to begin the process of recognizing a reality outside of the self, we might cultivate a sense of wonder and surprise, allowing the depths of reality to have their voice. We might also cultivate a sense of gratitude and respect, since these are based on an appreciation for an autonomous, but related, other. Lastly, we could encourage in ourselves and others an appreciation of art, which opens the space of wonder, and of language, which expresses both the limits and the possibilities of our yearning for transcendence.

Trust Nicholas Lash agrees with Hegel to the extent "that knowledge of God is not to be had by 'gazing' at some real or imaginary object or idea, but by participating in God's self-movement of utterance and love." Such knowledge is achieved by cultivating a basic trust, by actualizing the relational protocol revealed in the doctrine of the Trinity, and by working towards the authentic occurrence of community.

Prayer Evelyn Underhill relates how genuine prayer brings transcendence into one's life. "For genuine prayer in all its degrees, from the most naive to the most transcendental, opens up human personality to the all-penetrating Divine activity . . . For prayer is rooted in ontology. . . . It is genuine communication with Reality, or nothing." Such prayer makes it clear that "Your whole life hangs on a great Givenness." Likewise, the spirit of worship cultivates "the

---

[37] Such concentration on the nature of relationality as a "signal" of transcendence highlights and develops Jesus' identification of himself with "the least of these."

[38] He writes that "in reducing itself to a function for constituting objectivity, the subject [self] has lost all content of its own and been swallowed up by the all-encroaching objectivity of its own making. The historical period that has introduced the self as an absolute has concluded with the death of the self."

habit of looking up and out beyond the frontiers of the useful and the obvious, and finding beyond those frontiers a beloved Reality which gives significance to the useful and the obvious." Such a habit is particularly highlighted by the distinctive Catholic emphasis on sacramentality, the conviction that indivisible depths of reality are manifested in visible ways. (McBrien)

It's difficult to find a general critique of this "yearning for the transcendent," although several authors point out difficulties with Rahner's position. Nicholas Lash notes that Rahner's distinction between "spirit" and "matter," while allowing the difference between the world and God to be displayed in discourse, must not operate as if it referred to a division within the world. "Spirit" must not be reduced to a certain kind of matter. While Rahner never directly states these positions, Lash believes that he "tends to underplay the indispensability of taking actual human relations as the proper metaphor for the relation of God," and losing sight of the fact that all statements about the individual's relationship to God are abstract or formal statements about something concrete. Van Beeck also notes that what remains open to criticism in Rahner is his focus on the human person as the potential rather than the actual recipient of God's self-communication. Yves Congar and Walter Kasper both critiqued Rahner for failing to "take seriously the truth that through the incarnation the second divine person exists in history in a new way." (Kasper) There's an asymmetry between the theology and the economy of God's self-communication; God's self-communication "takes place in a mode that is not connatural with the being of the divine Persons[39] . . . [and] will not be a full self-communication until the end of time." (Congar) In a word, Rahner may be locating transcendence too much in anthropology, unwittingly becoming bound by the limits of his anthropological analysis. God's autonomy and God's radical historical presence through Jesus Christ must both be preserved.[40]

---

[39] He notes, for example, that the Father's omnipotence and the world's evil are both true and real. God remains "more" than fully realized in God's self-communication.

[40] Von Balthasar has argued that Rahner's anthropological turn reduces religious truth to the perspective of anthropology and thereby does less justice to other perspectives.

Consideration still needs to be given to the implications these aspects and dynamics of humankind's yearning for transcendence have for how we teach.

Dúpre insists that transcendence is, in fact, lost in today's secular culture. We need to primarily cultivate an attitude in which transcendence can be recognized again. In a world where the autonomy of the believer is presupposed and faith is a matter of personal decision, "religion has become what it never was before: a private affair. In secularized society the religious person has nowhere to turn but inward." To make the conversion from the priority of holding a conviction to that of being held by a reality other than our own is one that requires more than simple engineering.[41] And if our concern is making others capable for knowing God, receptive to revelation, then the task is even more daunting.[42] "The situation requires a new depth, the conveyance of another dimension to all life."

It's possible here only to list some of the operative commitments whereby education might participate in the task before it:

1) Christianity is finally not about ideas and concepts, but about the reality of a personal God. To be a Christian is not simply to believe and learn something, but to be someone. The truth at the heart of theology is someone to whom we must surrender. As part of a living tradition and in a living redemptive community, that reality is encountered as one participates in the Christian mystery.

2) "There are aspects of understanding which are the fruit, and not the precondition, of love." (Lash) Sympathy towards, and interiorization of, what is other than ourselves are the movements of love which shape true knowledge.

3) With Buber we might say, "I have no teaching, but I carry on a conversation." Basic trust in God and each other

---

[41] Dúpre: "What is needed is a conversion to an attitude in which existing is more than taking, acting more than making, meaning more than function - an attitude in which there is enough leisure for wonder and enough detachment for transcendence."

[42] Newman's comment applies: "...never do we seem so illogical to others, as when we are arguing under the continual influence of impressions to which they are insensible."

through small practical leaps of friendship or trust dispose us to address those important ideas which concern us in the present.

4) Art of various kinds evokes transcendence by the inadequacy of its form, evoking an openness and reach that make room for wonder, for reverence.

5) The religious attitude begins with an ability to detect the wonder of Being in each encounter with reality. Anything which engenders a new openness toward the real contributes to that attitude.

6) Creativity practices the giving of form and expression to deeper realities, introducing experiences of both limits and possibilities.

7) Making connections with things outside of the scope of immediate study widens horizons, enlarging the capacity for considering the nature of our capacities.

If people have a connaturality for transcendence, then they are trustworthy partners in the task of education. From long tradition, the word "education" has meant "to bring to an open developed mode of being what already existed in a hidden, undeveloped manner." (Dúpre) If one of the dimensions of that being is a mode that we have recognized as the ground of transcendence, then education also consists of bringing the tacit conviction of transcendence into the light of day. Community, relationality, trust, wonder, respect, art, and radical openness will all enhance the growth of a greater capacity for participating in the dynamics integral to transcendence's source. We may not fully understand or be able to grasp those internal dynamics, but we may come to know that they are trustworthy, that they reflect the kinds of dynamics we encounter when we encounter persons, and that they resonate with the internal dynamics, the yearning, that we find within our own depths.

Works Read & Cited

Books:

Buber, Martin. *I and Thou*. New York, NY: Scribner, 1970.

Dupré, Louis. *Transcendent Selfhood: The Loss and Rediscovery of the Inner Life*. New York, NY: Seabury Press, 1976.

Lash, Nicholas. *Easter in Ordinary*. Charlottesville, VA: University Press of Virginia, 1988.

Louth, Andrew. *Discerning the Mystery: An Essay on the Nature of Theology*. Oxford: Clarendon Press, 1989. 147.

Polanyi, Michael. *The Tacit Dimension*. Garden City, NY: Anchor Books, 1967.

Rahner, Karl. *Foundations of Christian Faith*. New York, NY: Crossroad, 1989. (Ch. 1 - The Hearer of the Message; Ch. 2 - Man in the Presence of Absolute Mystery.)

Underhill, Evelyn. *Life as Prayer*. Harrisburg, PA: Morehouse Publishing, 1991.

Essays:

Dupré, Louis. "Catholic Education and the Predicament of Modern Culture." *Living Light* (1987): 295-306.

Whitehead, Alfred North. "The Aims of Education." *The Aims of Education and Other Essays*. New York, NY: The Free Press, 1957.

          George Van Grieken, FSC

The Psychology of Transcendence and Carl Jung

Being largely unfamiliar with the Jungian world of interpretation, my reading of the literature was akin to walking into an unfamiliar house and staying awhile. Parts of the house that were at first somewhat mysterious became less so as they were put to use, while others which had seemed obvious became mysterious and questionable with time and use. Jung's terminology and interpretive framework is not one that is easily grasped, although many parts of it do appear consistent.[43] The point behind this caveat is that Jung's understanding of "transcendence" and how it operates in the psyche must be gleaned from his remarks on a particular dynamic in the psyche called the "transcendent function" and on his observations of religion's impact on individual psychic life. In other words, while Jung never speaks directly to "the psychology of transcendence," he does speak of psychological matters that reflect his understanding of "transcendence" and the way it impacts the psyche.

Jung first wrote of "the transcendent function" in a 1916 essay. When this essay was discovered and published in 1959, two years before his death, he provided an introduction that characterized this function as answering the question, "How does one come to terms in practice with the unconscious?" He saw this question as being asked indirectly by all religions and philosophies. "For the unconscious is not this thing or that; it is the Unknown as it immediately

---

[43] As Ann Ulanov has pointed out, Jung's concepts are both empirical (personifications of unconscious contents) and symbolic (mediations to consciousness of the nature, emotional quality, and effect of psychic data). This makes handling them all the more difficult. It's rather within Jung's interpretive framework that these concepts begin to take shape. Jung himself said: "The names are of little use by themselves." He called his work not a theory or method, but "a circumambulation of unknown factors" that constantly required new definitions and perspectives. It's a "metapsychology" in that it's a fiction in which we invent vocabulary to speak about the psyche as an aid to comprehension. Jung's model doesn't represent concrete reality but is rather a metaphor for it, according to Anthony Stevens: "The only way in which we can know the psyche is by living it. All else is inference."

affects us." Bringing that unknown to the fore through the use of active imagination is the role of this transcendent function.

A "function" for Jung is "a certain form of psychic activity that remains theoretically the same under varying circumstances." The kind of activity specified by the "transcendent" function is the reconciliation of polarities (matter/spirit, good/evil, male/female, etc.) within the psyche.[44] It is the activity by which the conscious awareness of the ego, the conscious "I," encounters the unconscious energies and through the creative capacities of the unconscious, channels (primarily through symbols) the energy of that confrontation into a common direction, one that leads to an "organic transition" from a lower attitude to a higher one (hence "transcendent"). It is based on the conviction that the psyche is a homeostatic system that strives perpetually to achieve a balance between opposing tendencies while also actively seeking its own individuation.[45] This "transcendent" activity, then, consists of a growing awareness of unconscious material which, as it become integrated into the ego, allows the true Self to emerge.[46] The transcendent function is the psyche's means of evolution and an aspect of its self-regulation. It is manifested symbolically and is experienced as a new attitude towards oneself and towards life.

The transcendent function of the psyche is one that is primarily mediated by an analyst who helps bring the conscious and

---

[44] The psyche is the totality of all psychological processes, both conscious and unconscious.

[45] "For Jung, individuation is an unending process of differentiation and integration that repeats itself on every-higher planes. The analytical capacities of the conscious mind allow us to distinguish, develop, and contrast the individual components of the psyche. The creative forces of the unconscious, on the other hand, provide symbols that bring these one-sided, opposing elements together again, on a higher level. These symbols direct the energy created by the temporarily incapacitating dividednesss of theses and antithesis into a common channel, and life flows on again, renewed and transformed (Jung, 1921, p.480)." (Wulff)

[46] Both "ego" and "Self" are loaded words. The ego resides on the level of the conscious, and consists of inherited character constituents, while the Self is an a priori archetype of wholeness / integration which is the regulating center of the psyche, "a transpersonal power that transcends the ego." (Sharp: Jung Lexicon)

unconscious together.[47] Often it is the emotional energy of some neurosis (a psychological crisis due to internal disunity among emotional forces / images) that activates this function, providing its "energy" and emotional momentum. Its dynamics are based on the evaluation of self-generated unconscious content which comes from dream-images (little energy tension) or, better yet, free fantasy (more energy tension). This unconscious material, however derived, forms one pole of the transcendent function, and has to be given some form and meaning before it can be brought into confrontation with the ego. Creative formulation and understanding will both be at work. After this, the ego takes the lead (while still allowing the unconscious to have its say), encountering the unconscious content and coming to terms with it. The energy generated by the tension of this confrontation creates a third essence. "From the activity of the unconscious there now emerges a new content, constellated by thesis and antithesis in equal measure and standing in a compensatory relation to both. It thus forms the middle ground on which the opposites can be united." (Jung)[48]

Such a "constellation" is usually expressed in symbols that reunite conflicting tendencies irreconcilable at the conscious level. True symbols carry the content of such reconciliation, perpetually calling for deeper personal engagement. True symbols, for Jung, are "an expression of an intuitive idea that cannot yet be formulated in any other or better way," "bridges thrown out towards an unseen shore," and "the intimation of a meaning beyond the level of our present powers of comprehension." In this symbolic approach to the psyche, Jung makes "his special contribution to depth psychology." (Ulanov) It's an approach that is commensurate with the

---

[47] The conscious refers to psychic contents of the ego, while the unconscious is the totality of all psychic phenomena that lack the quality of consciousness, i.e., that are not conscious. The unconscious compensates for the limitations of conscious attitudes, presenting to consciousness contents necessary for psychological health (balance) through dreams, impulses, etc. It is not superior to consciousness and must always be mediated by the ego.

[48] Anthony Stevens: "...[O]ne has to become aware of both poles of every conflict and endure, in full consciousness, the tension created between them; then, some radical shift occurs which leads to their transcendence. This comes about through the power of the unconscious to create a new symbolical synthesis out of the conflicting propensities."

intangible quality of the psyche, making the unconscious accessible, yet meeting it in terms of itself alone. To get to the nonrational, nonrational modes of apprehension must be used. And the transcendent function is one of these nonrational modes. Jung came to see that we can never solve life's most crucial problems, but that we can with patience transcend them by becoming aware of both poles of every conflict, enduring in full consciousness the tension created between them, and then engaging the new symbolic synthesis that emerges from the unconscious.

The result of this process is that consciousness is put in deeper touch with the rest of the psyche, enriching a person in his/her relationships with others and making him/her feel more fully in touch with life. This experience of reconciliation also brings with it "a sense of being guided by and related to the source and power of being. It is this kind of experience that is felt as religious. This native capacity of the psyche to produce symbols that have this reconciling effect and stirring presence is what Jung calls the religious function."[49] (Ulanov)

Religion for Jung is a necessary psychological function, "an instinctive attitude . . . [whose] purpose is to maintain the psychic balance."[50] While difficult personal decisions are "rendered safe by suitable measures of a religious nature [offerings, blessings, rites, etc.]," the attitude that defines religion comes about when individuals consciously experience the "numinous." Faith is a secondary phenomenon to an experience of the numinous (such as that of the transcendent function) that first instilled trust and loyalty in us. When the dynamic factors in the powerful, dangerous, helpful, grand, beautiful, and meaningful are carefully considered and observed (i.e., all those things that seize us, for whom we always seem its victim rather than its creator), individuals assume that those dynamic factors or powers exist apart from themselves. Jung, however, holds that their immediate source are the archetypes in the

---

[49] Recall that "function" refers to a "psychic activity." Jung speaks of religious phenomena as distinctive psychological realities.

[50] Unless otherwise noted, all quotations are from Jung's works.

collective unconscious.[51] These archetypes are instinctual ideational forms according to which human knowledge is shaped.[52] They are like the "inner release mechanism" which in animals becomes active with appropriate stimuli, bringing about a specific pattern of behavior such as nest-building. Their manifestation in religious contexts through symbolic means constitute the religious function. As long as one interprets religious ideas symbolically, appropriations are possible that neither conflict with knowledge nor impair the meaning of those ideas. But if allowed to become either a substitute for inner experience or literally accepted creeds, such ideas and symbols come "into insufferable conflict with [other] knowledge" and help us to escape from the responsibility of personal individuation. Conversely, the more of cultural and personal myth we are capable of making conscious through religious symbolism, the more of life and the unconscious we are able to integrate.

If I read Jung correctly, a person of faith is one who has begun this journey of individuation, this process of attaining ever more insightful incorporation's of unconscious content. The operative dynamics of religious experience (the numinous, symbols, rites, etc.) provide a way whereby archetypal psychic material becomes accessible, drawing the person towards ever greater integration of the conscious and the unconscious, and thus bringing to realization the authentic Self (the most important archetype and the most difficult to understand). This Self represents the harmony and balance of the various opposing qualities that constitute the psyche, and becomes symbolized in anything that the ego takes as a greater totality than itself (mandala, animals, Holy Grail, etc.). Jung would hold that the self archetype produces the same symbolism that has always expressed some sort of deity; it's impossible to distinguish between a

---

[51] The "collective unconscious" is distinct from the personal unconscious. It's a structural layer of the human psyche that contains inherited elements which, some say, derive from "common neurons" situated in the phylogenetically ancient cerebral regions of the midbrain and brainstem.

[52] Jung: "Human knowledge consists essentially in the constant adaptation of the primordial patterns of ideas that were given to us a priori." He likens these primordial patterns to the infra-red part of a spectrum, present yet invisible and effective. Archetypes are not representable in themselves, but their effects are discernible in archetypal images and motifs (The Great Mother, The Wise Old Man, etc.)

symbol of the self and a God image. Jung concludes that the self is the "God within us." For the person of faith, God (and Christ, Yahweh, Shiva, etc.) is representative of the self, and the task of individuation is to integrate the ego and the unconscious into awareness / realization of that self.

To many, Freud is seen as religion's foe and Jung is seen as religion's friend. Others, however, have suggested that Jung misrepresents the essential spirit and truth of religious traditions, denying to metaphysics and theology their self-definition. These note that Jung stepped out of the bounds of psychology in studying religious symbolism, maintaining that psychology and religion are not differentiated. His "empirical" psychology takes from religion only what confirms and illustrates his psychology. He is interested in religion primarily for its therapeutic value and substitutes psychological dogmas for the ecclesiastical ones that he dismisses. His identification of the numinous with religion, as one example, is contradicted both by numinous experiences outside of religious contexts (Cf. Jung's own studies of magic, art, poetry, neurosis, psychosis, etc.) and by religious experiences that are not numinous (Cf. religious biographies, committed faith, the mystic's "naked will," etc.). Martin Buber entered into direct conflict with Jung, finding the psychology of individuation and Yahwistic faith diametrically opposed orientations of the human spirit.[53] And there's a decidedly aristocratic element in Jung's individualism, emphasizing as it does a "higher way" for the privileged few. Among these general criticisms of Jung's psychology, there are a few specific ones worthy of note.

Ann Ulanov is generally sympathetic to Jung, but finds that while he opposes it, he may be contributing to the modern reduction of the nonrational to blind, uncomprehending faith "by narrowly interpreting it [faith] as an acceptance of something on the authority of tradition rather than on the authority of personal experience, or as a gift of grace in which truth is accepted but not really understood." On the opposite front, Ulanov defends Jung against feminist critics who find Jung sexist because he characterizes stereotypes

---

[53] There is no I-Thou relationship in Jung's psychology. The Self revolves around itself in isolation. "Jung is recommending an essentially private religiosity without institutional or communal membership." (Rieff) Jung's individuation overlooks any essential role for personal relations in attaining integration.

of gender as permanently written into human nature. This criticism, she holds, is based on a confusion between archetypes and the images employed by archetypes, and she goes on to show that Jungian psychology can enhance feminism by highlighting the exclusion of the feminine from religious symbolism and pointing out the individual / collective ills that have resulted. On the religious front, Jung holds that the Christ symbol is of great psychological importance because it is one of the most highly differentiated and developed symbols of the self. But Jung's viewpoint is here decidedly different from that of theology. "Jung's view of Christ is not the same as that of theology. For psychology, Christ points to the self; for theology, the self points to Christ."

Victor White, whose book's preface was written by Jung, urges a definition of religion that is more broad and balanced than Jung's. Where Jung speaks of "God" and "Christ" and "Yahweh" as human complexes[54] and representations, White points to the fact that persons of faith hold that God is nothing finite at all, although God is manifested through images and psychological processes. "God" is not the name of a class of somethings, like minerals, etc. Since the task of psychologists is that of helping us distinguish our images from reality, it's ironic that the same task cannot be accomplished in this case. "To the psychologist as such, there is no God independent of the imago or the complex." Therefore, the possibility of forming an adult, rational, voluntary relationship with God is a priori excluded. Even as phenomena, the "psychological fact is that to their respective devotees it is the differences rather than the similarities [between e.g. Yahweh and Shiva] which are of paramount importance . . . " Religion and psychology are inevitably divergent viewpoints. White concludes that the best approach is not to attack Jung's views but to meet the same facts with other relevant ones that the Jungians seem to have disregarded or minimized, and so to encounter basic human needs.

James Loder's most pointed critique addresses Jung's contention that Christ symbolizes the centered structure, the Self, by which the

---

[54] A complex is an emotionally charged group of ideas or images, a feeling-toned idea that over the years accumulates over certain archetypes such as "mother" or "father. "They are the building blocks of the psyche. Understanding their functioning within one's psychic life minimizes their negative unconscious effects.

personality is individuated. Jung's understanding of Christ is not sufficient because it implicitly confuses the order of being and knowing. " . . . [I]n Jung's position the symbol 'Jesus Christ' is one way of knowing one's self, but Christ's understanding makes Christ the revelation of being-itself. . . . Here it is all important that the truth not get confused with a structure for knowing it. If one is to understand Christ at all, Jung's order of being and knowing must be reversed." While the internal structure of the personality may indeed undergo radical decentering, the master image need not be one that combines existential opposites nor be one whose goal is the balanced self. " . . . [I]f Christ is a symbol of the self, then self structures will define Christ [Jung], but if the self is a symbol of Christ, then Christ will define the nature of the self. If the latter pertains, it will be marked not by anything resembling static balance, but by sacrificial love, the form that transformation takes in Christ."[55] Loder suggests that psychic structures that unite extreme opposites are fundamental to the imaginative vision of Jesus Christ, who himself unites God and humanity, etc. "However, Christ's being far exceeds any analysis of opposites because . . . it is Presence, personal and transfiguring the dark face of sheer balance . . . that makes the [Christian] difference."

Religious education can learn several things from all of this about its own exercise:

1) Psychological concerns are more readily considered than specifically religious ones by the majority of people today. They provide ways of considering the interior dimensions of human life and, as such, may begin the process of reflecting on religious concerns. Those religious concerns, however, must become central.

---

[55] Voicing echoes that I picked up in other critics, Loder writes that "To arrest transformation, making the balanced self its goal, is to abort the process in a kind of gnostic salvation that tends to create a cultic group of elite people possessed of this particular sort of wholeness. ..[T]he development of the ego may be relativized and recentered around a deeper psychic order. However, it does not meet the issue of Christ as Mediator in his terms. Otherwise it would have to take seriously his initiative, his revealed mediation, and his destiny, not only for the individual but for his World, the Kingdom of God."

2) The implicit impact of psychological assumptions in today's society is pervasive, especially vis-a-vis religious convictions. These assumptions must be recognized and addressed if they are to be challenged by Christian convictions.

3) Jung's psychology might provide insights for understanding human experience and intentional modes for compassionately dealing with experienced suffering, but it's a limited vehicle for encountering God, who will not be defined by such analysis.

4) Jung's perspective on symbolism and its psychological economy may be helpful. But his convictions regarding the nature and role of archetypes will have to be called into question if they are to be part of a Christian conversation.

5) Following James Loder, from the standpoint of Christian conviction, we can trust ourselves to step out of ourselves into a relationship with the Holy, because Christ is there; "we will be greeted not by empty silence but relief, joy, and the recognition that he is there." Christ is not a symbol, then or now; God is a living Presence.

6) Since religion and psychology are both concerned with interior movements of the human person, great care needs to be given that, on the one hand, religious concerns don't activate negative psychological movements and that, on the other hand, psychological concerns don't limit religious movements.

7) Religious education may correlate appropriate elements of psychology to faith while critically assessing their assumptions and goals.

Jung recognized that he was writing a highly personal statement when he set out to extrapolate his early reflections of personal psychological experiences. "He was writing, as it were, his own personal myth." (Wulff) After reading both his own words and those of others who critique him, I'm fascinated by his interpretive framework but also wary of it. It's as appealing as a box of candy, and perhaps as little satisfying in large quantities. Despite Jung's many caveats concerning the truth of his reflections (e.g., "I stand for no doctrine, but describe facts and put forth certain views which I hold worthy of discussion."), it is those reflections alone that are the final measure of his convictions. Following my earlier analogy, this house that he has built is certainly Jung's own , but I'm not sure if I could live within it. It doesn't seem to have any windows.

<u>WORKS READ & CITED</u>

<u>Books:</u>

Gorman, Margaret, ed. *Psychology and Religion: A Reader.* New York, NY: Paulist Press, 1985.

Jung, Carl. "The Undiscovered Self (Present and Future)." Trans. R.F.C. Hull. *Civilization in Transition.* Ed. Herbert Read, Michael Fordham and Gerhard Adler. 2nd ed. 20 vols. The Collected Works of C.G. Jung. New York, NY: Bollinger Foundation, 1964. 10: 245-308.

Jung, Carl. "On the Relation of Analytical Psychology to Poetry." and "Psychology and Literature." Trans. R.F.C. Hull. *The Spirit in Man, Art, and Literature.* Ed. Herbert Read, Michael Fordham and Gerhard Adler. 1st ed. 20 vols. The Collected Works of C.G. Jung. New York, NY: Bollinger Foundation, 1966. 15: 65-108.

Jung, Carl. "The Transcendent Function." Trans. R.F.C. Hull. *The Structure and Dynamics of the Psyche.* Ed. Herbert Read, Michael Fordham and Gerhard Adler. 1st ed. 20 vols. The Collected Works of C.G. Jung. Princeton, NJ: Princeton University Press, 1969. 8: 67-91.

Loder, James E. *The Transforming Moment: Understanding Convictional Experiences.* San Francisco: Harper & Row, 1981.

Stevens, Anthony. *On Jung.* New York, NY: Routledge, 1990. (Part I - Jung's Psychology)

Ulanov, Ann Belford. *The Feminine in Jungian Psychology and in Christian Theology.* Evanston, IL: Northwestern University Press, 1971. (Part I - Jung and the Psyche; Part II - Religion and the Psyche)

White, Victor. *Soul and Psyche: An Enquiry into the Relationship of Psychotherapy and Religion.* New York: Harper & Brothers, 1960. (Ch. 3 - The Jungian Approach to Religion)

Wulff, David. *Psychology of Religion: Classic and Contemporary Views.* New York, NY: Wiley, 1990. (Ch. 9 – C.G. Jung and the Analytical Tradition)

Constitutive Elements for Catholic Identity

Perhaps because the term "catholic" is literally translated as "universal," understandings of what the word means and how it applies to the church are widely held. The Church of England bristles at the notion that it is not catholic, and likewise the Orthodox and many Protestant denominations firmly hold that they are authentically catholic, albeit that each has its own nuanced interpretation of the term. Trying to elucidate the constitutive elements of Catholic identity involves an engagement of two distinct aspects of the word "catholic." The first concerns the generic meaning of the word and hearkens back to Ignatius of Antioch's first use of the term to describe the church's universal identity under wide-scale persecution. The second concerns the particular application of the word to those whose faith is united by convictions, basic operative commitments, practices, and social structure identified with the Roman Catholic Church. While the generic meaning and application of "catholic" is by no means unimportant, the scope of this essay will focus primarily on its meaning in terms of the Roman Catholic Church (hereafter, **C**atholic).

A number of authors have formulated interpretive frameworks for understanding the distinctive characteristics of Catholicism. It seems that the need to do so has become more evident in the modern world, with its tendency to reduce everything to certain kinds of particulars, than it might have been in the past.[56] Also, today's focus on the whole issue of identity, perhaps engendered by psychological consciousness, pervasive pluralism, and "the turn to the subject," has made the need for an effort to elucidate the distinctive nature of Catholicism all the more necessary and worthwhile. Such an effort will remain true to the catholic nature of the church by striving to engage the predominant needs and interests of modernity with the fullness of the Catholic church's reality. Three authors

---

[56] Up until the Reformation, the need to distinguish the Catholic church from the catholic church was not a priority. After the 1056 split from Orthodoxy, the Catholic church was that church which was not Orthodox. But after the Reformation, so many individual churches arose that the need for differentiation became more necessary as well; the thrust of faith's practice now concentrated on "We're different from..."

who have contributed to a contemporary understanding of what it means to be Catholic are Langdon Gilkey, Richard McBrien, and Avery Dulles.

Langdon Gilkey speaks of four traits that he sees as peculiarly Catholic, although my reading of him shows that he's really offering five traits. These traits are Catholicism's central attributes and sources of strength.

1) The unity and substantiality of the people as one community covering many nations, cultures, races, etc. This is authentically biblical and perhaps the most precious inheritance.

2) The reality, importance, and weight of tradition and history in the Catholic church's formation. This is reflected in her religious truths, religious experience, and general human wisdom.

3) A grace of *caritas* in her life and mission manifested in a tolerance and acceptance of the estranged, an acceptance of the other; making room for the imperfect aspects. Justice is always tempered by mercy.

4) A sacramental sense of life, of the living presence of God. God's presence and grace are mediated over the entire course of ordinary human life through concrete symbols.

5) A drive and insistence that the divine mystery "be insofar as possible penetrated, defended, and explicated by the most acute rational reflection."

Each of these creative principles has been embodied within traditional forms that are now made problematic by modernity, according to Gilkey. Catholicism's task today is to move from the supernaturalistic, absolutist, and extrinsic forms of her past life, and reinterpret both our common Christian symbols and their Catholic forms in terms that are nonsupernaturalistic so that the transcendent core upholding her life will continue to be a means of grace to our time.[57]

---

[57] Tom Groome has taken this schema and applied it to pedagogy. He characterizes the Catholic church as being distinctive in terms of sacramentality (God calls and we respond through the ordinary), anthropology (grace works through

Richard McBrien notes that on one level, only the Petrine doctrine sets the Catholic church apart from all other churches. On a deeper level, it is the precise configuration of certain characteristics that is distinctive to the Catholic church. And on a deeper level still, "Catholicism is characterized by a *radical openness to all truth and to every value. It is comprehensive* and *all-embracing* toward the totality of Christian experience and tradition, in all the theological, doctrinal, spiritual, liturgical, canonical, institutional, and social richness and diversity of that experience and tradition."[58] Philosophically, Catholicism integrates its theological and doctrinal orientations with a critical Christian realism that rejects both naive realism and idealism, reaching beyond what seems to be and taking historicity into account in the use and interpretation of ideas and principles. Theologically, the principle of sacramentality (the encounter with God as a mediated but real experience within a communal context) is most central and most characteristic of Catholicism. Generally speaking, " . . . there is within Catholicism a configuration of values which enjoy a normative character in discerning the Christian tradition as a whole." These include a sense of sacramentality, the principle of mediation, a sense of communion, a drive toward rationality, a critical realism, a respect for history / tradition / continuity, a conviction that we can have radical notions of sin and more radical grace, a high regard for authority / order and conscience / freedom, and a fundamental openness to all truth and to every value.

Avery Dulles affirms that it's impossible to analyze catholicity "without speaking of other traditional attributes of the Church: unity, holiness, and apostolicity." When we look at the Catholic center, we find a field of tension that endures, a continual balance that

---

nature; balance between self-sufficiency and dependency), community (we are most ourselves when in right relationship), Story and Vision (Christian faith over time and towards the future), and rationality (reason and revelation are mutually advantageous).

[58] This is manifested most directly its *both/and* rather than an *either/or* approach: graced nature, reason illuminated by faith, law inspired by Gospel, normative tradition within Scripture, faith from works and works expressing faith, authority in the service of freedom, present in continuity with the past, unity in diversity, etc.

demands spiritual strength.[59] "Catholicity" is an analogous rather than a univocal term; there is no precise definition for it. It's predicated of particular realities and implies a unitive relationship among diverse things, suggesting an organic whole that turns to a center to assure unity. Far from excluding differences, catholicity demands them, uniting opposites that seem incompatible; catholicity is "reconciled diversity." Catholicity designates a fullness of reality and life, especially divine life, that is actively communicating itself. The institutional / sacramental structure that mediates the truth and grace of Christ in the Church is necessary to sustain the various dimensions of catholicity. Episcopacy is how the Church actualizes its own essence as an organically structured whole and is part of her essence.[60]

Van Beeck states that "Vatican II . . . inaugurated a significant rearrangement of the themes and emphases of the Catholic faith and identity experience." After Vatican II, there was a lack of differentiation between the "distinguishing marks" that identified Catholic experience (is fish on Friday the same as Mass on Sunday?). An authentic renewal of the Catholic church "must go back to the original and abiding realization that Christ is alive and present in the Spirit." Such renewal engenders a new sense of identity and a new style of openness in a global church where worship and witness together shape the touchstones of faith. Restoring the traditional distinction between a doctrine's certainty and its rank in the hierarchy of truths, Vatican II affirmed the understanding that faith is best secured by insight into its structure. While not explicitly stating the core of the Christian faith, the council did make reference to the Trinity and the Incarnation in the article following the one on the hierarchy of truths; truths that "vary in their relation to the foundation of the Christian faith." (Decree on Ecumenism, n. 11) It is to within this

---

[59] Dulles: "The Catholic insistence on mediation as against false mysticism, on communion as against individualism, and on plenitude as against sectarianism or reductionism, must be a matter of principle."

[60] Dulles: "Rome is the centre, the principle of unity; Catholic is the periphery, the principle of diversity. There can be no centre without a circumference, no circumference without a centre ... Roman primacy and Catholic communion...are dialectical opposites which exist and flourish in mutual relatedness."

context that I now turn to outlining a "structure" permeating the constitutive elements of Catholic identity.[61]

My "systematic" will be to take the perspective of the religious educator (primarily of adolescents, but by extrapolation of others too): If we are to educate people for Catholic identity, what are the aspects that are essential? Among the hierarchy of truths, which of those truths are most accessible and vital for engaging the faith of students? And how might one structure them so that they mediate the reality that they represent?

Erickson has confirmed that the issue of identity is the foremost task and challenge of the adolescent, focusing - epigenetically - concerns that are spread throughout the span of life.[62] Adolescents are primarily concerned with what it means to be a person, both generally speaking and specifically applied to themselves. "Whom do I say that I am." Catholic identity, I propose, speaks most authentically to that concern.

Catholicism strives to remain faithful to Christianity's commitment to the personal nature of God's reality. The most adequate way to indicate, as created humans, the nature of God (both God's mysterious, pervasive presence within our horizon and God's fullness in history through Christ and the Holy Spirit) is to speak of God as Person. "To speak of God as mystery is another way of saying that God is 'personal.'" (Catherine LaCugna) The most secure basis for Christian identity is the person of Christ.[63] As David Tracy has written, we should begin with an analysis of God's self-revelation in Jesus Christ, not the nature of God and his attributes, if we want to be faithful to the *Christian* understanding of God. It is the person of God, the person of Jesus Christ, and the person of the Holy

---

[61] It will be good to keep in mind Dulles' *caveat*: "Catholics must be on guard against defining the Church solely in terms of what is distinctive to Catholicism. Catholicism, taken in a 'Catholicist' sense, could be the enemy of catholicity."

[62] One might ask if it is possible to similarly delineate "Catholic identity" concerns over the span of one's life that epigenetically predominate during particular life stages. But that's not the foremost task here.

[63] Van Beeck: "neither the tradition of the Church's doctrine, worship, and discipline, nor the urgency of the imitation of Christ in the concerns of actual life provide, in and of themselves, a secure basis for Christian identity; only the *person* of Christ does."

Spirit who will impact the student most profoundly, since the student is most radically concerned with what it means to be a person and is searching for models of personhood. Catholicism, insofar as it mediates characteristics of God's personal knowledge and love for each human person, shapes Catholic identity by providing both the context and the stepping-stones for the formation of individual integrity as truly sons and daughters of God.

Students engage, are shaped by, and share in the life of Catholicism through both relational encounter (worship), behavior (conduct), and reflection (creed).

<u>Worship</u>: "The heart of Christianity is not the redemption of humanity . . . . The essence of the Christian faith is humanity's worshipful *encounter with the living God*." (Van Beeck) Students long for the kind of touch encountered in worship yet neither experience it nor are able to engender it in themselves in any fulfilling way. They are fascinated with their growing capacity to know and love, yet are most blown away by the apparent incapacity to integrate the two - to match what they know (or think they know; i.e., mostly socially formed knowledge) with what they experience as love (or think they experience as love; i.e., mostly ambivalent feelings and emotions). Catholicism may introduce them, through both its sacramental consciousness and its sacramental life, to the ways in which the encounter with God is accessible and forms the human person into the authentic human person.[64] The *both/and* nature of Catholicism's continual spiritual tension as experienced throughout history and today models the kinds of tensions that make up the human person. These cannot be, and should not be, avoided but should rather be engaged and brought to unity in the person of Christ and the living reality of his presence in the Holy Spirit. Such sacramental consciousness and formation is accomplished through specifically Catholic practices such as participation in the sacraments (especially those most immediately of interest: Sunday Mass and

---

[64] McBrien: "To be Catholic is, before all else, to be human....For the Christian, the ultimate dimension of human experience is a triune God: a God who creates and sustains us, a God who draws near to us and identifies with out historical condition, and a God who empowers us to live according to the vocation to which we have been called. More specifically, the God of Christians is the God of Jesus Christ."

Confirmation) and peripheral religious practices (classroom prayer; intercession of Mary and the Saints; participation in parish life), and is also accomplished through a pervasive attitude which looks beyond apparent realities to their ground and sustenance. This latter aspect is manifest in ways whereby reverence is displayed in approaching school subjects, discipline, and organization; in paying regular attention to both "the bigger picture" and "the deeper picture" of our concerns.[65]

<u>Conduct</u>: Students are always asking questions - mostly about behavior of one type or another. Students are also always making observations - mostly about behavior of one type or another. Their personal identity becomes shaped as these questions and observations about behavior become integrated with their own behavior. Their most difficult task often consists in differentiating how they behave from how others behave, being tugged both by the desire to fit in and by the desire to become themselves. Catholicism may contribute to their identity by presenting both a sounding-board and a model. Catholic identity, while often challenged, is rarely accused of being ambiguous (at least on the level of general religious experience). Its awareness of both the human person's teleology and the human person's weaknesses provide a forum wherein the integration of behavior and belief that identifies ethics has a chance to develop. Gilkey's comments about Catholicism's *caritas* highlight the opportunity Catholicism has of being the context within which students may come to practice and enrich their capacities for authentically human behavior. Students look to something (anything!) definite and apparently unchanging for guidance, despite their protestations to the contrary (in itself an indication of the opposite concern). Catholic ethics, as manifested both in particular ethical situations within schools (interpersonal and structural) and in specific ethical considerations in classes (and NOT only religion classes), provides ways in which the students' personal conduct might be shaped along catholic and Catholic lives.

---

[65] Catholicism always asks how God is made manifest (the bigger picture) and how the individual person is respected and called forth (the deeper picture). In school situations, I suspect that the latter perspective will often be the more accessible entry-point to the student's personal life.

<u>Creed</u>: Schools are places where reflection on truth is intentionally pursued; where books, discussion, and curriculum are actively engaged. Persons stretch their intellectual horizons even as their emotional horizons seem to be gaining the upper hand. Knowledge begins to be more than something memorized, making a bloody entrance (Dante?) and appearing invincible once attained. Formal and informal knowledge is shared about subject matter, things, and people (people-knowledge is most coveted and remembered). Personal identity is formed as all this knowledge becomes differentiated and integrated according to particular categories that arise out of outside structures (science, society, culture) or inside structures (emotional needs, personal convictions, individual proclivities). Catholic identity may be formed insofar as Catholicism's convictions regarding reason & faith, nature and revelation, etc. are introduced and integrated into that process. While sacramental life forms a person's religious sensibilities (for lack of a better term), an intellectual life informed by Catholic convictions shapes a person's intellectual Catholic sensibilities. Reflection need not be theological reflection, but it should be like it.[66] Inasmuch as the characteristic concerns of Catholicism are involved in all intellectual aspects of school life, Catholic identity has a chance of shaping the reflections of those who embody the school.

Specifically, distinctive characteristics of Catholicism, then, are manifest in schools to the extent to which Catholicism's traditional concerns are integrated into its life. Within the hierarchy of truths, in terms of education, I would break it down as follows:

1) God is personally engaged with the world, both as Ground and Presence, and as historically mediated through Jesus Christ and the Holy Spirit.

2) The church mediates and bears responsibility for carrying forth the reality of God's salvific presence among humanity.

---

[66] Lash: "Serious theological reflection is always hard work, and its outcome fragmentary, tentative, and (often) quite technical in its quest for appropriate imaginative and conceptual accuracy, not because *God* is complicated, but because we are - and so is the world in which we live."

3) Human persons, by participating in the life of the church, discover and uncover their deepest longings as human persons, finding fulfillment in their relationship with God.

4) Catholic schools participate in this dynamic to the extent that they embody, incorporate, and integrate concerns that are in continuity with Catholic sensibilities and concerns. Their concentration on personal identity and formation is a challenge and a distinctive opportunity for forming personal Catholic identity insofar as Catholic concerns shape the relational encounters, behavior, and reflection of the persons who make up the school.

   - Relational encounters: recognizing the depths and integrity of personhood, both of others and of oneself; participation in the sacraments and in a sacramental consciousness / appreciation of symbol / cultivation of wonder; learning to pray as individuals; becoming responsible for others.

   - Behavior: becoming aware of the ethical demands that undergird Church law; discovering correlations between contemporary / immediate ethical concerns and historical church concerns; discovering in Mary and the saints models of authentic human fulfillment.

   - Reflection: not letting dogma of any kind "become the most exalted form of invulnerability against revelation [of any kind]." (Buber); discovering both the possibilities and limitations of language, "the house of being" (Heidegger); applying new categories to classic Church concerns while remaining committed to those concerns; relating what is known to what is loved (e.g., "There are aspects of understanding which are the fruit, and not the precondition, of love." - Lash).

God's personhood defines what it means to love, to do, and to know. That personhood is made manifest in Jesus Christ and in the Catholic church through the Holy Spirit. If relational love is God's highest ontological category (Walter Kasper), then the world of relationships is where God is to be encountered. The most constitutive element of Catholic identity is finally a personal reality: the living Spirit of Christ. As such, it shares in the nature of all persons who "become, in their measure, 'mysterious,' not insofar as we *fail* to understand them, but rather in so far as, in lovingly relating to them, we succeed in doing so." (Lash) Through such a loving relationship to the mystery of the Church, the Body of Christ, Catholic identity will best emerge, increase, and flourish.

WORKS READ & CITED

<u>Books</u>:

Dulles, Avery. *The Catholicity of the Church*. New York, NY: Oxford University Press, 1989.

Gilkey, Langdon. *Catholicism Confronts Modernity: A Protestant View*. New York, NY: Seabury Press, 1975.

Lash, Nicholas. *Easter in Ordinary*. Charlottesville, VA: University Press of Virginia, 1988.

McBrien, Richard P. *Catholicism*. San Francisco, CA: Harper & Row, 1981. 1169-86. (Ch. 30 - Catholicism: A Synthesis.)

Schussler-Fiorenza, Francis, and John P. Galvin, ed. *Systematic Theology: Roman Catholic Perspectives*. Minneapolis, MN: Fortress Press, 1991.

Van Beeck, Frans Josef. *Catholic Identity After Vatican II*. Chicago, IL: Loyola University Press, 1985.

Van Beeck, Frans Josef. *God Encountered: A Contemporary Catholic Systematic Theology*. San Francisco: Harper & Row, 1989.

<u>Essays</u>:

Groome, Thomas H. "Catholic Teachers for Catholic Schools." Boston, MA: Boston College Institute for Religious Education and Pastoral Ministry, 1992.

A SHORT INTRODUCTION
TO DEVELOPMENTAL THEORIES

(Geared for High School Teachers)

<u>Introduction</u>

Do you recall what you were like as a child, as an adolescence, as a young adult, or as a thirty-something? Think a moment about the world-view you had at those times - what you spent your time and energy on, how you faced problems and chose pleasures, where your attention was drawn to and what things influenced your decisions. Would it be fair to say that there are some memories which provoke a smile and others which provoke a silent shaking of the head? Do we not look back with a certain kind of wisdom which recognizes the good and the bad, the helpful and the hurtful, the challenges and the disappointments? What we in fact recognize when we do so, is the reality of our own growth, our own maturation, our own development as persons.

One might beneficially spend time identifying and articulating those elements in our past experience which seem to be important, those that emerge as significant developments, since by such a process we begin to know ourselves more deeply. And knowing ourselves more deeply can only lead us to a deeper understanding of life around us and the possibilities we hold to encounter that life. In a school context, we can certainly recognize the fact that the give-and-take experience among students and teachers is influenced by the degrees to which each has grown and developed. Greater awareness of such developmental aspects will allow for a wiser and more effective sense of involvement. As Charles Shelton writes, "The behavior, life challenges, and developmental issues that adolescents experience necessitate a personally-oriented pastoral approach that recognizes the unique developmental level (and needs) of each adolescent."[1]

---

[1] Shelton, Charles M. <u>Adolescent Spirituality</u>. Chicago: Loyola University Press, 1983, Pg. 23

But such an understanding of developmental levels need not emerge wholly independently, like a tree in the desert, based solely on individual ruminations or personal reflections. We are not alone in our trials and joys, our visions and temptations, our questions and attempted answers. Others have gone before and others will follow. Developmental theory grows out of a common experience of the past and the insights which have emerged based on that experience. This brief essay serves as a short introduction to a few of those insights.

It is not immediately important to know the names of the developmental theorists except insofar as those names are quick references for clusters of ideas among people who know the theories well. For our purposes, their names will be used only as a matter of convenience and reference. If you wish to delve into their ideas in detail, many resources are available. The point here is to see if their insights resonate with your experience. Does what they say make sense when you think about your own life and look at the lives of those around you? If they do, then they may be a guide, their ideas will show us well-worn paths from which we can view the world of growth with confidence and reasonable clarity. At the least, their thoughts will give us the basis from which to wander off into our own reflections, if such is our need. At best, their models will articulate our experience and empower our appropriation of that experience. The ideas are there for our benefit; we don't have to squeeze ourselves into the ideas.

The spectrum of human experience is vast and has many facets. Likewise, the possible areas of developmental growth are widely divergent, ranging from biology to spirituality. And many of them overlap and interrelate. The present concern is general non-biological development and growth[2], especially those domains which

---

[2] Although even biology offers many insights into the structure of our general development. For example, we retain early biological (and non-biological?) characteristics into adulthood because of a significant slowdown of physical development rates. "Primates are slow developers among mammals, but we have accentuated the trend to a degree matched by no other mammal. The morphological [i.e., form and structure] features of eternal youth have served us well. Our enlarged brain is, at least in part, a result of extending rapid prenatal growth rates to later ages. (In all mammals, the brain grows rapidly in utero but often very

effect educational pedagogy within a religious setting. Within those parameters, human beings may be understood as individuals who develop cognitively, morally, spiritually, psychologically, and socially. These aspects of a person may each be studied separately while recognizing that they, in fact, form an integrated and coherent whole. [3] Our concentration on any one dimension of personal growth is done solely to facilitate a more focused understanding. Ultimately, as will become evident, developmental growth proceeds among various personal dimensions in parallel fashion.

Jean Piaget's work has concentrated on the cognitive dimension; Lawrence Kohlberg's studies have examined the moral dimension; James Fowler has looked at the spiritual or faith dimension; Erik Erikson has outlined the psychological dimension; and Robert Selman has offered some patterns regarding social dimensions of development. An overview of these models will provide a framework for understanding both the complexity of human development and the tendencies which identify common aspects of our experience (something which will be termed as "stages"). The object is to begin to see some consistency and commonality among the various paradigms of development.

These are leisurely strolls along forest paths. Notice the scenery and the places where the paths merge together. You may find yourself growing in appreciation and familiarity as you move more

---

little after birth. We have extended this fetal phase into postnatal life.) But the changes in timing themselves have been just as important. We are preeminently learning animals, and our extended childhood permits the transference of culture by education. Many animals display flexibility and play in childhood, but follow rigidly programmed patterns as adults. [Konrad] Lorenz writes, in ... ['Entirety and part in animal and human society', 1950] 'The characteristic which is so vital for the human peculiarity of the true man - that of always remaining in a state of development - is quite certainly a gift which we owe to the neotenous nature of mankind [i.e., the retention of early characteristics into adulthood].'" Gould, Stephen Jay. <u>The Panda's Thumb</u>. New York: W.W. Norton, 1982. Pg. 106-107

[3] This observation is also noticed in studies such as that done by Virginia Axline in <u>Dibs In Search of Self.</u> (Ballantine Books, 1964) "...the complexity of human motivation and behavior is demonstrated over and over again. There is no single isolated experience or feeling that triggers reaction patterns. There is always an accumulation of experiences intertwined with highly personal emotions, goals, values, that motivate the person and that determine his reaction." Pg. 91

deeply into the world of human experience and growth. [4]

Cognitive Development - Jean Piaget

> "Every time we teach a child something, we keep
> him from reinventing it. On the other hand, every
> time a child discovers it for himself, it remains with
> him for the rest of his life. "[5]

Jean Piaget formulated a theory of cognitive growth based on extensive research with small groups of children, concentrating not so much on the correctness of given answers as on the reasons behind those answers. Piaget held that structural changes which move towards an equilibrium between various factors of cognitive operations are a function of development. He stipulated a series of qualitative changes in thought processes called "stages" which were both universal, increasingly complex, sequential and invariant.[6] Biological organic growth provided a model of organization (structuring processes) and adaptation (balancing assimilation and accommodation) which appeared equally applicable to cognitive growth. With such a model, structures of memory and perception are the basis for a dynamic system whereby new information is "digested" into continuously deeper and more complex levels of acquired meaning and future potential for acquiring meaning. Here, too, as biological functions are inseparable in fact, so also are cognitive dimensions an integrated and interdependent whole.

Piaget identified four distinct stages, or clusters of common experience, in the development of cognitive capacities. For this overview of developmental theory, the age-ranges for each stage will be

---

[4] The two major resources will be Muus, Rolf E. <u>Theories of Adolescence</u>. Random House, 1988 and Charles Shelton's book cited above.

[5] A frequently quoted phrase from Piaget. Muus, op.cit. Pg. 179

[6] "The order of succession of these stages has been shown to be extremely regular and comparable to the stages of an embryogenesis. The speed of development may vary from one individual to another and also from one social environment to another...but this does not change the order of succession of the stages through which they pass." Piaget, Jean., "Intellectual evolution from adolescence to adulthood." In R.E. Muus, ed. <u>Adolescent Behavior and Society: A Book of Readings.</u> New York: Random House, 1980. Pg. 70 - 71

left out so that you might match each description with your experience of others and of yourself without adding age factors. In this
way, your own observations will begin to be engaged and you will
proceed steadily into an awareness of developmental contexts.
[Brief behavioral examples will be included in brackets.]

1) **<u>Sensimotor Stage.</u>**

There are several submovements which are observable in this
stage. Physical reflexes modify to meet new demands [sucking]
and are slowly replaced by voluntary movements [grasping]. Objects and events unrelated to the self are pursued intentionally
[following toy movements], leading to associating certain means
to certain ends and the recognition of permanence [searching for
hidden toys]. Foresight and symbolic representation begin to be
evident in behaviors such as seeing if something will work before
actually doing so [fitting toys through openings].

2) **<u>Preoperational Stage.</u>**

This stage is divided into two distinguishable phases during
which there is a transition from egocentric and motor activities to
early social and conceptual behavior. In the first phase, sensory
experiences is the sole basis for any concept formation. [A chocolate bar broken in half is more chocolate because it looks like
more.] Language develops rapidly and aids conceptual growth.
In the second phase, more complex issues may be investigated
although they are still heavily based on the senses and one-dimensional. [Equal volumes in different shapes are inconceivable.
Also, Boston and Massachusetts or a blue wooden bead and a
white wooden bead are each sets of entirely different things.]

3) **<u>Concrete operational stage.</u>**

Basic logical and mathematical operations are mastered. Based
on definite experiences, situations, and objects, such operations
result in a more mobile and flexible equilibrium of cognitive ability. A hierarchy of classes may be applied to such concrete objects
or experiences [cities in Massachusetts or differently colored

beads], and an order of relationships may be applied to them [arranging objects according to height, weight, size, etc.].[7] Shape does not change mass, weight, or volume [a ball of clay vs. a pancake of the same clay], and actions are able to be reversed or compensated for [reversing the pattern in a chain of beads]. There a genuine effort to understand and communicate with others, as well as an ability to view things from another perspective [another person's point of view or curiosity about the "other side" of the moon].

4) <u>Formal operations stage.</u>

What matters now is form rather than content. Thought processes are refined in terms of the way that methods of thinking are applied and controlled. Abstract reasoning and combinational analyses are brought to bear on problems so that gradually trial-and-error reasoning is reduced and systematic, rigorous, even elegant proofs increase in the face of greater logical reflection and more inclusive laws or generalizations [explanations of why wood floats and a key doesn't]. [8] Reasoning and symbolic operations [If . . . , then. . . statements] may be based on verbal propositions instead of objects or concrete events. Thinking about thinking is both possible and inviting [religious, philosophical, scientific, and political theories].[9] Stage 3's inferences *based on* concrete experience become theoretical syntheses *applied to* concrete

---

[7] The way thought processes at this stage can manipulate classes and relations are identified by Piaget as belonging to four categories: 1) Classes may be combined into a more comprehensive class [all men and all women = all adults], 2) Thought processes may be reversed [all adults except all women = all men], 3) The same goals may be reached by different mental processes [(3+1)+5=9 is the same as 3+(1+5)=9], and 4) Operations may be nullified by combining them with their opposite [adding and then subtracting or multiplying and then dividing].

[8] Formal thinking also prompts intellectual posturing in which arguments are pursued for their own sake, and "pseudostupid" questions in which an individual "ask complex questions and seek answers beyond his or her ability to comprehend." such that no answer is satisfactory. Shelton, op. cit., Pg. 33

[9] There is often a desire to change society based on a "new" model resulting from personal speculation, and there are often "ideal" personal futures constructed. The world of ideas and the possible may easily become more real to them than the objective and categorical.

experience.[10] Reality and possibility are reversed in cognitive operations and thereby become more balanced in overall developmental growth.

Piaget's schema, although valuable, isn't entirely water-tight. It has been argued that the later forms of Stage 4 reasoning are actually not consistently found in either adolescents or adults, and that both the math/science orientation and the lack of standardized procedures of evaluation limit the normative status of Piaget's model. Formal reasoning among different tests which were structurally equivalent has sometimes proven to show little correlation in overall cognitive approach. Finally, it is unclear how Stage 4 characteristics are manifested in the literary or artistic (analogy, metaphor, symbol) areas of cognitive growth. Some suggest that formal operations in fact interfere with their development.

Piaget's key insights, however, remains significant. Muus summarizes them in this way:

> "Apparently, the subject's cognitive structure determines the degree of understanding that the individual can bring to the solution of a problem. . . [Individuals] seem incapable of being guided even through careful questioning beyond [the limits of their understanding]. And even if correct answers with explicit explanations are provided, [individuals] appear to return to their own level of cognitive functioning as indicated by their earlier responses rather than to produce any generalized cognitive growth that would readily transcend the earlier established limits. . . [Regarding the long range influence of teaching strategies,] the knowledge that [an individual] might acquire before developing the corresponding cognitive structures either disappears very rapidly or, if it is retained, is retained as rote memorization without real understanding. . . If the gaps in the presentation of educational material are too large or too advanced . . . ,

---

[10] David Elkind has observed how, particularly in adolescents, this fascination with and application of thinking leads to the creation of both an "imaginary audience" as interested in me as I am, as well as a "personal fable" of my own mystique and invulnerability. Cf. <u>All Grown Up & No Place to Go.</u> Addison-Wesley, 1984.

the individual cannot accommodate. [Piaget's] objection to what he referred to as the American question, 'How can we accelerate the child's progression through your developmental stages?' is that to do things faster or earlier is not necessarily a desirable thing and may be even worse than doing nothing."[11]

Others, notably H. Aebli and Jerome Bruner, have shown that the choice and sequence of curriculum material as well as methods of teaching may in fact successfully accelerate cognitive growth when adapted to fit an individual's current logical structures. In other words, the way learning and teaching are ordered and arranged, especially insofar as both recognize the cognitive limitations and abilities of student groups, effect the overall educational impact of the endeavor. This is not a new insight. But Piaget's work in what others have called "genetic epistemology" has offered a structural context from which to address the phenomenon of cognitive development, maintaining all along that individuals actively and autonomously participate in their cognitive growth. His concerns would be beneficially addressed by all who are engaged in the ministry of education.

> There are two basic and correlated principles from which an educator inspired by psychology can never depart: (1) That the only real truths are those that one builds freely oneself and not those received from others, and (2) that moral good is essentially autonomous and cannot be prescribed.[12]

---

[11] Muus, op. cit. Pg. 200 - 202.

[12] Piaget, Jean. "The moral development of the adolescent in two types of society, primitive and 'modern.' " This was a lecture given to the United Nations Educational, Scientific and Cultural Organization, Paris, 1947. Pg. 248.

Moral Development - Lawrence Kohlberg

"A moral choice involves choosing between two (or more) . . . values [such as punishment, property, roles and concerns of affection, roles and concerns of authority, law, life, liberty, distributive justice, truth, and sex] as they conflict in concrete situations of choice."[13]

Piaget and Kohlberg both addressed the human dimension of moral judgment [not moral behavior]. Piaget believed moral judgments to be based on existing cognitive structures and dynamics. Stage 2 "preoperational" morality looked entirely to an outside authority [parents, etc.] for justice and was fully based on the "objective" damage inflicted [amount over intent], having no ability to either consider alternatives or see another's point of view. [You break a rule and something bad will happen to you.] Stage 3 "concrete operational" morality brought in societal dynamics; i.e., concern about motivation and others' perspectives. [You break a rule and you break a consensus of behavior among a group.] Stage 4 "formal operational" morality brought abstract thought into the consideration of possible alternatives and the development of responsibility based on moral principles. [You break a rule and you break a personal moral principle.] Kohlberg expanded Piaget's ideas into a more inclusive and systematic theory, focusing on the critical adolescent years.[14] Piaget concentrated on the reasons behind logical problems, and Kohlberg similarly examined the ways individuals resolved constructed moral dilemmas. As Piaget focus-ed on the cognitive structures behind the reasonings, Kohlberg's concentrated on the moral structures underlying the various responses. Note, therefore, that different "stage" classifications are meant to be consistent with verbal reasonings and do not necessarily reflect actual or

---

[13] A statement of Kohlberg's as quoted by Shelton, op. cit., Pg. 46.

[14] His initial studies with 72 male subjects [aged 10, 13, and 16] has been critiqued most notable by Carol Gilligan in terms of gender prejudice. See Ch. 10 in Muus' book cited above and Carol Gilligan's <u>In a Different Voice: Psychological Theory and Women's Development.</u> Cambridge, Mass.: Harvard University Press, 1984. As Muus points out: "Kohlberg's system appears to penalize women for their greater sensitivity to others and their caring attitude and to reward males for their ability to abstract principles of justice." (Pg.224-225) Kohlberg terminates the moral development of most women at stage 3.

potential moral behavior.[15] Also, the various stages or structures reflect patterns of reasonings, not values.

Kohlberg identified six distinct stages of moral philosophy among 3 basic levels of moral development, moving from egocentric through sociocentric to universal principles of judgment.

Level 1 - Preconventional

Moral reasons are based on external, concrete consequences to the self. I respond out of fear of punishment or anticipation of reward. My immediate needs are primary.

Stage 1. Obedience and Punishment Orientation

I must submit to the greater power and value others insofar as I personally benefit from them. Physical damage and gratification determine the moral parameters. Good and bad mean obeying or disobeying. There is no other moral guideline.

Stage 2. Instrumental Relativism Orientation.

The needs of others are considered only insofar as they will effect my own. Being nice to others is important insofar as it will lead to the gratification of personal needs or desires. Good and bad mean doing those things which will bring about what I want for myself. Moral guidelines are a little wider than in stage 1. Others' needs are now part of the picture.

---

[15] In fact, it's been proven that there's little correlation between moral judgment and moral behavior (Cf. Muus, op.cit., Pg. 206). Only in the higher stages does there appear to be some correlation. It's also been pointed out that Kohlberg's moral dilemmas do not consider typical adolescent conflicts and issues. (Cf. Muus, op.cit., Pg. 209)

Level 2 - Conventional

Moral reasons are based on external social expectations. I respond out of an adherence to the social order and a recognition of the rights of others. Conventional justifications are primary.

Stage 3. Interpersonal Concordance Orientation.

Personal needs no longer define morality, but group approval does. Living up to expectations and greater interpersonal connectivity determine what should be done. Good and bad mean doing or thinking what others do or think. Harmony and group integrity must be preserved. Intentionality underlies moral guidelines; as long as you "mean well" it's okay.

Stage 4. Orientation toward Authority, Law, and Duty.

Obeying the rules of my society are the best way to have my rights respected and to respect the rights of others. If I don't, I'll feel guilty and others would rightly impose penalties. Good and bad mean following society's laws and doing your duty. The principles and laws of society are the moral guidelines.

Level 3 - Postconventional

Moral reasons are based on autonomous, deliberately chosen, universal principles of justice. I respond not because of laws, social conventions, or personal needs, but because of comprehensive and integrated convictions. Universal standards are primary.

Stage 5. The Social Contract Orientation.

Principles of equality, mutual obligation, and individual rights are the foundation of my morality. Laws reflect those principles or else should be changed to do so. Good and bad mean whatever will benefit individual rights and the larger community. Moral philosophy determines moral guidelines.

<u>Stage 6. Universal Ethical Principles Orientation.</u> [16]

Consistent abstract standards that equally apply always and everywhere, in support of life and dignity, determine the dynamics of my moral reasoning. Concern for both immediate others and society will impel me to expose unjust laws through open disobedience and acceptance of the resulting consequences. Good and bad mean whatever will follow universal ethical principles. Principled convictions of conscience determine moral guidelines.

Kohlberg holds that these stages, like Piaget's, are universal, sequential and invariant.[17] Moral reasonings within any one stage or at a level between two sequential stages will be highly consistent within the parameters of those stages. According to others, however, observations of "skipping" stages and regression have been noted. Offering a unique perspective, Margaret Gorman has outlined a proposal whereby all the stages are active within an individual. Varieties of relative emphases among the stages along with the dominating influence of one is seen as defining the moral reasonings of individuals or age-groups. [18]

Further cross-cultural studies by Kohlberg have supported the universality of most of his outline. But these studies also adjusted the model according to the potential impact from cultural and situational factors such as social behavior systems, education, economics, and politics. Generally, however, "Education plays a major role in the development of moral reasoning, and individuals who terminate their formal education tend to remain at the level of moral

---

[16] This stage has been omitted in recent writings because it is more a consequence of Kohlberg's theoretical thrust than a conclusion from empirical data. It also appears to lean towards Western democratic societal structures. Calling this the inevitable "highest" level has also not been sufficiently documented.

[17] Appendix A breaks the levels down into various conceptual foci.

[18] See Appendix A. Taken from course handbook for "Youth Religious Development" Boston College, Fall, 1990. Pg. 64

reasoning they attained while in school. . . [And also,] moral development is slower and less likely to reach the more advanced level of moral reasoning in primitive, less educated, rural, more traditional, and lower-class communities."[19]   Clearly, Kohlberg's structural paradigm based on cognitive development remains an inviting model for understanding the dynamic development of moral judgment.[20]

The educational implications range from the classroom to the school environment. To the question "How can one teach morality?" Kohlberg once answered: "You must think I am very fortunate to know how virtue is acquired. The fact is that far from knowing whether it can be taught, I have no idea of what virtue really is."[21] Certain factors, however, can make a difference in classroom situations: 1) social peer group interactions, especially among individuals on different levels of moral reasoning stimulates assimilation and the reorganization of moral reasoning,[22] 2) role-playing activities encourage development of techniques of incorporation and the restructuring of moral thinking, and 3) creating a "cognitive dissonance" between personal points of view and moral conflicts calls forth dynamics of re-organization and re-adaptation which assimilate the views of others and accommodate to more comprehensive models of moral judgment. On a school-wide level, morality is practiced in fact through behaviors, practices, and policies among administration, faculty, students and parents. The stages exhibited in a school environment are often neither very highly developed nor educative, in the sense of "drawing out" developmental growth,

---

[19] Muus, op. cit. Pg. 216 - 217

[20] William Perry has added further perspective to moral development by studying the dynamics of commitment and its influence on relativism among college students. His nine positions range from the simple duality of adolescents to the developed commitment wedded to personal identity characteristic of late adolescence.

[21] Muus, op. cit., Pg. 221

[22] Students can rarely comprehend arguments that originate more than one stage ahead of their own and prefer arguments from stages preceding their own. ibid. Pg. 222

especially in the area of moral judgment. [23]

Faith Development - James Fowler

Whereas Kohlberg reasons that theological conceptualizations are derived from and are grounded on moral structures of reflection but take longer to develop, and holds that moral principles cannot be based on faith because of faith's historical variety, James Fowler maintains the opposite; that a moral viewpoint is supported by cherished convictions and attachments.[24] His studies in faith development, in ways similar to Piaget and Kohlberg, focuses on how the structure of a faith view comes to be conceptualized and develops. But he cautions that inasmuch as faith is a process which encounters lived experiences, content in this case does make a significant contribution to faith's development. He also includes both cognition and affection as foundational aspects of faith development, moving away from the previous exclusive concentration on cognitive dimensions of development while at the same time maintaining the notion of religion as "meaning-making. " This complementary basis on cognition and affection is necessary because "faith is an irreducibly relational phenomenon. . . faith is a person's way of seeing him- or herself in relation to others against a background of shared meaning and purpose."[25] Faith is a sense of commitment based on trust in both a transcendent and an immanent aspect of our lived experience, moving through gradual structures or stages by which we know, value, and relate to others. Affective factors, therefore, carry at least as much weight as cognitive ones. Along the same vein, it is important to remember that transitions between apparent levels of faith are often difficult and prolonged. "Pigeon-

---

[23] It would be curious to see on which stage or combination of stages you would place your school in terms of Kohlberg's moral "spectrum." One might also apply similar analysis to one's own teaching style, etc.

[24] An worthwhile overview of the relationship between religious and moral education might be found in John L. Elias' Moral Education: Secular and Religious. Chapter 5. (Malabar, Florida: Krieger Publishing Company, 1989)

[25] As quoted by Shelton, op. cit., Pg. 67

holing" people's behavior would probably be a more accurate indication of one's own stage than that of another [26]

Fowler presents six stages of faith development. The double names protect against their easy categorization or simplistic application.

Stage 1. Intuitive - Projective

Others are the most important influences on my life, both for religious authority and factual information. I depend on them. Symbols or images are what they represent, fact and fantasy are virtually the same, and I have little understanding of cause-and-effect. God is HUGE and has emotions like mine. The future is not part of my world.

Stage 2. Mythic - Literal

Religious belief and ritual provide a sense of order and dependability because there's such a big world out there that I'm powerless against. I depend on them for security. I know that there is a difference between my private world and the world out there. I can't reflect abstractly about things but I can find personal meaning in true Bible stories and I can begin to see someone else's perspective, as long as they are like me in some way. God is faithful and lawful.

Stage 3. Synthetic - Conventional

Everything is and must be personal. I want to deepen relationships and internalize the views of others so that I can begin to encounter this increasingly ambiguous, complex world, filled with groups I like or don't like. My family made me what I am, now I'll do the rest. People must be sincere if they want to influence

---

[26] This last observation is my own, rather than Fowler's, although he does caution against judging another's faith level. As a side comment, it seems to me that faith development, more than moral or cognitive development, becomes defined and actualized precisely in the processes of transition between stages, since relationships by nature are all fully reconfigured each time a new element is added.

me. Rituals and symbols allow me to stretch my thinking and to focus my struggle with identity. God is a friend in the person of Jesus. Things look firm [I'm trying my best] but they feel like Jello.[27]

Stage 4. Individuative - Reflective

I am responsible for myself. My faith is my own, personal but consistent with my experiences and encounters with others. It has resulted from critical reflection on the meaning of my life and can be seen in my lifestyle, commitments, and attitudes. Any outside authority's views must resonate with my own in order to be adopted. The meaning behind symbol or ritual is what's most important. God is greater than anyone's capacity to comprehend. I value my expressions of faith.

Stage 5. Conjunctive Faith (Paradoxical - Consolidative)

My experience of lived tensions draws me into greater identification with others as I find deeper aspects of myself and realign priorities and convictions. Commitment is obviously required. I don't know if I can do that, but I must remain open to the possibility of making commitments. Politics and ethics are a part of my life because suffering, loss, and injustice have demanded a more universal view of what I'm part of; not just my friends or acquaintances but also the rest of the world and people from the past. Symbol and ritual call up central dimensions of my being. God is a deep part of who I am and who others are. My serious interaction with others and my personal situation determine my faith.

---

[27] The break-up of this stage may be initiated by "cognitive dissonances" with significant others [Mother and I disagree], previously reliable structures [What does the Church say now?], or personal reflection patterns [Why do I think this way?].

<u>Stage 6. Universalizing Faith</u>

Love and justice demand my involvement. My desire to help others cannot be contained in myself. Personal difficulties are unimportant in the face of the great need of others. All human beings, all nature, all reality are one with me and I with them. Symbols live. God is present in the depths of existence, manifested in every nook and cranny of daily life [people and situations], especially in the distressing disguise of the suffering and marginalized. My life in unimportant except insofar as I encounter my situation, embracing its challenges and challenging its attachments. My faith and my life are one.

Again like Piaget and Kohlberg, each "stage" builds on the previous one, grows increasingly more complex, occurs in sequence, and follow another invariantly.[28] He departs from their premises when he adds the affective dimension to the cognitive one. Fowler does not claim that the stages are universal across all cultures and experiences since his studies are as yet incomplete in this respect. His developmental outline nevertheless does provide a convenient and comprehensive structure from which to view the human dimension in the growth of "faithing."

Charles Shelton places the adolescent years between Fowler's stages of 3 and 4. If such is the case, he suggests that ministering strategies should include the following:[29]

---

[28] C. Ellis Nelson, in an evaluation of Fowler's position, points out discrepancies in terms of normative and descriptive elements among the stages. Fowler's concern lies with the human dynamics of faith. Nelson points out that "Somewhere in the growth process human faith becomes fused with religious beliefs...beliefs overwhelm human faith...If stages are determined, do we not have our attention diverted to where we are on a predetermined course rather than on what we should be and do in particular life situations?...I am inclined to believe that people with religious faith have experiences to which they respond. The way they think about these experiences and the way they live and evaluate their beliefs as they live strengthens or weakens their faith in God." From an article: "Does Faith Develop? An Evaluation of Fowler's Position," <u>The Living Light</u>, Vol. 19, No. 2, Summer 1982. Pgs.171-173

[29] Shelton, op. cit., Pg. 75-78

1) Encourage adults to share personal life experiences along themes of personal commitment and ways of relating to others.

2) Have students identify and prioritize the various roles s/he is experiencing.

3) Pursue many "Why" questions related to experienced group dynamics.

4) Expose students to other consistent, coherent, legitimate perspectives.

5) Apply understanding of God or Jesus as friend to intellectual, affective, and moral dimensions of life.

6) Pursue reflection on deeper personal relationships, relating them to commitments, values, and beliefs. Move towards issues of true responsibility.

7) Foster a reflective technique regarding personal and social values along with an openness towards future encounters along with their concomitant call for a realignment of priorities, beliefs, etc.

Looking back at Stages 3 and 4, notice how these strategies develop strengths and stretch limitations. On top of these suggestions, you may come up with several others which would be equally helpful. In fact, you and others are probably using quite a few techniques borne out of experience which effectively address students' developmental concerns. What Fowler has provided is a schema within which to examine and articulate those techniques while also providing a context within which further intentional ministerial strategies might be pursued or evaluated.

Psychological Development - Erik Erikson

The adolescent or young adult, in beginning to pursue abstract thinking most vigorously (Piaget), in grappling with social expectations vis-a-vis peer group, family, and society (Kohlberg), and in entering and moving through the kind of faith where personal or "person" concerns are dominant (Fowler), focuses his/her attention and new-found capacities for reflection on the one issue which is always on stage in our lives but which now takes on the central role; Identity.[30] The future, and its continuity with the past and present, is becoming very real. Life seems very complex and multidimensional. There is a demanding need both for a larger capacity for assimilating a whirlwind of new information, relationships, personal issues, etc., and for an individually grounded sense of self in the eye of that whirlwind. The need for security on many levels struggles with the need for growth on those same levels in a constant interplay which is, of course, ever present and never truly leaves the stage of life. In this respect, educators mirror and focus the emergence of a life-long identity-forming dynamic, providing both security and challenge in such a way that genuine growth becomes possible.

Erik Erikson has done the most extensive studies on identity formation, or the acquisition of ego-identity, modifying Freud's theories of psychosexual development to an anthropologically-based theory of psychosocial development. Central to his identity-formation theory is a biologically-based principle of growth which he describes as "epigenetic." This principle states "that anything that grows has a ground plan, and that out of this ground plan the parts arise, each part having its time of special ascendancy, until all parts have risen to form a functional whole."[31] In effect, specific aspects of identity-acquisition surface at specific times and according to a certain order, but all aspects are present and active in some way all the time, with the pivotal focus on identity per sé happening during adolescence. Each of Erikson's "Eight Stages of Man" proceeds

---

[30] Shelton quotes Josselson: "Identity formation may be the 'star' of adolescence, but it has been rehearsing and will continue to act throughout the life cycle." op.cit., Pg. 82

[31] Erikson, E.H. <u>Identity: Youth and crisis.</u> New York: Norton, 1968. Pg. 92.

along a line of increasing psychosocial differentiation - meaning an increasing sense of individual identity - and each stage is characterized by some kind of developmental conflict whose outcome may be one of two opposite qualities. Whichever quality is adopted becomes part of the personality structure and either helps or hinders further developmental responsibilities. Each crisis or conflict seems most pronounced at certain age levels; they are never really and fully "solved." Specific situational crises during one's life may also momentarily highlight and focus on one particular stage, or aspect of identity-formation. But the overall pattern appears to be universal, sequential, and invariant, as we have seen with other developmental models.

Erikson identified eight aspects of psychosocial identity-acquisition which stand out during particular phases of one's life.

1) Trust Vs. Mistrust

The conviction emerges that "I am what I am given." Regular satisfaction of bodily and emotional needs build both trust of others and trust of self. First through the mouth [eating] and then through the body [grasping, reaching, crawling, walking], individuals experience a predictability and security that form the basis for a capacity to experience faith as well as a basic stance of confidence and optimism. The developing capacity for mutual recognition contributes to the later growth of empathy. The achievement of trust at this stage leads to autonomy.

2) Autonomy Vs. Shame and Doubt

The conviction emerges that "I am what I will be." Increasing intellectual and motor capacities lead to an awareness of being "different from" others, a differentiated personal self. Ability to control both the body [toilet training] and the mind [temper tandrums] builds towards a sense of self-certainty, a will to be oneself. The autonomy balance achieved at this point will strongly re-emerge during adolescence as either confidence in one's ability to be independent or low self-esteem, doubt, and scattered dependency. The achievement of autonomy at this stage leads to taking initiative.

3) Initiative Vs. Guilt

The conviction emerges that "I am what I can imagine I will be." Aggressive manipulation becomes a learning tool; in terms of objects [taking things apart], language [asking 'what' and 'why' questions], and bodies [examining one's own and others]. Intrusion is the key dynamic. The individual thrusts the self forward into his/her world, exploring the environment, relationships, and roles. Responses from others will define the degree to which later initiatives in identity formation become empowered or immobilized.[32]   The achievement of initiative at this stage leads to engagement and industry.

4) Industry Vs. Inferiority

The conviction emerges that "I am what I will learn or can learn to make work." An apprenticeship to life involving the mastery of physical, intellectual, and social skills builds pride and confidence in one's ability to be successful, recognized, and legitimate. Structured cooperation activities and an anticipation of others' perspectives call forth a desire for success in the eyes of others along with a willingness to work towards such success. Without the enjoyment and esteem that result from approval, futility and work paralysis become a dominating influence - especially in terms of the next stage. The achievement of industry at this stage heralds and prepares for the central task of identity achievement.

---

[32] Even sexual identity has some roots in developments made during this period. "The sexual self-image and the differentiation between masculine (making) and feminine (catching) initiative become important prerequisites for the sexual identity crisis during adolescence." Muus, op.cit., Pg. 59

5) Identity[33] Vs. Identity Confusion

The conviction emerges that "I am what I am " Bodily changes trigger a whole new world of concern wherein previous identity concerns run rampant among biologically diffuse signals. With trust and autonomy, personal identity must be worked at; it takes industry and initiative. Peer groups and "first loves" replace parents as primary sounding boards. Past [psychosocial history], present [hormonal manifestations], and future [vocational concerns] become integrated into a philosophy of life which reaches for continuity and coherence.[34]   Individuals may easily become "stuck" and prefer the dubious security of escape, diffusion, and/or dependency to the challenge of commitment.   The achievement of identity at this stage leads to the pursuit of intimacy.

6) Intimacy Vs. Isolation

The conviction emerges that "We are what we love." If ego-identity has emerged, individuals will seek emotional intimacy with another, pursuing enduring relationships. Dependence on peer group gives way to interdependence among individuals. Genuine friendship and intimacy or isolation and loneliness result. One might even detach and distance oneself from others in order to remain secure without commitment, protecting one's acquired,

---

[33] Identity here is defined as "the establishment and reestablishment of sameness with one's previous experiences and a conscious attempt to make the future a part of one's personal life plan." ibid., Pg. 62

[34] Today's society isn't very helpful for such an endeavor. Rapid social change undermines adequate role models and the goal of socialization [socializing for what kind of society?]. Competing ideologies and fluid philosophies undermine attempts at a consistent personal, committed philosophy. Along the same vein, David Elkind has pointed out in the work cited above that "American society has struck teenagers a double blow. It has rendered them more vulnerable to stress while at the same time exposing them to new and more powerful stresses." (Pg. 6) He also suggests stress management techniques for the four types of stress, 1) Foreseeable and Avoidable Dangers [classwork and relationships], 2) Unforeseeable and Unavoidable Stress [death & accidents], 3) Foreseeable and Unavoidable Stress [responsibilities], and 4) Unforeseeable but Avoidable Stress [burnout, tensions]. (Cf. Pgs. 210-216)

vulnerable self-image.[35] Mutuality of relationship is the goal and marriage [or commitment] becomes a real possibility. The achievement of intimacy at this stage leads to a desire to manifest oneself to others, or generativity.

7) Generativity Vs. Stagnation

The conviction emerges that "I am what I create or can produce." Productive creativity at work and at home, for myself, others, and society is the driving force. One wants to be needed, to give of oneself, to expand one's interests beyond one's own. One's contributions must make a difference. Without that, routine repetition and self-indulgence terminate development at stagnation, where one expects not to be bothered and not to "bother" others. The only worthwhile "product" becomes the self. For this stage, further ego-expansion is the goal and ego-absorption is the danger. The achievement of generativity at this stage leads to a concern about "the big picture," the integrity of one's entire life, its acceptance and appreciation.

8) Integrity Vs. Despair

The conviction emerges that "I am what survives of me." Acceptance of one's past in all its complexity and ambivalence stands against a basic discontentment with one's life. Appreciation or bitterness becomes dominant. One either comes to terms with death with an integrated identity or fears death and regresses to childhood dependency. All previous stages resolve into an integrated totality whose thrust remains positive or negative. Life was worthwhile or wasted. The goal is full and content integration.

---

[35] Genuine others become a threat because they challenge the security of one's self-concept. Hence, the world is seen with eyes which are blind to the reality of others' lives and developmental growth stagnates or proceeds unevenly.

Identity Development – Erik Erikson

Erikson's general focus, and the primary focus for anyone involved in education, is the issue of identity. Some additional research into the confusing time of adolescence and young adulthood has made some helpful observations. James Marcia expanded Erikson's concern with identity vs. role diffusion (particularly focused at Stage 5 but experienced throughout life) by examining two essential variables in the attainment of a mature identity, crisis and commitment. Based on the presence or absence of crisis and commitment in various combinations, he formulated four separate identity statuses. These may prove to be insightful in the assessment of adolescent educational stances. They are not necessarily sequential and may be found in combination. Each may also be individually terminal.[36]

1. Identity-diffused or identity-confused

This subject has not yet experienced an identity crisis nor made any commitment to a vocation or a set of beliefs.

2. Foreclosure

This subject has not yet experienced an identity crisis but has made commitments. However, these commitments are not the result of personal searching and exploring; rather, they are handed, ready-made, to the individual by others, frequently parents. These superimposed commitments are accepted without the individual's raising of fundamental and searching questions about them.

3. Moratorium

This subject is in an acute state of crisis; he [she] is exploring and actively searching for values to eventually call his [her] own. In other words, this individual is actively struggling to find his [her]

---

[36] Muus' summary is as compact as possible and will therefore be presented in toto. Cf. op. cit., Pg. 66

identity but has not yet made a commitment or has only developed very temporary kinds of commitments.

4. Identity-achieved

This subject has experienced personal crises but has resolved them on his [her] own terms. As a result of the resolution of these crises the individual has made a personal commitment to an occupation, a religious belief, and a personal value system and has resolved his attitude toward sexuality.

There have been many cross-studies between levels of Marcia's identity statuses and the developmental stages described by Piaget and Kohlberg. Other studies have compared Marcia's identity statuses and variables of gender[37], personality, self-esteem, intelligence quotients, etc. Both Erikson and Marcia, however, for our overview purposes, present plenty of focused insights into the dynamics of an educational endeavor.

If identity concerns are clearly primary during the adolescent and young adult years, are they being addressed with corresponding vigor, or are educational environments organized so that the dynamics of identity concerns work "against the grain"? Most high schools appear to rather exemplify and reward foreclosure behavior when, in fact, moratorium issues predominate. Educators walk a fine line between their structures of external control and the students' structures of internal motivation; between rules, obedience, duty, curriculum, etc. and self-understanding, identity integration, interpersonal relationships, and values. With social role definitions and their implementation [e.g., puberty rites] virtually absent, the school becomes a major locus for identity formation. Educators have a pivotal influence both in developing the students' tolerance for meaningful frustration [e.g., through the practice of solving social, literal, or math problems] and in gently challenging the

---

[37] These studies are proving to be the most fascinating, noting for example that Erikson's stages for girls are probably more merged and occur on deeper, less tangible levels, in quieter and more subtle ways. Also that achievement and foreclosure are "stable" statuses for women as achievement and moratorium are "stable" for men, who also seem to hover around either diffusion and foreclosure ore moratorium and achievement. (Cf.Muus, op.cit.Pg.80 - 82)

students' identity status towards greater integration and achievement [e.g., including identity-relevant topics as part of the curriculum]. Erikson's and Marcia's schema distinctly situate these issues of identity development and offer an articulated structure from which to address them.

Social Development - Robert Selman

A last dimension of human development to consider is that of "social reasoning" or the capacity to be aware of and understand others. This is a more generalized aspect of growth since it involves a host of behaviors and concepts which together form an attitudinal engagement with all that lies outside of the self. In that sense, all of the developmental aspects considered above influence the way that an individual relates with the perceived world in which s/he dwells [38] Robert Selman crystallizes the phenomena of social reasoning in what he calls "role-taking," a process by which personal perspectives and those of others interact.[39] His studies have identified role-taking stages, sequential and invariant, which develop structures of perspective that move from physical events to social events to moral events. Again, like Piaget and Kohlberg, Selman addresses the structure of social reasoning, not its content. In fact, he locates social reasoning structures, as manifested in role-taking perspectives, between logical reasoning structures (Piaget) and moral reasoning structures (Kohlberg).[40] An individual gradually becomes aware of, and influenced by, another's way of seeing things, moving towards ever-more comprehensive, complex, and

---

[38] Certainly all developmental dimensions influence each other, and no one of them stands by itself, as has been pointed out earlier. In considering social reasoning, however, the particular focus is on how the totality of a person interacts with all that is encountered outside of that person. In that respect, personally oriented developmental factors contribute to that totality and socially reasoning result from their particular influences.

[39] Social role-taking skills are defined as skills "in differentiating between the perspective of self and others and accurate perception of the thinking of others." Muus, op. cit., Pg. 245

[40] "Conceptually, role taking can be described as a form of social cognition intermediate between logical and moral thought." Selman, R.L. "Social-cognitive understanding: A guide to educational and clinical practice." In T. Lickona, ed., <u>Moral development and behavior: Theory, research and social issues.</u> New York: Holt, Rinehart & Winston, 1976. Pg. 307. As quoted by Muus, op.cit., Pg. 245

in-depth viewpoints or perspectives structures. Marching in step with increased role-taking capacities are increasing capacities for understanding the relationship between the perspectives of the self and of others [The more I can take on the role of another, the more I can understand how other viewpoints relate to mine. Then I will be able to take on a more complex role, etc.] Selman highlights the importance of adolescent development changes in terms of their effect on the direction of social reasoning and perspective-taking. His model is therefore particularly relevant to educators.

Selman delineates five stages or levels which appear to have distinct characteristics.

Stage 0. Egocentric, undifferentiated, social perspective taking

I know that there are immediate differences between myself and others, but I can't distinguish between different motives. Things are only physical. Actions are more important than the reasons behind them. My perspective is the only one possible [the only one I can think of] and therefore true. Feeling = Behavior. Intentional behavior is no different from unintentional behavior. Others effect me in solely physical terms.

Everybody likes jelly beans because I do (They're things that are liked). If people do things that I don't like, I can tell to go away or hit (physically limited). And I know when I do wrong things because I get punished.

Stage 1. Differential or subjective perspective-taking.
(Also called Social-informational role-taking)

I know that there are physical and psychological differences between myself and others (through physical observations), but I can't think of two different perspectives. (Things have reasons that I think of). Things are more complicated, still but physically-based. Feeling remains closely attached to behavior. I can understand that somebody might have a different viewpoint, or act unintentionally, but I can't see how others see me.

People like jellybeans for different reasons. If people do things that I don't like, somebody can do something to fix it. And there are good reasons for punishing me, but my reaction makes no difference.

Stage 2. Self-reflective thinking or reciprocal perspective taking.

I know that there are motivational differences between myself and others [and I know that others can know that too], but I can only think of each of these sets of motivations [which even have a hierarchy], not both at the same time. The outer realities can hide the inner ones. Thoughts and feelings are different, so people's behavior may not follow their intentions. I know that others are able to walk in my shoes, and I walk in theirs in order to see how I'm coming across.

People can like jellybeans for opposite reasons. If people do things that I don't like, I have to think of how we can work it out together, one-on-one, since we caused it together (no mutual consensus, however) . And punishment is something that others do to help me be better the next time (or else I'll be punished again).

Stage 3. Third-person or mutual perspective-taking.

I know that there is are relational differences between myself and others. I can observe myself, the other person, and the relationship at the same time. I can both be active in the relationship and view it objectively (motivations, thoughts, feelings, etc.). My point of view, the other person's point of view, and an outside "neutral" point of view may all be different, but I can study and understand the dynamics of each. Feelings, thoughts, and behaviors may all be different and inconsistent with each other. Others see me in all sorts of ways; the important thing is to have a mutual relationship of trust, friendship, and loyalty.

People can like jellybeans for the wrong reasons (they may only think that they do). If people do things that I don't like, we have to look at the problem together from all sides, working it through and making personal changes so that everyone is satisfied. (After all, conflicts do happen and may even lead to stronger commitments and individual growth.) . And punishment is okay for those who need it, but there are better ways of addressing my behavior.

Stage 4. In-depth societal perspective taking.

I know that there are complex developmental differences between myself and others. Different people have different perspectives and think about those perspectives in different ways; i.e., according to their own particular perspective. Everyone is part of a social point of view which enables communication and mutual understanding. Unconscious processes and psychological factors influence behavior and intentionality. Others see me in ways consistent with their developmental perspective.

People can like jellybeans for no reason that they can see. If people do things that I don't like, I have to consider their personality and psychological profile, making mutual adjustments that will allow for maximum growth on both our parts. And punishment is really a way whereby, unconsciously, psychological control over others is maintained.

Charles Shelton has suggested that educational ministry, especially in regard to spirituality, might include certain approaches which would recognize and empower developing structures of social reasoning and role-taking.[41] These would include 1) examining Jesus' perspective and its relationship to my own, 2) considering others' needs and attitudes, especially broad social groups, 3) reflecting on adolescent relationships from a third-party perspective (providing variety of perspectives, including the Christian one), and 4) role-playing relevant, experienced situations, focusing on understandings, emotional reactions, coping strategies, and the influence of Christian values.[42]

---

[41] Shelton, op.cit., Pg. 100 - 101

[42] Note that these need not be confined to "Religion Class." Social reasoning structures are a pervasive presence within individual development. They might be profitably be addressed within almost any particular educational context or subject area.

In further studies, the previously mentioned intermediate function of the development of role-taking, or social reasoning, between those of logical reasoning and moral reasoning has been supported. [43] A certain developmental level of logical reasoning is the necessary prerequisite for either social role-taking or moral judgment, although high levels of logical reasoning are possible without much progress in either social role-taking or moral judgment. Also, high levels of social role-taking are possible without equivalent progress in moral judgment, but along with high moral judgment are found similarly high levels of social role-taking. [44]

Cognitive emphasis in education often side-steps the significant potential present in the pursuit of understanding interpersonal dynamics. Skills such as thinking of alternative solutions and of following their consequences contribute to an educational approach in which there is a recognition and inclusion of the dynamics of social reasoning. Explaining things has never been as effective as discussion or debate. Eliminating structures or behavioral attitudes which assume early developmental levels of social reasoning, and encouraging the involvement of higher levels of social cognition will both lead to a more authentic engagement with the students' own developmental dynamics as well as prepare the foundations for the further development of moral judgment. The expectations, goals, and limitations inherent in the educational endeavor are more clearly understood and more consistently applied when developmental concerns become an integral part of its ministry. Such a focus cannot but be part of what education is all about.

Conclusion

Developmental studies are descriptions of perceived characteristics. They are significant insofar as they contribute to a greater understanding of, and participation in, the dynamics of human growth.

---

[43] Muus, op.cit, Pg. 261

[44] Studies have also been done correlating moral and religious development. Results here indicate that variations between moral and religious levels appear to be based on psychological maturity and degrees of genuine religious committed vs. religiosity. Cf. review of doctoral dissertation in 'Moral Education Forum" Vol. 14, No. 3, Fall 1989, Pg. 23. (Cullman, Elaine Grace, Ph.D. University of Cincinnati, 1988. "Morality and Religion in Adult Development.")

Recalling our "forest path" analogy, the paths which these theorists have followed offer distinctive viewpoints that correlate certain aspects of our common experience but never really either see the same thing or see the whole thing. Each path offers its own insights and possibilities, has its own strengths and limitations. Each time we travel a particular path, we will notice new things and new connections with things we remember from other paths. But the more we travel any path, the more we will come to appreciate the depths and complexities of the forest, realizing more and more that we can comprehend it less and less.[45]

Walking the more abstract paths of developmental theory may be more difficult than its physical counterpart, but it is no less valuable or revelatory. In our maturity, we learn that greater understanding brings with it a greater capacity for appreciating depth, totality, and distinction [46] The more we see of the forest by entering in and engaging its life, the more we are able to see and participate in the forest's dynamics. The more we commit ourselves to understanding [i.e., seeing] human development by entering into and engaging life, the more we learn to see and participate in human development's dynamics. (This is why is it unnecessary to have a degree in developmental psychology in order to participate in human development.) The paths formed by Piaget, Kohlberg, Fowler, Erikson, Marcia, and Selman are helpful in that they provide well-established patterns and observations. The degree to which we appropriate, apply, compare, contrast, etc. their models [i.e., "walk with" their descriptions] will determine the degree to which we enter into and engage the world of understanding human development.

The nature of learning, it seems to me, is itself an epigenetic mystery. Developmental understanding may always be a concern and

---

[45] Margaret Gorman has commented "More mature persons can choose to be committed to the uncertainties of a faith or vision which can never quite encompass the mystery seen as underlying all life and all relationships." (Article on "Life-Long Moral Development" in Knowled & McLean, eds. Psychological Foundations of Moral Education and Character Development. Boston: University Press of America, 1986. Pg. 271) Such complexities are found in whatever we pursue, and such commitment remains a necessary prerequisite for greater understanding or engagement.

[46] The $20 description for this would be a conative dialectical hermeneutic.

profitable pursuit, but it has its ascendancy and eventual integrates itself into the totality of a person's individual growth-momentum (which, I hasten to add, may be directed towards the study of development). Certain concerns and capacities highlight certain common situational combinations of age, experience, and environment.

Greater correlation between these common situational combinations of various factors among large groups of individuals allows for the genesis of descriptive articulations of their common experiences and the proposal of specific models vis-a-vis the dynamics which define their combination. In other words, it's easy to talk about people who are alike. And the more they are alike, the more they reveal and the easier it is to talk about them.

The process of learning is a process of becoming more aware of, and involved in, the world around us. It is epigenetic in that, at certain times, certain things will grab our awareness or involvement and others will not. As educators, it is the learning dimension itself which remains constantly in our field of vision. For us, the more we become involved in this process of learning, approaching it from the other side [teaching], the more we come to know the complexity and depth of the endeavor. In fact, we find that a greater understanding of education leads to a greater appreciation of individual uniqueness. People are less and less alike, and it becomes increasingly more difficult to talk about them as a group. At that point, it is important to step back into the forest of common experience, of human growth, and to walk once more the paths forged by developmental theorists. One may find there the map which will enable confident engagement and significant progress.

Their map will only be useful if it is used, and it will only be valuable if it enables greater, more confident, successful, and deliberate movement around the territory of human growth and development. It is to that end that this introduction to development theory, this "trail map and camping guide," is offered.

"Everything depends on the person who stands in the front of the classroom. The teacher is not an automatic fountain from which intellectual beverages may be obtained. He is either a witness or a stranger. To guide a pupil into the promised land, he must have been there himself. When asking himself: Do I stand for what I teach? Do I believe what I say? he must be able to answer in the affirmative.

What we need more than anything else is not textbooks but textpeople. It is the personality of the teacher which is the text that the pupils read; the text that they will never forget."[47]

================================

	Piaget Cognitive	Erickson Psycho-social	Kohlberg Moral	Fowler Faith	Westerhoff Faith
Ages 3-5	Concrete thinking	age of fantasy; Virtue: autonomy egocentric; grows via identification with adults	Fear of getting caught	**Imaginative-Projective Faith:** highly imaginative; fluidity between reality and fantasy	**Experienced Faith:** observes & imitates; responds to experiences explores and tests
Ages 6-8	Concrete thinking; begins to categorize & classify; begins to be able to take another's perspective	Ego-centric to social awareness & strong peer group Virtue: initiative Developing personal values; friendships important	*From* Stage 2-self-interested concern (I'll scratch your back, if you scratch mine) *to* Stage 3 (Pleasing Others) recognizing feelings & meeting expectations of others	**Mythic-Literal Faith:** literal approach to stories of faith; incapable of reflecting on meaning of stories; symbols & myths taken at face value	**Affiliative Faith:** Belonging; feelings primary—"heart before the head;" authority-- knowing what your way or story is
Ages 9-12	Uses both concrete & abstract logic (but needs experience in using abstract concepts & deductive logic)	Physically awkward, self-conscious, prone to moodiness; Virtue: industry strong peer pressure age of searching needs understanding & sense of autonomy; wants freedom to make decisions	*From* Stage 3-meeting expectations of others; beginning to think about intent of act; Rules of group important *to* Stage 4-beginning to see importance of adhering to acceptable standards; justice seen as uniform for all (lacking sense of mercy)	**Synthetic-Conventional Faith:** ability to reflect on one's own thinking; begins to pull together important images & values; images of God as extensions of inter-personal relationships (e.g. God as Friend, Companion, etc.)	(Continuation of the above)
Ages 13-18	Abstract concepts & deductive logic	identity formation; interpersonal relationships very important Virtue: Identity	Stage 2-Stage 5 questions injustices & moral issues; concerned with good vs. evil may become rebellious	**Individuative-Reflective Faith:** begins to reflect on self and faith apart from groups & shared worldview held up to that point; authenticity	**Searching Faith:** struggles with doubts & questions; challenges authority; commitment to causes & related actions; experimentation
Young Adult 20s	Abstract/logical	Intimacy needs; isolation & loneliness Possible; seeking Stable and personal Relationships Virtue: intimacy	*From* Stage 2 (brought on by insecurities) *to* Stage 5		**Owned Faith:** open to others who are different since one knows & is secure in one's own faith & identity; feels compelled to witness; "walks the talk;" integrates beliefs into one's style of living
Adult 35+	Abstract/logical	Search for personal identity with God that gives special meaning to life Virtue: Generativity & Integrity	Stage 5—respect for rights, life, and dignity of all	**Conjunctive Faith:** awareness of unconscious; deepened readiness for relationship to God that includes mystery; more comfortable with paradox	
Adult 35+			Stage 6—willing to forfeit one's life for the sake of one's beliefs & others	**Universalizing Faith:** Few people experience a shift from the self as center of experience to participation in God or Ultimate Reality; more lucid, simple, liberated	

---

[47] Heschel, Abraham Joshua, <u>I Asked for Wonder</u>, Samuel H. Dresner Ed., Crossroad, 1985. Pg. 62.

SOUL FOR SOUL – THE VOCATION OF THE CHILD IN LASALLIAN PEDAGOGY

Introduction

"The end of the Institute is to give a Christian education to children." *(Rule of 1705)*[1] Since its foundation, the Brothers of the Christian Schools[2] have aimed their educational ministry towards children. The educational principles and practices that emerged from this tradition are ones that have stood the test of time through 325 years of daily experience in the classroom.

To speak today of the "vocation" of the child is to immediately endow childhood with a dignity and an incipient but substantial decision-making potential that would be readily recognized by anyone associated with the educational tradition of John Baptist de La Salle and the educational movement he created. From the time the movement began in 1680 with a small tuition-free parish-school for poor boys in Reims, France, up to this very day when there are some thousand schools in 80 countries teaching over 1,000,000 students, the consistent thread and the unfailing motivation of the teaching-encounter have revolved around the daily recognition of the dignity of each student along with the conviction that each student grows by exercising his or her ability to make and act on choices small and large. In other words, children by definition are growing into their vocation for living, and the school is one privileged and formative context for doing so.

---

[1] The entire paragraph from 1705 Rule of the Brothers of the Christian Schools reads:" The end of this Institute is to give a Christian education to children; it is for this purpose the Brothers keep schools, so that, having the children under their care from morning until evening, they may teach them to lead good lives, by instructing them in the mysteries of our holy religion and by inspiring them with Christian maxims; and thus give them a suitable education." *Rule of 1705*: 1,3 - Manuscript Copy. Note that the word "Christian" on a practical level meant "Catholic" in 17th century France.

[2] The congregation is also known more popularly as "Christian Brothers," or "De La Salle Brothers," or "De La Salle Christian Brothers" (the last to distinguish them from the Congregation of Christian Brothers, formerly known as the Irish Christian Brothers).

Although the notion of a child's vocation has been part of the life-blood of our particular educational heritage for over three centuries, this tradition – called a "Lasallian" tradition in honor of its founder – has consistently remained somewhat under the radar when it comes to the larger educational world. Few seem to be aware of the foundational perspectives and influential writings of De La Salle, or the role that his writings and heritage played in the formation of the various teaching congregations that others founded in the 18th and 19th centuries. The Roman Catholic Church highlighted his role in education when, in 1950 on the fiftieth anniversary of his canonization, he was declared the Patron Saint of All teachers of Youth,[3] and his statue – posed in company with a student - stands in the main nave of St. Peter's in Rome. Judging from the experience of the last twenty years, once educators of all stripes are exposed to the writings of De La Salle and the practices these writings shaped, they are uniformly captured by the same genuine, caring, and professional spirit that continues to inspire more teachers today than ever before.[4]

De La Salle and His Context

De La Salle grew up in a second half of the 17th century. This was the age of King Louis XIV, the "Sun King" who ruled France with an iron, if clever, fist. It was an age when social standing, good manners, benefices, political intrigue, and grand living were the rule. And that was just in the church. The State had all of this plus it was engaged in one war after another, taxed the populace as much as it could tolerate, followed a system of governance and justice that had as many exceptions as it had applications, and for a time built up France's status to that of a "superpower."

---

[3] Pius XII declared him the Special Patron of all teachers of Youth on May 15, 1950). (*Circular No. 331*. Rome: teachers of the Christian Schools, 1950. pp. 13 - 16.)

[4] One testament to the enduring character of De La Salle's educational movement consists in the variety of formational programs that continue to flourish. Among these in the United States are the three-year Buttimer Institute of Lasallian Studies that studies his life, pedagogy, and spirituality, and the Lasallian Leadership Institute geared towards developing educational leaders in the schools.

France had a well-established school system geared mostly for the non-poor, consisting of schools, colleges, and universities run by religious orders, secular priests, and lay professors. Education in France was under church control, essentially religious in content, inspiration, and direction. The bishop was the local superintendent of public instruction, acting through an appointed superintendent of schools who saw mainly to the financial concerns of the individual teachers under his patronage.[5]

By the time De La Salle became involved in primary education in 1680, primary schools were plentiful, although widely divergent in style and quality.[6] Without intending to, nor actually really wanting to, De La Salle, as a newly ordained priest with a PhD in Theology

---

[5] The Council of Trent (1545 - 1563) had mandated free parish schools (on the primary level) for the poor, establishing the parish priest as the new authority overseeing the poor's religious instruction and schooling. In response to the Council of Trent's mandate of free parish schools for the poor, numerous "charity schools" were established with mixed success. Parish priests could now open their own schools, but anyone else had to have the superintendent's permission to open or teach in a primary school. Qualifications among teachers varied widely. Often they were tradesmen (cobblers, tailors, ropemakers, and so on) who gave some daily time to instructing children. Most parish schools continued to suffer from a lack of adequately trained full-time teachers, sufficient money, and appropriate school buildings.

[6] Among the choices of the time were the following: *Being tutored at home.* This was the preferred option of the wealthy. It was also the way that De La Salle himself was educated; *Attending a grammar school.* These were primary schools connected with some university. It was presumed that education would be continued there; *Attending choir school.* Those singing in the cathedral choir attended their own school on the cathedral grounds; *Attending a "Little School."* These were taught by schoolmasters who belonged to the Guild of Schoolmasters. They were paid a modest fee by the parents and were supervised by the diocesan superintendent of schools; *Attending a convent school.* These were boarding and day schools taught by nuns. Such schools were almost always the exclusive domain for girls; *Attending a writing school.* These schools were taught by the Guild of Writing Masters, officially protected by the civil authorities. Along with other writing and reading, such schools also taught bookkeeping; *Attending a charity school.* These schools, operated by the poor house or by a parish, were for the destitute; that is, those listed on the parish list of the poor. Today, we would consider these people as paupers or welfare cases. The poor in the towns and cities would rarely attend any of these schools. A non-working child represented a lack of income to the family, and there was little relationship between the subjects studied in most schools and the daily concerns of working people.

and a very bright future in the church ahead of him, gradually became involved with a dedicated layman from Rouen who was determined to start schools for poor boys in Reims. De La Salle helped him become established in a local parish, and then gave some advice and help with the first teachers that were recruited. Retreats followed, regular school visits, meals at his home, and finally an invitation to have the teachers come and live with him. What had started out as pure charity turned into a life's vocation.[7] As he wrote later in his life:

> "I had imagined that the care which I assumed of the schools and the masters would amount only to a marginal involvement committing me to no more than providing for the subsistence of the masters and assuring that they acquitted themselves of their tasks with piety and devotedness. . . . Indeed, if I had ever thought that the care I was taking of the schoolmasters out of pure charity would ever have made it my duty to live with them, I would have dropped the whole project; for, as naturally I set below my manservant those I was obliged, especially in the beginning, to employ in the schools, the mere thought that I might have to live with them would have been unbearable. . . .It was apparently for this reason that God, who guides all things with wisdom and gentleness, and is not in the habit of forcing the inclinations of men, wishing to encourage me to take full responsibility for the schools, did so in a most imperceptible manner and over a period of time; so that one involvement led me into another, without my having foreseen it in the beginning."[8]

---

[7] A very good description of this personal journey over a period of five critical years is given in Sauvage, Michel. "The Gospel Journey of John Baptist de La Salle." John Baptist de La Salle Today. Edited by William Mann. Manila, Philippines: De La Salle University Press, 1992. p. 24-57.

[8] Blain, Jean-Baptiste. *The Life of John Baptist de La Salle, Founder of the teachers of the Christian Schools.* Translated by Richard Arnandez. Romeoville, IL: Christian teachers Conference, 1983. Vol. 1, Bk. 1: 60 - 61.

Br. Luke Salm, FSC, provides a summary of De La Salle's educational contributions that succinctly completes the story.

> The Christian Schools might not have been established at all if De La Salle had not been willing to put his own spiritual formation and advanced education at the service of those in need. In the process, he created a new type of school system for the elementary education of the poor, a new set of standards that would transform teaching school into a profession and a vocation, and a new community of consecrated lay teachers as a new form of religious life in the Church.

> To achieve all of this, to enter into the world of the poor with creativity and authenticity, Father De La Salle had to sacrifice all of his personal ambition, his family fortune, his ecclesiastical honors, his comfortable lifestyle, and even his personal reputation. People thought that he was crazy. His own family disowned him. The educational authorities of the time had him hauled into court, condemned, and fined because the educational policies he introduced threatened to break down the established social barriers. In his determination to give rich and poor the same education in the same classroom, and all for free, he had to act against the law.

> Then there were the Church authorities. Pastors, bishops, and even the Cardinal Archbishop of Paris, hounded De La Salle relentlessly. They could neither understand nor control this persistent innovator who didn't want his Brothers to be priests, who had his own ideas about how to run a school, and how to make the Christian message appealing to those who rarely heard good news of any kind.

> De La Salle did not limit his educational vision to gratuitous elementary schools for the poor. He realized that there were other needs. Well trained teachers were high on his list of priorities. On three distinct occasions he was able to establish experimental training schools for lay teachers. Aware that there was no provision at the time for working teenagers to continue their education, De La Salle founded a

Sunday program of advanced courses in practical subjects just for them. He opened a boarding school with offerings in advanced technical and pre-professional courses, unavailable, unheard of, and unthinkable in colleges and universities. He pioneered in what we now call programs of special education to backward students. He opened one of the first institutions in France to specialize in the care and education of young delinquents.[9]

When De La Salle died in 1719, after 40 years of labor, there were only 100 Brothers in 23 communities who operated some 34 schools in various parts of France - very small, compared for example with Saint Francis of Assisi, who in 22 years gathered some 10,000 disciples. Yet the influence of De La Salle's convictions, as evidenced in both his writings and in the practices that they led to, came to be the inspiration for generations of educators and other religious teaching orders. De La Salle succeeded where so many had failed because, in the words of the French historian Georges Compayré, De La Salle launched an educational "movement," and it is one that is more alive today than at any other time in its history.

The Lasallian Perception of Children

John Baptist de La Salle was first and foremost concerned about the education of children. That became his passion and his life's work. He knew children, related to children, spoke about children, and prayed for children as individuals who reflected God's presence and were growing and learning persons with a dignity of their own. He realized that they were struggling with real-life issues both inside and outside of the classroom, and the best thing that their teachers could do for them was to take them seriously, both professionally and personally, and to care for them as older brothers would.

First, it should be said that he came to have a very honest assessment of the state of affairs that the poor of his day found themselves in. He writes:

> " . . . Consider that it is only too common for the working class and the poor to allow their children to live on their own, roaming all over like vagabonds until they are able to

---

[9] Salm, Luke. *Who is Saint John Baptist de La Salle.* Pg. 2. Unpublished article

be put to some work. These parents have no concern to send their children to school because their poverty does not allow them to pay teachers, or else, obliged to look for work outside their homes, they have to abandon their children to themselves.

The results of this condition are regrettable, for these poor children, accustomed to lead an idle life for many years, have great difficulty adjusting when it comes time for them to go to work. In addition, through association with bad companions they learn to commit many sins which later on are very difficult to stop, the bad habits having been contracted over so long a period of time.

God has had the goodness to remedy so great a misfortune by the establishment of the Christian Schools, where the teaching is offered free of charge and entirely for the glory of God, where children are kept all day, learn to read, to write, and their religion, and are always kept busy, so that when their parents want them to go to work, they are prepared for employment." (M 194.1)[10]

The school's focus was on the salvation of these students on two levels, both on the spiritual level (which was not insignificant at the time), and on the practical level (which was probably much more to the interest of parents, however, even then). From this viewpoint, the vocation of children would seem to be rather objective, uniform, and indiscriminating as to personal interests, talents, and the like. But as we shall see, the lived experience of De La Salle's schools support a notion of the child's vocation that has much warmer, compassionate, and personally sensitive overtones.

The Identity of Children

Throughout his meditations, De La Salle rarely uses the term *students* (*élève*) for the children that came to the schools, but he most often

---

[10] *Meditations by St. John Baptist de La Salle*. Translated by Richard Arnandez, FSC, and Augustine Loes, FSC. Edited by Augustine Loes, FSC, and Francis Huether, FSC. Landover, MD: Christian Brothers Conference, 1994. Pg. 434 – 435.

uses the term *disciple*.[11] While this referred directly to the mission or vocation of the teacher to make these children disciples of Jesus Christ, it also informed the relationship between teacher and pupil. Popular education in the 17th century being what it was, the relationship between teacher and pupil was, in most cases, hardly ever more than a commercial one at best. Teachers largely worked to earn a living, dispensing their knowledge for a fee. Young students, especially poor ones, were often looked upon as undisciplined, ignorant, and wholly uncultured necessities for the teacher's livelihood. By describing them as disciples, De La Salle not only established a fundamentally religious component in the relationship between teacher and pupil but also introduced an element of responsibility that gave students a central place in the educational enterprise.

De La Salle highlights the value that children in the schools have by articulating the nature of their religious identity. "[L]ook upon the children God has entrusted to you as the children of God himself." (M 133.2)[12] For De La Salle, all students were a proximate incarnation of Jesus Christ. "Recognize Jesus beneath the poor rags of the children whom you have to instruct. Adore him in them." (M 96.3) Yet they are also described as "weary and exhausted travelers" (M 37.1), "abandoned orphans" (M 37.3) on the road of life seeking direction, support, and guidance in a confusing world. Children, for De La Salle, carry a dignity that belies their practical circumstances and that reaches beyond the popular perception of childhood. Although the word "vocation" is not used by De La Salle in reference

---

[11] The word *disciple* is used 230 times in all of his writings — 133 times in his meditations, and not once in the *Conduct of Schools* school handbook. The term *enfant* (child) is used 324 times — 177 times in his meditations, and not one in the *Conduct of Schools* school handbook. For an analysis of these terms and their contexts, see Morales, Alfredo. "Child – Pupil - Disciple" in *Lasallian Themes*, Volume 1. Rome: Brothers of the Christian Schools, 1994. Pg. 66.

[12] *Meditations by St. John Baptist de La Salle.* Translated by Richard Arnandez, FSC, and Augustine Loes, FSC. Edited by Augustine Loes, FSC, and Francis Huether, FSC. Landover, MD: Christian Brothers Conference, 1994. PG. 245. All references from De La Salle's will follow the numbering standardized published in this text. This reference is to meditation number 133, section 2. Subsequent references in the paper will only give the number of the meditation along with its relevant section.

to children, clearly his perspective on childhood combines a unique, essentially religious identity with very practical experience. Their "vocation" is to grow into the mature fulfillment of who they are, and they do so in concert with their educational progress and with the guidance of "older brothers," their teachers.

Children are the most innocent part of the Church and are usually best disposed to receive the impressions of grace. (M 205.3) But the "innocence" of which he speaks is not the sentimental and distorting kind of innocence referred to by William Werpehowski, whereby "they come to bear virtues and values serving, preferred, and protected by adults."[13] It is a notion of innocence rooted firmly in a deeper, longer, faith perspective that looks beyond and behind the challenging and often disturbing realities prevalent outside, and sometimes inside, the classrooms of the time. De La Salle was all too conscious of the fact that teachers in schools had to deal with a wide variety of children. He knew firsthand the kinds of characteristics and behaviors that children of the poor were likely to have. This was simply the way things were, and this was the substance of one's prayer (and work). "You have two sorts of children to instruct: some are disorderly and inclined to evil; the others are good, or at least inclined to good. Pray continually for both . . ." (M186.3)

The teachers in De La Salle's schools, through their lifestyle, association, and religious commitment, participated in an endeavor whereby one looked both solidly at, and through, the realities of children's lives. Rather than viewing children with a sentimental or distorted perspective, these "older brothers" were likely to be the first adults who considered them with more serious attention than they had previously encountered in either their families or society,[14] a care and attention from teachers who saw themselves as fully and finally responsible. "Consider that the account you will have to give to God will not be inconsequential, because it concerns the salvation of the souls of children whom God has entrusted to your care,

---

[13] Werpehowski, William. "The Search of Real Children: Innocence, Absence, and Becoming a Self in Christ." *The Vocation of the Child.* Patrick M. Brennan, William B. Eerdmans Pub. Co., 2008, 53-74.

[14] H.D. Baer, in this volume, illustrates this through the example of Mister Rogers, recognizing that "even the very young are seriously at work understanding the world and their place within it."

for on the day of judgment, you will answer for them as much as for yourself." (M 205.2)[15]

"Best Practices" for Children

Identifying children in this way has clear implications in how they should be treated. The respect and sense of discipleship that emerge from De La Salle's meditations are backed up by specific practices that may be found in the "handbook" for the schools, *Conduite des Ecoles* (The Conduct of Schools; hereafter the *Conduct*).[16] This practical reference work came to be produced through years of experimentation and practice, and it systematized the "best practices" that had become most successful in the many schools and situations that the Brothers had encountered.[17]

Among the *Conduct*'s practices were the following: large groups of students divided into sections based on ability and level, a highly structured method of questions and sub-questions, and communication beyond teacher questions and student answers through an elaborate set of "signals" with a pointer / clicker designed for the purpose.[18] A significant portion of the text is devoted to the means

---

[15] "You must be convinced of this, that God will begin by making you given an account of their souls before making you give an account of your own. For when you took responsibility for them, you committed yourself at the same time to procure their salvation with as much diligence as your own, for you engaged yourself to work entirely for the salvation of their souls." (M 205.2)

[16] De La Salle, John Baptist. *Conduct of Christian Schools.* Translated by Richard Arnandez and F. de la Fontainerie. Edited by Richard Arnandez and William Mann. Landover, MD. 1996.

[17] The first copy dates from 1706, with the first printed edition appears in 1720, the year after De La Salle's death.

[18] Each classroom consisted of a number of levels and grades together, and each group of students following its own program of activities. Each group would be addressed in turn by the teacher, with the other groups quietly working on their own material. In reading, for example, one student reads while all are reading the same material to themselves, the teacher calling on students out of turn in order to make sure that they are following the same section. In arithmetic, individual pupils do examples of particular lessons for the class, being questioned by the teacher to make sure that each concept and term is fully understood. Everything explained to the pupil should be repeated by the pupil before moving on. If the one doing the example failed in any respect, another student doing the same

for maintaining order. Looking beyond the common notions of punishment that were popularly in effect at the time, even as part of the upbringing of Louis XIV, De La Salle's innovation lay in how these means for maintaining order were seen as part of the overall educational picture.

De La Salle knew that neither piety or learning would be fostered by punishment. The overall atmosphere of the school created by its organized methodology, the seriousness of its teachers, the religious character of all its operations, the standard, pervasive silence of its buildings, all contributed to a situation where the use of punishment was a clear exception to common practice.[19]

He also knew, however, that on the practical level punishment was a reality in elementary education. A class full of young boys, no matter how silent or how well-organized, would need correcting. Experience had shown him that teachers must act in a manner both gentle and firm, and they must never letting passion or anger have part in the correction. (CS 2.5)[20] A detailed section in the *Conduct* deals with the kinds of children who should and who should not be punished. Discrimination in this case is essential, since everyone is not alike.

It is important to see that such discrimination is not a faceless categorization simply based on external behavior. It is a discrimination that respects the child's character while addressing his behavior. William Werpehowski addresses the dangers inherent in categorizing children based simply on their behavior, activities that

---

lesson was called on to make the correction, or failing that, a student doing a more advanced lesson was called on. After each correction, the original student repeated the correct answer. Every single student was to do an example on the board of the lesson being covered with the teacher paying close attention to both what the student does and says. Integral to De La Salle's method was the policy of personally involving each student every day.

[19] "To avoid frequent correction, which is a source of great disorder in a school, it is necessary to note well that it is silence, restraint, and watchfulness on the part of the teacher that establish and maintain good order in a class. It is not harshness and blows that establish and maintain good order. A constant effort must be made to act with skill and ingenuity in order to keep the students in order while making almost no use of correction." (CS 2.5.2)

[20] These references indicate the specific chapter and subsection of *The Conduct of Christian Schools*. Op. Cit.

"immunize grownups from considering the general social circumstances and conditions that do and do not support children's lives, and their responsibility for them."[21] This kind of categorization limits both what children can do and how we subsequently see ourselves related to them. These dynamics become especially critical in the area of correction, as most of us are able to attest from early educational experience; e.g., one of the more serious "sins" that teachers can make is to misjudge a situation and make a false judgment about a student. De La Salle takes steps to prevent such mistakes by emphasizing the critical importance of discerning the individual character of students.

> "Jesus Christ compares those who have charge of souls to a good shepherd who has great care for the sheep. One quality he must possess, according to our Savior, is to know each of them individually. This should also be one of the main concerns of those who instruct others: to be able to understand their pupils and to discern the right way to guide them.
>
> They must show more mildness toward some, more firmness toward others. There are those who call for much patience, those who need to be stimulated and spurred on, some who need to be reproved and punished to correct them of their faults, others who must be constantly watched over to prevent them from being lost or going astray.
>
> This guidance requires understanding and discernment of spirits, qualities you should frequently and earnestly ask of God, for they are most necessary for you in the guidance of those placed in your care." (M 33.1)

De La Salle shows a keen eye for the emotional dynamics that children are subject to. He wants to make sure that corrections indeed accomplish what they should; i.e., help student recognize and correct wrong behavior. Children are never to be publicly humiliated, and punishments are given only when students recognize and accept the reason for them. Correction also included the immediate

---

[21] See Werpehowski, William. "The Search of Real Children: Innocence, Absence, and Becoming a Self in Christ", Op. Cit.

opportunity to make the appropriate correct response. The focus was on the child's capacity to change his behavior for the better.[22]

Nothing was left to chance in the administration of school discipline. The *Conduct* is filled with sound advice in this respect. In fact, some of the advice that he gives is extremely unusual for the historical time period, revealing an educational wisdom that deeply respects the integrity of both teachers and students. A striking example of this is the list of six ways in which the *teacher* can be unbearable to the students. Some examples: "[W]hen the teacher is too insistent in urging upon a child some performance which the child is not disposed to do, and the teacher does not permit the child the leisure or the time to reflect. . . .[W]hen the teacher exacts little things and big things alike with the same ardor. . . . [W]hen the teacher immediately rejects the reasons and excuses of children and is not willing to listen to them at all."[23] Instead of putting the burden on the children, it is the teachers who must look at how they make themselves or their actions unbearable to those entrusted to their care.

---

[22] One example: "By their modesty and restraint, teachers will give an example of the manner in which the students should walk. In order that the teachers may more easily see the students and observe how they behave themselves on the way to holy Mass, teachers will walk on the opposite side of the street from them, ahead of the line, with their faces sufficiently turned toward their students to be able to see them all. While on the street, teachers will not admonish students for any faults of which they may be guilty, but will wait until the next day, just before going to holy Mass, to correct them. (CS 8.1)

[23] First, the teacher's penances are too rigorous and the yoke which the teacher imposes upon the students is too heavy. This state of affairs is frequently due to lack of discretion and judgment on the part of the teacher. It often happens that students do not have enough strength of body or of mind to bear the burdens which many times overwhelm them. Second, when the teacher enjoins, commands, or exacts something of the children with words too harsh and in a manner too domineering. Above all, the teacher's conduct is unbearable when it arises from unrestrained impatience or anger. ... Sixth, when the teacher not mindful enough of personal faults that he does not know how to sympathize with the weaknesses of children and so exaggerates their faults too much. This is the situation when the teacher reprimands them or punishes them and acts as though dealing with an insensible instrument rather than with a creature capable of reason. (CS 2.5)

The Experience of Children

De La Salle was deeply aware of the experience of children among the poor and the working class of the cities of 17th century France. He knew that they were subject to difficult challenges on a daily basis. "It often happens that students do not have enough strength of body or of mind to bear the burdens which many times overwhelm them."(CS 2.5) The children of the poor were largely neglected or ignored, allowed to amuse themselves in whatever way they wished until they were able to begin working at some trade or craft. De La Salle came to see that children were being educated into forms of thinking and behaving that would remain with them throughout their lives. That was why it was so important to shape their character in a Christian fashion at an early age.

Two meditations are particularly revelatory of De La Salle's viewpoint regarding the situation within which students found themselves. In one of them, he notes the ease with which children can be taken captive by a habit of doing wrong.

> "People are naturally so inclined to sin that they seem to find no other pleasure than committing it. This is seen especially in children, because their minds have not developed yet and they are not capable of much serious reflection. They seem to have no other inclination than to please their passions and their senses, and to satisfy their nature. . . . [I]f they are abandoned to their own will, they will run the risk of ruining themselves and causing much sorrow to their parents. The reason for this is because the faults turn into a habit which will be very difficult to correct. The good and bad habits contracted in childhood and maintained over a period of time ordinarily become part of nature . . . .It can be said with reason that a child who has acquired a habit of sin has in some sense lost his freedom and has made himself a miserable captive." (M 203.2)[24]

---

[24] This meditation retains greater relevance today in terms of its insights into the formative status of habits than it does in terms of its theology. It reflects the 17th century's pessimistic outlook on human nature.

This observation about the captivity of sin and the loss of freedom echo modern observations regarding compulsive or addictive behaviors and their tenacious hold over individual lives, limiting one's interests, options, and horizons. The freedom of which De La Salle speaks is based on what he had seen in his own schools, places where structure, vigilance, and good example allowed children to relax enough, as children, so as to benefit from all of the child-centered instruction, cognitive and behavioral, that the school provided. It's the kind of relaxed freedom that any teacher would immediately recognize in a well-run class. And while he undoubtedly was subject to the influences of Jansenism and its negative perceptions of human behavior vis-à-vis salvation, De La Salle came to know children well and has an empathy for the kinds of troubles children can bring onto themselves, describing with perfect candor and keen insight the process by which they proceed to make themselves captive.[25]

It would accurate to say that he did not have any romantic or idealistic ideas about children. Forty years with the poor would quickly erode the best of intentions in that regard. Instead, De La Salle gave children their due, recognizing both their limitations and their strengths, and setting their vocation firmly in the midst of their experience. Children have a vocation to see themselves as part of the world around them, and they have a God-given right to be treated with a respect that reaches beyond their years, drawing them forward to live into the deeper version of their vocation as a child of God.

In this connection, De La Salle's notion of childhood bears strong resemblance to Vigen Guroian's description of the "office of child" – including both the responsibilities and graces associated with that office.[26] The essentially spiritual identity of children and childhood highlighted by Guroian's references from St. Peter Chrysologos, John Henry Newman, George MacDonald, and Karl Rahner are

---

[25] De La Salle knew that there was many a boy in the Christian School who "has walked the way of sin, seeking to satisfy his passions in the world, and has found there nothing but vice and vanity, misery and disappointment." (M 37.1)

[26] Guroian, Vigen. "The Office of Child in the Christian Faith: A Theology of Childhood." *The Vocation of the Child.* Patrick M. Brennan, William B. Eerdmans Pub. Co., 2008, 104-126.

ones with which De La Salle would resonate. His deep familiarity with the Fathers of the Church, found throughout his meditations, and his lengthy exposure to the realities of urban education among the poor, led De La Salle to develop a profoundly spiritual, yet practical, appreciation of children. While there was a fundamentally spiritual identity at their core, children still needed to be taught reading, writing, math, and manners. The content, context, and method of that teaching, personalized in no small measure in the teacher, identified that spiritual identity and brought it to the fore. If De La Salle had not viewed children in this light, he clearly would not have dedicated his life to their welfare.

The anthropological foundation for De La Salle's educational perspective, on the other hand, may appear to be somewhat condescending or paternalistic and is seen in another one of his meditations. However, given the popular movements of 17th century France (Jansenism, Quietism, Gallicanism, etc.) and De La Salle's own wide-ranging educational experience, it should still be also seen as remarkably insightful and direct.

> "It can be said that children at birth are like a mass of flesh. Their minds do not seem to emerge from the matter in them except with time, becoming refined only little by little. As an unavoidable consequence, those who are ordinarily instructed in the schools are not yet able by themselves to understand easily the Christian truths and maxims. . . . Christian truths are hidden from the human mind. If this is true of all men, it is incomparably more true of children, whose minds are more unrefined because they are less free of their senses and of matter. Children, then, need someone to develop the Christian truths for them in a more concrete fashion, one that is harmonious with the limitations of their minds, for these truths are hidden from the human mind. If this help is not given, they often remain all their lives insensitive and opposed to thoughts of God and incapable of knowing and appreciating them [1 Cor 2:14]. For this purpose the goodness of God has provided children with

teachers who will instruct them in all these things." (M 197.1)[27]

The limitations that poor children carry become the occasion for the teacher's ministry. De La Salle highlights the distinctions between children and adults. They are neither "little adults" nor fully developed persons of any particular kind. They are children, individuals subject to their senses and to concrete, immediate things who only gradually "emerge" and "become refined." Therefore, their instruction must be appropriate to their nature. Their vocation as children includes the development of reason, judgment, and moral behavior – things that De La Salle's schools, through their structure, teachers, and environment, were established to provide. And while De La Salle's emphasis on reason and critical stance towards most things dealing with passion, feeling, or emotional attachments might seem uncaring or stunted, it's clear from everything he writes that he grew to develop a great love for children and their needs, and he became as empathetic and as practically responsive to the real needs of poor children as anyone of his time could be.[28]

Two of the practical ways that the experience of children was addressed inside and outside of the classroom were through a communal sense of school ownership, in today's terms, that was cultivated by having a plethora of student responsibilities, and through the individual care demonstrated by the keeping of individual student records.

It seems that most, if not all, students had some responsibility or job in the classroom, from the student who would open the doors

---

[27] De La Salle observed that many children of the time "are little accustomed to use their reason, because nature is more lively in them and strongly inclined to enjoy the pleasures of the senses." (M 56.2)

[28] There are sections of De La Salle's writings, especially those dealing with the religious life of his followers, that place an emphasis on obedience, mortification, sacrifice, and humility that sounds overblown to our contemporary ears. And some of that 17th century religious sensibility was certainly as aspect of his educational outlook. This makes it all the more remarkable that the educational practices in the *Conduct* and the educational perspectives from his meditations can stand on their own even today.

to the school – *before* the teacher arrived – to prayer leaders, bell ringers, and street supervisors. It seems that if there was a job to be done in school, there was a student to do it.[29] And these jobs were given with a full understanding of the ways that children might behave, if left totally unsupervised. For example, a "class inspector" oversaw the arrival of students prior to the arrival of the teacher, reporting anything observed and never interfering with anything that happened. But there were two further monitors, unknown to the class inspector or to one another, who would validate the reports of that inspector. "Trust, but verify" has a long history.

An attention to, and respect for, individual student experience is also demonstrated by the fact that each teacher drew up a record for each student in class. This record began with an interview when the pupil was admitted, recording his family, background, home-life, particular traits, and other significant data. During the year, the teacher would enter pertinent information about the student, passing it one to the next teacher at the end of the year. When the student left, they would be filed for future reference. The value of such acquired insights into an individual student, despite the risk of acquiring a skewed viewpoint based on a single teacher's experience, make personal attention a realistic possibility. One example:

> "Francis Delevieux: 8 1/2, two years at school, in 3rd section of Writing since July 1st. Somewhat turbulent; little piety at church or prayers unless supervised. Lacks reserve. Conduct satisfactory; needs encouragement to effort; punishment of no avail; light-headed. Rarely absent except when with bad companions; often late. Application moderate but he learns with ease. Twice nearly dismissed for

---

[29] Such duties with their qualifications and terms of office were carefully described, rotated among the pupils either as a reward or as an incentive towards developing responsibility. Some examples: Leaders of prayers did so throughout the day, distinctly and without distraction. Holy water bearers made holy water available when entering or leaving church. The rosary keeper and his assistants gave rosaries out in class and in church, distributing them and counting them when returned. The bell ringer had to be vigilant, exact, and punctual, ringing the bell each half hour and at the beginning and end of the school day. Papers were given out and returned by students who followed a set routine. The sweeper kept the classroom clean, and the doorkeeper saw to it that only Brothers, pupils, and the parish priest were admitted.

negligence. Submissive to a strong hand. Not a difficult character. Must be won over. Spoiled at home. Parents resent his being punished."[30]

If any one of us received such an overview of a student, we would quickly have a good basis upon which to proceed both inside and outside of the classroom. Such a summary also indicates the kinds of traits that teachers found significant in developing the child's individual character.

The Guidance of Children

Recognizing both the challenging situations within which many students dwell and the eminent value that they have in the sight of God, De La Salle specifies particular dimensions for approaching their Christian formation and practical education.

In summary fashion, De La Salle points out the need to teach the young both spiritual and practical realities with a view towards cultivating piety.[31]

> "You will procure the good of the Church by making them true Christians and docile to the truths of faith and the maxims of the holy Gospel. You will procure the good of the state by teaching them how to read and write and everything else that pertains to your ministry in regard to exterior things. But piety should be joined to exterior things, otherwise your work would be of little use." (M 160.3)

He insists that the teacher's first care should be "to make sure they grasp fully the doctrine of the holy apostles, to give them the spirit

---

[30] De La Salle, Jean-Baptiste. Œuvres Complètes. Rome: Frères des Ecoles Chrétiennes, 1993. p. 657.

[31] "*piété* (n.): piety. For De La Salle the word *piété* had a much broader and key meaning than the word piety in English today, which at times can carry a connotation of childish or superficial devotion. De La Salle uses the word 149 times in the meditations to signify a range of meaning. It can refer to conversation on religious or spiritual topics, to the practice of prayer, or acts of devotion, to a solid spirit of religion, or the practice of one's religion." (Augustine Loes, ed. in De La Salle, *Meditations*, tr. Arnandez.)

of religion, and to make them practice what Jesus Christ has left us in the holy Gospel." (M 116.2) This is done by interpreting Christian truths in more concrete ways, ones that resonates with their ways of thinking.[32]

At the same time, the practical goals of education are never far behind; i.e., a knowledge of all the practical truths and skills that will enable the students to become responsible members of society — reading, writing, calculating, good manners, and pious example.

Success will have been reached if "they often think of Jesus, their good and only Lord, that they often speak of Jesus, that they long only for Jesus, and live only for Jesus." (M 102.2) All their actions will be united with Jesus Christ. They "practice what Jesus Christ has left us in the holy Gospel" (M 116.2) and grasp the doctrine of the apostles.

Emphasis is placed on docility to the truths of faith and the maxims of the Gospel, along with piety and the spirit of religion. Piety "is the principal object and the purpose of your work . . . .The trouble you take to give them this piety will in the end make your students docile and truly submissive to their parents . . . , self-controlled and well-behaved in public, pious in church, and in all that refers to God, to holy things, and to everything that relates to religion." (M 186.1) While on the one hand it may seem that such an emphasis would confirm the suspicion that the only real goal in this entire enterprise is to render children docile to the prevalent social structure of the day — and there would be evidence to support at least a partial validation of this — it is far more true to recognize the

---

[32] It is not enough to procure for children the Christian spirit and teach them the mysteries and doctrines of our religion. You must also teach them the practical maxims that are found throughout the holy Gospel. But since their minds are not yet sufficiently able to understand and practice these maxims by themselves, you must serve as visible angels for them in two things: 1) You must help them understand the maxims as they are set forth in the holy Gospel, 2) You must guide their steps along the way that leads them to put these maxims into practice.... You must win them to practice the maxims of the holy Gospel, and to this end you must give them means which are easy and accommodation to their age. Gradually accustomed to this practice in their childhood, they will be able when older to have acquired them as a kind of habit and practice them without great difficulty. (M 197.1)

authentic context and import of this result as representing a genuine appreciation and desire to see children deepen their identity as children of God.

The role of personal example in the attainment of these educational goals is key. It speaks to both the nature of the child's vocation and the nature of the teacher's role as mentor, guide, and "older brother."[33] De La Salle has observed at numerous times that the "tendencies of the young are easily guided, so that they accept without great difficulty the impressions we seek to give them." (M 186.1)[34] This is why it is so important that teachers "act so wisely in their regard that nothing in themselves or in their conduct could give these youths any dislike for the service of God, or cause them to deviate even slightly from their duties." (M 115.1) Their approach to students must be one of constant example, since this addresses their recognized learning patterns and confirms the content of one's teaching.

> "Example makes a much greater impression on the mind and heart than words. This is especially true of children, since they do not yet have the minds sufficiently able to reflect, and they ordinarily model themselves on the example of their teachers. They are led more readily to do what they see done for them than to carry out what they hear told to them, particularly when the words they hear are not in harmony with the actions they see." (M 202.3)

> "Do you wish your disciples to do what is right? Do it yourself. You will persuade them much more readily through your example of wise and prudent behavior than through all the words you could speak to them. Do you want them

---

[33] One could make an argument for saying that this role is a version of William Werpehowski's dictum that "a child ought to have teachers and exemplars of integrity."

[34] These sentiments seem to contrast with his earlier remarks regarding the difficulty children have of forming good habits and the ease with which they fall into sin. His overall understanding seems to be that children are readily formed by whatever influences surround them. If these are bad influences, the child will develop bad habits. If these are good influences, the child will develop good habits. The teacher must insure that the child is surrounded by good influences so that good habits, and piety, may be developed.

> to keep silence? Keep it yourself. You will make them pru-
> dent and self-controlled only in so far as you act that way
> yourself." (M 33.2)

Instruction supported by example is one of the chief characteristics of the teacher's zeal. Without it, one's zeal "would not go very far and would not have much result or success." Zeal must be realized within one's behavior as a model to the students. This is the only way in which "the instructions you give to those whom you have to instruct" will become "effective in drawing them to the practice of good." (M 193.3) "Is it enough for them to see you in order to be well behaved? Is your behavior sufficient to encourage them to practice virtue? … This is the main benefit which you should impart to them, the best gift you can give them when they leave you." (M 98.3) One contemporary Lasallian scholar has noted: "In light of this, it is very obvious that De La Salle believed in the moral redemption of the child, and he placed his confidence in Christian education as an effective means for obtaining it."[35]

John Coons gives contemporary substance to this impression when he asks, "how does an obtending child proceed in this world of which she knows so little?" and then answers that she must "look for the most reliable (or more experienced) older navigator who is available and follow such authority so long as her own ignorance persists… It is an act of a pilgrim who puts confidence in a more experienced and discerning fellow human…"[36] In the life of virtue, as it is encountered by the child, De La Salle would have us realize both the grave responsibility given to teachers vis-à-vis those who may only recently have made forays into the world of obedience and the pivotal effect that teachers have in influencing the present and future direction of a child's life by virtue of their example.[37]

---

[35] Morales, Alfredo, Op. Cit. Pg. 69.

[36] Coons, John E. "Luck, Obedience, and the Vocation of Childhood" in Brennan, Patrick M. *The Vocation of the Child*. William B. Eerdmans Pub. Co., 2008.

[37] It was striking to read in the essay by John Coons that Karl Barth referred to "an ultimate state of the parents as 'ambassadors' of the good." De La Salle, in a key section of his meditations, refers to his teachers in a similar way, although focused specifically within the Christian context: "Since you are ambassadors and ministers of

For De La Salle, there was another means by which the importance of example, the practice of virtue, and effective communication of values came about, and that was through a genuine interest in, and practice of, Christian decorum and politeness. Social graces were more than an optional component in the stratified and socially conscious society of 17th century France. Good manners were seen as both a component of acceptable integration in society and a dimension of one's faith life. As such, proper manners were a component in the way that children were approached by teachers, and by such example such manners should become part of how they might, in turn, treat others both now and in the future.

For De La Salle, civility was the practical manifestation of a person's faith life, the way in which Christianity became part of one's everyday existence. He defines civility, or Christian politeness, as " . . . a sensible and regulated mode of behavior that one exhibits in one's speech and outward actions through an attitude of due moderation, or of respect, or of union and charity toward one's neighbor, paying attention to the times, places and persons with whom one is dealing."[38] De La Salle recognized and respected the traditional relationships that existed between the various social classes, classes that also extended to children, but he also gives these relationships wider application by extending the scope of politeness to include all those within one's social sphere.[39] It wasn't enough to be polite only to those who were members of one's own social class. Christian sensibilities demanded that one also was polite to those of other social classes. The popularity of De La Salle contribution to politeness

---

Jesus Christ in the work that you do, you must act as representing Jesus Christ himself. He wants your disciples to see him in you and receive your teaching as if he were teaching them. They must be convinced that the truth of Jesus Christ comes from your mouth, that it is only in his name that you teach, that he has given you authority over them." (M195.2)

[38] Calcutt, *De La Salle*, p. 435.

[39] For example, where other texts will specify the proper way to disagree with someone of a higher social standing, or the proper way to knock on the door of a lord, De La Salle extends those same standards universally. These are proper ways of disagreeing with anyone, or that the proper way to knock when visiting anyone. See Calcutt, *De la Salle*, p. 436.

education is attested to by the fact that over 150 editions of his book have been published since 1703.[40]

Since it was one of the "textbooks" for teaching reading, *The Rules of Christian Decorum and Politeness* was published in an elaborate script form, so that when students were ready to read it, they would not only learn societal conventions of behavior but would be further challenged by a formal writing style that they would encounter as adults.

But besides being a resource text for teaching reading, the contents of the book highlight the essentially religious outlook that governed all of De La Salle's perspective about children and their relationship to the world around them. He writes:

> "It is surprising that most Christians look upon decorum and politeness as merely human and worldly qualities and to not think of raising their minds to any higher views by considering them as virtues that have reference to God, to their neighbor, and to themselves."[41]

These social graces were not merely conventional practices of social propriety, they were manifestations of an awareness of God's presence in the world, of respect for oneself and for others. It was a means of growing into one's faith, to "live like true Christians." Through them, a child's vocation was once more invited to mature along authentic lines and in real life. Such development could not be a passive acceptance of society's rules. This was not a nominal faith. It was also a form of discipleship, a practicing of one's faith, and seeing social graces and politeness from the viewpoint of one's

---

[40] According to Alfred Calcutt, with this text De "La Salle provided the most important contribution to this form of social education in the schools of France for the next two centuries." (Calcutt, *De La Salle*, p. 433.) The latest edition of this text, a translation of the original edition of 1703, was published in 1990. *The Rules of Christian Decorum and Politeness.* Op. Cit.) For an overview of the work, see the preface of the English edition. Also see Wright, Gregory. "Why Read the Rules of Christian Decorum and Politeness." *Lasalliana* 24.May (1992): 3-4.

[41] De La Salle, John Baptist. *The Rules of Christian Decorum and Politeness.* Translated by Richard Arnandez. Romeoville, IL: Lasallian Publications, 1990. Pg. 3. For a modern reflection on this work see Wright, Gregory. "Why Read the Rules of Christian Decorum and Politeness." *Lasalliana* 24.May (1992): 3, 4.

faith was something that De La Salle also recommended to parents.[42]

In fact, through these teachings on politeness, as well as through other activities at the school, parents came to be instructed by way of their children. Writing classes used Christian maxims as models, and these writings were brought home each day. "They portrayed in great measure a humanitarian and cultural ideal, and moral and social values which the parents, even the illiterate ones, enjoyed hearing their children read aloud."[43] Similarly, children at home would have prepared the reading they would do in class the next day, or a short speech on a topic in the catechism or the politeness book, and in doing so they shared their religious and social formation and with their parents.

Specific instructions in the book on politeness would have a positive influence on both children and parents. Some examples: "It is impolite to wipe one's nose with the fingers and then clean them on one's clothes … which should always be clean no matter how poor they are since they are the adornments of a servant of God." "Good behavior demands that before a meal one should wash one's hands and bless the food … When there is a child present, it often happens that such a person is given this task." "Children especially should make it a rule to be the last to start and first to finish a meal … Children should always leave the table first, excusing themselves appropriately."

The breadth of practices and activities covered by the politeness book is evident in the chapter headings, all of which represent topics relevant to the present and future social life of young, untrained, inner-city boys: Three further examples from the text illustrate the variety of situations that the book addresses:

---

[42] "Fathers and mothers … far from telling the children for whom they are responsible that if they do such-and-such a thing, they will be blamed, and no one will like them, people will laugh at them … when they want them to adopt exterior practices regarding bodily welfare … will take care to motivate them through the presence of God … If they teach them and get them to practice politeness to their neighbor, they will teach them always to treat people with politeness and respect as the members of Jesus Christ." Preface of *Politeness*, Op. Cit., Pg. 3, as translated in Poutet, Op. Cit., Pg. 148.

[43] Poutet. Op. Cit. Pg. 132.

- It is against decorum to spit in front of yourself while with others, or to spit too far, so that you have to go looking for the spittle in order to step on it. In places that are usually kept clean, turn aside slightly and spit into your handkerchief, then fold it immediately without looking at it, and replace it in your pocket.

- You should remove your hat: 1) in a place where there are important people; 2) when you greet someone; 3) when you give or receive anything; 4) when you are being seated at table; 5) when you hear the names of Jesus or Mary; 6) when you are in the presence of persons to whom you owe great respect.

- It is entirely contrary to decorum to grow overexcited when you play. Still, you should not play in a careless manner nor lose deliberately as a way of flattering your opponent. This would make the person with whom you are playing think that you care little about contributing to his enjoyment in a well-played match.

What a child does has consequences that are immediate and that are long-term. In the situation itself, the child's behavior is a vehicle for the expression of one's religious convictions – one's faith – and deepens that faith life through the thoughtful practices involved. But more importantly, by behaving in a specific way – according to the convictions of faith – children are building their relationship with God through their relationship with others. Common interactions become a "school of Christian life" and children deepen their vocation as human individuals outside of the classroom as they had been doing, hopefully, inside of the classroom, where their teacher, their classroom protocols, their interactions with other students, and their exposure to a highly structured environment geared towards their growth has established the basis upon which their other experiences might be judged.[44]

---

[44] An especially compelling illustration of this was recently demonstrated to me through a French film documentary entitled "Etre e Avoir" that covers a year in the life of a small French country school. Numerous scenes echoed sections from

Conclusion

A child's vocation may be seen, through De La Salle's educational vision and practice, as a sort of apprenticeship to life. The primary components of this apprenticeship are the child and the teacher and their relationship to one another. Not only is the teacher a "Brother" in title, he is also to be an older brother to the child, demonstrating a care and concern that allows the child to both be at ease and to confidently move forward in academic studies, the life of faith, and individual identity.[45] The teachers' solicitude for the students' welfare and the care with which they attended to their duties resembled those of a serious older brother more than those of a schoolmaster.

As much as the teachers came to know their students in a variety of daily situations, the students also came to know their teachers. Such a relationship as De La Salle advocated became established over a long period of time through a wide variety of activities, ranging from direct teaching experiences during class to supervision at school meals, at recreation, and at church. A certain kind of relationship along with the particular teaching drew students to the practice of their faith. The combination of firmness and gentleness,[46] teaching and example, applied to all the subjects taught in

---

De La Salle's writings or practices and attitudes illustrated in both the *Conduct* and the *Meditations*. Many, of course, are now commonly appreciated in all sorts of schools. Still, it was gratifying to once again note how the best teaching has universal appeal.

[45] It is at least parenthetically significant that the Brothers were, and are, identified by their first names – as in Brother James or Brother Charles – by the students and parents, and not by their last names – as in Brother Kennedy or Brother McMann – which is the case in most other religious orders involved in education. This aspect of "formal familiarity" reveals an educational relationship similar to that which is so well described in William Werpehowski's essay in Patrick Brennan's *The Vocation of the Child*. (William B. Eerdmans Pub. Co., 2008) when he speaks about the relationship between Scout and Atticus Finch from *To Kill a Mockingbird*.

[46] Do you have these sentiments of charity and tenderness toward the poor children whom you have to educate? Do you take advantage of their affection for you to lead them to God? If you have for them the firmness of a father to restrain and withdraw them from misbehavior, you must also have for them the tenderness of a mother to draw them to you, and to do for them all the good that depends on you. (M 101.3)

the school and pervading all aspects of school life, was the vehicle for Christian instruction and the means for developing the child's vocation, a vocation that was based on, was aimed at, and was centered on God.

The teacher, in a curious and rather dramatic twist, has offered himself to God in place of the children that he educates. Similar to Jesus Christ himself and echoing the religious experience of other traditions, the "master" takes on full responsibility for his "disciples."[47] De La Salle writes: "You have committed yourselves to God in the place of those whom you instruct. By taking upon yourselves the responsibility for their souls, you have, so to speak, offered to him soul for soul. [Ex. 21:23]" (M 137.3) It is as if the vocation of the child is subsumed into the vocation of the teacher. One proceeds in concert with the other. There can hardly be a more religiously intimate responsibility than the one taken up under this conviction.[48]

Finally, the task of fostering the vocation of children is a divine work, according to De La Salle. "You carry out a work that requires you to touch hearts, but this you cannot do except by the Spirit of God." (M 43.3) "You must . . . imitate God to some extent, for he . . . loved the souls he created." (M 100.3) That imitation of God becomes incarnated in the teacher's daily relationship with students. "Every day you have poor children to instruct. Love them tenderly . . . following in this the example of Jesus Christ." (M 166.2) Through such fraternal devotion and deep attachment to the good of their students, teachers are able to draw down God's graces upon

---

[47] The idea of discipleship that defines the relationship between teacher and student is one that is informed by Jesus Christ's own example. De La Salle recommends the model of Jesus in the Gospels as the perfect example of the kind of teacher appropriate in a Christian School. By looking at the ways that Jesus used in leading his disciples to understand and practice the Gospel's truths, teachers will discover how they might similarly lead their own disciples towards the same goal. For that, the teacher's example for their students is again key, as Jesus' example is key to the teacher.

[48] For teachers, the students will be their glory; "the glory that you have procured for them will reflect on you." (M 207.1) In heaven, the students will then fully appreciate the work that has been done on their behalf and will beseech God to bestow upon their teachers the fullness of heaven's rewards. In this way, the vocation of both the teacher and the student will have been brought to maturity.

those entrusted to their care. The child's vocation flourishes by way of the graces that the teacher makes possible through his prayer and his daily efforts on the child's behalf.

De La Salle's favorite image for the activity of teaching, or of forming a child's vocation, is the winning and this touching of hearts. (M 43.3) "Do you have such faith that it is able to touch the hearts of your students and to inspire them with the Christian spirit? This is the greatest miracle you could perform, and the one that God asks of you, since this is the purpose of your work." (M 139.3) Such an image captures the essentially interior nature of forming a child's vocation. Facts and figures neither have the formative power nor comprise the major component of the activity of teaching. True personal formation involves dynamics of the heart, as salvation itself does. The salvation of souls is a matter of touching hearts (M 57.2), of leading children to live in a Christian manner through winning their hearts. Failing to do this will not only fail to draw them to God but will instead drive them away. (M 115.3) Therefore, teachers have the duty "of learning how to touch hearts" (M 129.2) through earnest application to interior prayer and the conscientious performance of their teaching responsibilities.

Children "themselves are a letter which Christ dictates to you, which you write each day in their hearts, not with ink, but by the Spirit of the living God." (M 195.2) Children have an openness, a capacity for learning and for inspiration, and an identity all their own. They are like a letter waiting to be written, ready for the kind of personal encounter from God that the teacher provides. The light that is enkindled in the hearts of students through the inspiration of the teacher brings about the warmth of soul and the intimacy that a letter often brings. Such teachers may be the first instance that children experience of God's loving concern for them. In a very real way, along with learning how to write, students come to know the foundation out of which writing receives its power. By touching their hearts, writing Christ's Gospel with the Spirit of the living God, teachers awaken and enkindle in the hearts of students their capacity to participate in their heritage as children of God; i.e., they fulfill their vocation as children.

THE FIVE CORE PRINCIPLES: THEIR ORIGINS, INTEGRATION WITH CATHOLIC IDENTITY, AND RESONANCE TODAY

"The things which really come first are the things which we are accustomed to think come last."[1] (G.K. Chesterton)

Introduction

The question of identity is one that defies an easy answer, whether it is asked about persons or about institutions. While identity may primarily be an operative, dynamic element that is only active in daily experience, it is also one of those things that becomes more understood as it is engaged, as it is reflectively and responsibly engaged. The identity of a person emerges during the course of conversations, shared experiences, and time. Similarly, the identity of groups of persons who share a common interest, purpose, or set of goals emerges gradually and over time, according to one's exposure to, and within, that particular group.

The essential substance of specific identity is something that is ultimately a mystery. It may be there first, but it is usually understood last. As with any mystery, identity deals with what might be called "depths of meaning." By nature, such depths defy being easily understood, because such is part of their nature. The theologian Herbert McCabe is helpful when he compares this sort of thing to the appreciation of Shakespeare's plays. Depths of meaning, he says, are not found " . . . in a play when you watched it for the first time; you have to learn to understand it, and you cannot take short cuts to the depth. . . . [A]s we understand a mystery it enlarges our capacity for understanding. . . . [W]hen it comes to reaching down to the deeper meanings, there is no substitute for watching or taking part in the play itself. The mystery reveals itself in the actual enactment of the play. It is very hard to put the meaning of Macbeth into

---

[1] Chesterton, G. K. "The Philosophy of Islands." Accessed September 24, 2018. https://www.chesterton.org/the-philosophy-of-islands.

any other words, and that is why literary critics are always harder to read than plays; it all seems so much more complicated. This is not because critics are trying to make things difficult nor is it that the deep meaning is itself something complicated. It is something simple; the difficulty lies in bringing it up from its depth. When you try to bring deep simplicities to the surface you have to be complicated about them. If you are not, then you will simply have substituted slogans ... for the truth."[2]

The identity of a Lasallian School deals with such "deep simplicities", more acquired through experience than through description. They have to be brought to the surface with some complexity so as to insure that they won't simply be slogans instead of genuine invitations into an engagement with a truthful reality. In this brief paper, I will survey some of the history of attempts to do just that – describe the identity of Lasallian schools – along with the emergence of the most popular set of identity markers in the District of San Francisco New Orleans, commonly called the "Five Core Principles of Lasallian schools." These five core principles will then be viewed in relationship with similar Catholic school identity markers that come from relatively recent Catholic Church documents. We will then see that the five Lasallian core principles have also come to articulate an accessible set of pathways for Lasallian students, teachers, administrators, parents, and others to recognize, appreciate, and promote their personal experiences in a Catholic Lasallian school. Finally, some observations and questions will be shared for future consideration by both students and scholars.

The History

It is important to know something of the context within which the five Lasallian core principles came about. While this is not an exhaustive survey, even a brief overview will be helpful.

The first major contemporary effort to articulate defining characteristics of Lasallian schools came from the Regional Education Committee of Christian Brothers (RECCB) in 1984, when they "determined to synthesize his [De La Salle's] concepts in one document

---

2 McCabe, Herbert. "A Long Sermon for Holy Week." *New Blackfriars* 67, no. 788 (1986): 56-69.

which would be brief, clear, informative, and challenging."[3] Two years of work, with input from scholars and educators from eighty institutions, culminating in a 1985 workshop with 150 participants, led to the 1986 document "Characteristics of Lasallian Schools." In that document, three major components – The Teacher as Minister of Grace, Association, and The Management of Schools – were described through statements based on quotations from De La Salle, specific articulated goals, and suggested activities for implementation.

A year later, in 1987, the Brothers' *Secretariate for Education* in Rome published a document entitled "Characteristics of a Lasallian School Today." It was "intended for the whole Institute." It was written by a group of 21 assembled European Brothers and consisted of eight sections, each of which began with a global statement which was then followed by specific numbered relevant points. The section titles were: *1) Attentive to the Needs of the Young, 2) Especially the Poor…, 3) They Associate, 4) In a Fraternal Atmosphere, 5) In Order That the School "Should Function Well," 6) And in Order to Exercise Their Educational Ministry, 7) In the Church, 8) In Creative Fidelity to the Charism of the Founder…*

Five years later, in 1992, the basic elements of what came to be known as the *Five Lasallian Core Principles* made their appearance at a workshop for student leaders of the San Francisco District, and by 1993 the Five Core Principles in their present form were documented. A more detailed history of this will come in the next section of the paper.

In 1994, Br. John Johnston, FSC, the Superior General of the Brothers, gave an address at the Lasallian European Congress in Strasbourg, Germany. In it, he states that "De La Salle did not leave a definitive list of the characteristics he considered essential for the Christian schools he founded. For this reason published lists of characteristics can vary somewhat in content, order and number. I have made a list of seven and, for practical purposes, have placed them in a certain order. In practice the characteristics are inter-

---

[3] York, Gary, Michael McKenery, Robert Kealey, and Nicholas Grahmann. "Characteristics of Lasallian Schools." Romeoville, IL: Regional Education Committee of the Christian Brothers, 1986.

related. It is the integration of these characteristics which gives the school its 'Lasallian' identity."[4] The seven that Br. John highlights are these: *1) Respect for each person as a unique person, 2) Spirit of Community, 3) School of Quality, 4) A School that is Christian, 5) Solidarity with the Poor, 6) Teachers: Men and Women of Faith and Zeal,* and *7) Organized Around the Story of De La Salle.* Each characteristic is well developed in the talk, with citations from De La Salle himself, Institute documents, and other sources.

In 1995, Br. George Van Grieken, FSC, in his Boston College dissertation articulated ten operative commitments of Lasallian schools, based on an analysis of De La Salle's *Meditations* and of the early operational handbook for the schools, as it were, *The Conduct of Schools.* These results were subsequently made more generally available in the 1999 book, *Touching the Hearts of Students.*

In 1997, Br. Luke Salm, FSC, wrote an essay called "Characteristics of Lasallian Schools" in which he speaks about some of the history behind this topic, including mentioning his own initial list of six characteristics enumerated in 1980 at a lecture at Manhattan College. He states, "In the conviction that the six characteristics proposed in 1980 have yet something to contribute to the ongoing discussion, this present essay will review and to some extent update the reflections that were made at that time."[5] The six characteristics are then enumerated and explained in Br. Luke's unique and thorough style. The characteristics he identifies are these: *1) Sensitivity to Social Needs, 2) Importance Given to Religious Education, 3) Commitment, in Association, to Teaching as a Vocation, 4) Quality Education, 5) Emphasis on the Practical,* and *6) A Unique Role in the Catholic Church.* He ends his essay by stating that "Other schools, no doubt, manifest many of these same qualities. But taken together they seem to describe that elusive something that we call a Lasallian school."[6]

---

4 Johnston, John, FSC. "Seven Hallmarks of a Lasallian School." AXIS: Journal of Lasallian Higher Education 2, no. 2 (2011). Presentation at the Lasallian European Congress, Strasbourg, March 1994. Pg. 3.

5 Salm, Luke, FSC. "Characteristics of Lasallian Schools." AXIS: Journal of Lasallian Higher Education 8, no. 1 (Institute for Lasallian Studies at Saint Mary's University of Minnesota: 2017). Pg. 1

6 Ibid., Pg. 100.

In 2005 the Christian Brothers Conference assembled a regional group of Lasallian representatives to articulate what came to be called the *Goals of Lasallian Ministries*. Previous documents and resources on the topic were studied, reviewed, adapted, and newly articulated in this document. The results became the basis for similar documents developed by each of the individual Districts of the region. After a general statement highlighting the fact that Lasallian ministries "respond to the needs of those entrusted to our care," the document provides five statements: *1) We are animated by and foster a spirit of faith and zeal, 2) We create and sustain respectful human relationships in community, 3) We exercise a preferential option for the poor, 4) We instill Gospel values,* and *5) We develop and maintain diverse programs meeting recognized standards of excellence.* Each goal is followed by a list of specific implications in each area for a Lasallian ministry.

In 2006, there was a MEL bulletin from Rome, written by Br. Frederick Mueller, FSC, entitled *Lasallian Schools and Teachers: A United States Perspective.* After an overview of the historical elements and contexts that have been part of the effort to deal with this topic of characteristics in the Lasallian world, he includes nine "basic Lasallian guidelines which, taken as a whole, would define Lasallian: (a) concern for the young as unique persons with real needs, (b) preferential option for the poor, (c) communion with the Church, (d) social conscience and advocacy of social change with an emphasis on the rights of the child, (e) inspiration in the Gospel, (f) spirit of faith and zeal, (g) formation of a community of faith, (h) programs of excellence, and (h) an educational plan linking evangelization and sound human development and emphasizing catechesis and pastoral work in multiple contexts open to ecumenical and interreligious dialogue."[7]

There have been further documents from schools, Districts, and other Lasallian entities that speak about the unique characteristics of a Lasallian institution. But these will be sufficient for for better understanding the development of the Five Core Principles.

---

[7] Mueller, Frederick, FSC. "Lasallian Schools and Teachers: A United States Perspective." *MEL - Brothers of the Christian Schools*, no. 32 (2006): 9.

The Five Lasallian Core Principles

The genesis of the five Lasallian core principles came from a student leaders' workshop that was held in March of 1992 at the Christian Brothers Retreat House in St. Helena, CA, for 41 high school Juniors and their school moderators from nine Lasallian schools in the District of San Francisco. Organized by the Office of Education, the workshop was directed by Gery Short, who at that time was the District's Coordinator for Lasallian School Programs. As part of the three-day program, there were sessions about leadership styles, communication skills, planning skills, and a panel discussion with high school seniors and with Directors of Student Activities.

There was one other session, called "Lasallian Characteristics," that was held on the morning of the second day. For this session, Br. Ronald Isetti, FSC, [8] a history professor at Saint Mary's College of California, had been invited. Referencing a pivotal 1967 document, *The Brother of the Christian Schools in the World Today: A Declaration*,[9] he identified six characteristic and listed them in a handout[10] for the student leaders. Each characteristic was accompanied by a short explanatory paragraph:

1. CONCERN FOR THE INDIVIDUAL
    Needs of the individual are primary and precede rules and regulations.

2. ACADEMIC AND INTELLECTUAL FREEDOM
    An atmosphere of freedom is present that encourages each student to take responsibility for his or her own growth and to take an active part in the life of the school. Especially with regard to religious instruction, no student is coerced but expected to follow one's own conscience.

---

[8] Br. Ronald Isetti, FSC, left the Institute in 1995 but remained as a professor at Saint Mary's College. Now retired, he has written extensively about the history of the San Francisco District and biographies of significant Brothers.

[9] Brothers of the Christian Schools. *The Brother of the Christian Schools in the World Today: A Declaration*. Rome: 1967.

[10] Available at the Archives of the San Francisco New Orleans District, Napa, CA.

3. INCLUSIVE COMMUNITY
    A united community where diversity is respected, where no
    one is left out, and everyone finds a place. Individuals
    within the school community recognize and accept one an-
    other's limitations.

4. RESPECT FOR ALL PERSONS
    A concerted effort by the school, especially with regard to
    curriculum and school policies, to address all forms of prej-
    udice and to respect the dignity of all persons.

5. CONCERN FOR THE POOR AND SOCIAL JUSTICE
    Especially through the curriculum and outreach programs,
    the school demonstrates sensitivity toward the poor and
    those suffering from injustices. In general, the community,
    especially the students, are encouraged to get involved in
    assisting the marginalized.

6. QUALITY EDUCATION
    An education is provided that prepared the student not only
    for a job and college, but for life.

This presentation was well received by the students. An April 6,
1992, letter from Gery Short to Br. Ronald says: "As the evaluations
indicate, your presentation was greatly appreciated. Your presentation was concise, clear, and your invitation to dialogue with the students was well appreciated. As was evident by the exchange, you
created much food for thought. I hope that a follow-up poster or
summary, that of the characteristics of the Declaration which your
highlighted, will serve as a reference for student leaders in the District throughout the upcoming school year."[11]

The same workshop for student leaders was held in 1993 at St. Joseph's Camp on the Russian River. While Br. Ronald was not on
the schedule, "Lasallian Characteristics" were. They were scheduled

---

[11] Gery Short to Br. Ronald Isetti, FSC. April 6, 1992. De La Salle Institute, Napa,
CA. Copy of the letter is available at the Archives of the San Francisco New
Orleans District, Napa, CA.

to be reviewed with the students at a preliminary meeting.[12] It was in a handout for that workshop that the Five Core Principles in their present form were first articulated, with each core principle including a short explanatory paragraph, as in the 1992 handout, and again citing the *Declaration* as its source.

CORE PRINCIPLES OF A LASALLIAN SCHOOL

1. FAITH IN THE PRESENCE OF GOD
   Belief in the living presence of God in our world. Prayer and regular reminders of God's presence is a prevailing spirit of the school. All are taught to discover how God is active in one's life and to learn to see the world with the "eyes of faith."

2. RESPECT FOR ALL PERSONS
   A concerted effort by the school to respect the dignity of all persons.

3. INCLUSIVE COMMUNITY
   A united community where diversity is respected, where no one is left out, and everyone finds a place. Individuals within the school community recognize and accept one another's limitations.

4. QUALITY EDUCATION
   An education is provided that prepares students not only for a job and college, but for life. This education advances the students' abilities to use their talents to critically examine the world, contemporary culture, etc., in light of the message of the Gospels, and to take greater responsibility for their own education.

---

[12] See the Agenda for the "Preliminary Meeting with Students" – March 4-7, 1993. Available at the Archives of the San Francisco New Orleans District, Napa, CA.

5. CONCERN FOR THE POOR AND SOCIAL JUSTICE
    The school demonstrates a sensitivity toward the poor and
    those suffering from injustices. In general, the community,
    especially the students, are encouraged to get involved in
    assisting the marginalized.

    (Reference: *A Declaration: The Brothers of the Christian Schools
    in the World Today.*)

This second iteration is largely the same as the list provided by Br.
Ronald Isetti in 1992. The descriptions for the four characteristics
that remained had been somewhat changed, with some shortened
and others expanded. Two characteristics from that previous list,
"Concern for the Individual" and "Academic and Intellectual Freedom," had been eliminated and a new characteristic, "Faith in the
Presence of God," had been added. This change was the result of a
conversation between Lawrence Puck, who oversaw the student
leadership program along with Br. John Montgomery, and a group
of students. They identified the phrase "Let us remember that we
are in the holy presence of God" as a key element of our Lasallian
identity – something that everyone recognized as a 'Lasallian'
marker – and they made the changes to reflect that reality.[13]

These five Lasallian core principles that first appeared in this 1993
handout have remained the same and have been used consistently
as part of District publications and activities for the last twenty-five
years. The descriptive paragraphs have also remained the same, with
some slight variations. It was only much later that the descriptions
were adapted by others according to context and use. But the core
statements themselves have remained the same throughout.[14]

It should be noted that besides their use at the student leadership
workshops, these core principles were initially largely unknown
throughout the wider District except insofar as student leaders

---

[13] Phone conversation on February 19, 2019, with Mr. Lawrence Puck, President
of Saint Mary's College High School, Berkeley, CA.

[14] The student leadership workshops continued to be held through 2004, using
the same handout as the one used in 1993, after which there was a transition to
annual week-long gatherings of Lasallian Student Leaders during the summer instead of leadership workshops during the school year.

brought them back to their home schools. A year after the introduction of the 1993 format, the students from La Salle High School in Milwaukie, Oregon [15] who had attended the workshop returned and after meeting with their principal decided to create five banners for the main hallway of the school.[16] On those banners were short phrases that represented the five Lasallian characteristics they had learned about.[17] These hallway banners quickly became popular at the school and began to show up in school photographs and in District videos. Gradually, other Lasallian schools began to pay attention to these five Lasallian core principles and regular reference to them gained momentum. Within ten years, not only were other Lasallian institutions in the District of San Francisco using the same core principles as a reference, but they were beginning to be applied in creative ways by others.[18]

---

[15] Today the name of the schools is La Salle Catholic College Preparatory.

[16] The leadership of one of the students, Kathy Fisher, is to be noted. In a letter to her from Gery Short on October 31, 1994, he writes "Since the Student Leadership Workshop, I have been receiving reports of your regular meetings with Mr. Edwards, your presentation to the faculty last spring, your influence in changing the Helping Hands program, and the addition of a second event. Last week when I visited, I noted the banners in the main hall which Mr. Edwards indicated you are greatly responsible for developing." Letter available at the Archives of the San Francisco New Orleans District, Napa, CA.

[17] Gery Short to Michael Krussel. June 10, 2013. De La Salle Institute, Napa, CA. Copy of the letter is available at the Archives of the San Francisco New Orleans District, Napa, CA.

[18] The Mission Council for the New Orleans-Santa Fe District, as a result of brainstorming ways for parents to learn more about the Lasallian charism and mission, came up with "The Five Core Meal" and held such a meal at Christian Brothers School in New Orleans in 2004, with parents from all four Lasallian schools of the New Orleans area in attendance. This was a public meal during which each core principle corresponded with the appropriate food item(s): Appetizer (Faith in the Presence of God), Salad (Inclusive Community), Bread (Concern for the Poor and Social Justice), Main Course (Quality Education), and Desert (Respect for All Persons). A reflection, Scripture readings, Lasallian quotations, and conversation pointers/questions was associated with each course, such that it became a time for sharing a meal, stories, and ideas on how to live as members of the Lasallian community.[18] These meals have expanded and have proven to be both effective and popular, both at the high school and at the college level.

These particular five statements have persisted because they reso-
nated with the experience of teachers and students in the schools.
They rose to the top and have stayed there. The five Lasallian core
principles handout from 1993 was not a document that was corpo-
rately endorsed and subsequently integrated into an organizational
structure. Instead, their popularity grew within the Lasallian organizational culture because they provided generally accessible focal
points, meaning clusters, or touch stones for something that has
always been very difficult to adequately describe or contain. As
Gery Short, who has witnessed their development over the last 25
years, wrote, "I was never insistent that these characteristics become the norm for the school's or students. My attitude was that it
was a tool, made sense, but if someone found another set that was
better, so be it. As we know from history these characteristics or a
close version persisted. The students especially connected to them
and found them useful. Even though several others . . . had published their set and all were valid, for some reason our set proved
helpful with minor edits over the first few years."[19] Gery also insisted that they be simply called "core principles" and not "the core
principles," which would imply that they were definitive, comprehensive, or complete.

In the last section of this paper, some examples of their wider adoption and further expansion will be provided. At this point, however,
it is appropriate to connect these five Lasallian core principles with
the essentially Catholic nature of the Lasallian school, especially
since their labels, on the face of it, do not include identifiable Catholic terminology. The mission vectors represented by the core principles, however, will be shown to be remarkably consistent with
those found in Catholic identity characteristics expressed within
Catholic Church documents.

Integration with Catholic Identity

A Lasallian school is a Catholic school, a school that expresses its
Catholic identity through the lens of the Spirit-led educational
movement initiated and sustained by the life, vision, and spirituality
of St. John Baptist de La Salle, Patron of All Teachers of Youth.

---

[19] Gery Short to Br. George Van Grieken, FSC. September 12, 2018. De La Salle
Institute, Napa, CA.

The foundational documents, basic operative commitments, and consistent practices that define De La Salle's pedagogical spirituality continue to inspire and guide educators around the world in an authentically Catholic way and as part of our Catholic living tradition.[20]

The five Lasallian core principles identified in the last section have come to express and describe the experience of many who are part of Lasallian educational communities, and in so doing they have led to questions as to whether these same core principles have any significant relationship to what it means to be an authentically Catholic institution. It is a valid question and a valid concern. The answer to the question must recognize two things: 1) that descriptions of similar things may be provided through different language expressions, and 2) that differences of degree are not the same as differences in kind. One may describe a flower through poetry, or biology, or biochemistry. All are accurate. And while the differences are in the kinds of observations made and languages used, the thing that is described, the flower, remains the same. It is not a better or larger or greater flower, except perhaps in the mind and heart of the observer or listener.

The language used in the core principle labels is, except for the first one, relatively generic. The description underneath each label begins to concretize that short phrase within a Lasallian Catholic context. In so doing, what might be called their "mission vector" is given apostolic shape, degree of importance, and intentional direction. A closer examination of the five Lasallian core principles and their descriptors will show that they synchronize remarkably well with similar clusters of identity that have come from a publication that intentionally highlights Catholic educational identity markers based on relevant Catholic Church documents.

In the booklet "The Holy See's Teaching on Catholic Schools,"[21] Archbishop Michael J. Miller, CSB, former Secretary of the

---

[20] Van Grieken, G. (1995). "To touch hearts": the pedagogical spirituality of John Baptist de La Salle. An unpublished doctoral dissertation, UMI Dissertation Services, Boston College, Boston, MA.

[21] Miller, Michael J. *The Holy See's Teaching on Catholic Schools.* Sophia Institute Press, 2006.

Congregation for Catholic Education in Rome (2003-2007) and member of the Secretary of State Office (1992-1997), presently Archbishop of Vancouver, Canada, provides a succinct summary of Vatican documents on the topic of Catholic education. The booklet highlights "the major concerns found in post-conciliar Vatican publications on the subject"[22] and are organized around five essential marks of an authentically Catholic school. These five marks are measurable benchmarks, based on church documents, that form the backbone and inspire a Catholic school's mission. They "help to answer the critical question: *Is this a Catholic school according to the mind of the Church?*"[23]

The author sets the larger context by quoting Saint John Paul II, who told a group of bishops that the Church's institutions must be "Catholic in their self-understanding and Catholic in their identity."[24]

The five specific marks, or characteristics, of a Catholic school highlighted in the book are these:

- Inspired by a Supernatural Vision
- Founded on Christian Anthropology
- Animated by Communion and Community
- Imbued with a Catholic Worldview Throughout Its Curriculum
- Sustained by Gospel Witness

These marks of a Catholic school, upon closer examination, appear to align—in the thoughtful, focused and well-nuanced language of the Church—with mission vectors that are part and parcel of the *Lasallian Five Core Principles.* We will look at each one in turn.

<u>Inspired by a Supernatural Vision</u> This essential Catholic school mark appears to align with the Lasallian core principle of *Faith in the Presence of God.*

Education is described by the Church as a process that forms the whole child towards being good citizens of the world, loving God

---

22 Ibid, viii.

23 Ibid, 17.

24 Ibid. 18-19.

and neighbor, enriching society with the leaven of the gospel, and fulfilling their destiny to become saints. Catholic schools must transmit the full truth about the human person, created in God's image and called to life in Christ through the Holy Spirit. There is an emphasis on the dignity and the spiritual dimension of the human person.[25]

The Lasallian core principle of *Faith in the Presence of God* includes in its 1993 descriptor, "All are taught to discover how God is active in one's life and to learn to see the world with the 'eyes of faith.'"[26] This is a supernatural vision of the human person, expressed regularly in the invocation "Let us remember that we are in the Holy presence of God." It lives out the deeply-held Catholic Christian belief in sacramentality and has implications for what we teach, how we teach, how we interact with our students and each other, the environment we create in our schools, and how we attend to the religious and spiritual lives of our colleagues and students.[27]

<u>Founded on Christian Anthropology</u> This essential Catholic school mark appears to align with the Lasallian core principle of *Respect for All Persons*

Archbishop Miller writes that "Repeatedly the Holy See's documents emphasize the need for an educational philosophy built on a correct understanding of who the human person is.[28] The Christian concept of the person "attributes to the human person the dignity of a child of God. . . . It calls for the fullest development of all that is human."[29] The Catholic school "sets out to be a school for the

---

[25] Ibid., 20-21.

[26] 1993 Handout at the Student Leadership Workshop of the District of San Francisco. Available at the Archives of the District of San Francisco New Orleans, Napa, CA.

[27] SFNO District, *Lasallian Catholic Characteristics & Practices*, 2016-2017, 1. The Lasallian Catholic Assessment Process. Available at the Archives of the District of San Francisco New Orleans, Napa, CA.

[28] Michael Miller, *Holy See's Teaching*, 22.

[29] *Lay Catholics in Schools: Witnesses to Faith*. Cited in Michael Miller, *Holy See's Teaching*, 23.

human person and of human persons"[30] centered around the model and presence of Christ.

The Lasallian core principle of *Respect for All Persons* includes in its 1993 descriptor, "A concerted effort by the school to respect the dignity of all persons.'"[31] De La Salle in his meditations tells his teachers to "recognize Jesus beneath the poor rags of the children whom you have to instruct. Adore him in them."[32] All share in being created in God's image. Lasallian pedagogy has its basis in Christian anthropology, and its educational endeavors are designed and implemented with this in mind. All have an essential dignity befitting a daughter or son of God, and deserve to treated as such.[33]

<u>Animated by Communion and Community</u> This essential Catholic school mark appears to align with the Lasallian core principle of *Inclusive Community*

The Church highlights that as a community of persons and a community of faith, Catholic schools propose an alternative model to that of an individualist society. It is "rooted both in the social nature of the human person and in the reality of the Church as the home and the school of communion."[34] Such a community is chiefly manifested in four areas: the teamwork manifested within a warm, familial school climate, especially in schools with consecrated religious, who are seen as "experts in communion"; the cooperation, mutual trust, and ongoing dialogue between educators and Church leaders; the personal accompaniment of, and rapport with, students in a friendly atmosphere; and a pleasant and familial physical environment illuminated by the light of faith (chapel, prayer, etc.).

---

[30] *The Catholic School on the Threshold of the Third Millenium.* Cited in Michael Miller, *Holy See's Teaching*, 24.

[31] 1993 Handout at the Student Leadership Workshop of the District of San Francisco. Available at the Archives of the District of San Francisco New Orleans, Napa, CA.

[32] Loes, A. & Huether, F. (Eds.). (1994). Meditations by John Baptist de La Salle. (R. Arnandez & A. Loes, Trans.),
179. Landover, MD: Christian Brothers Conference.

[33] SFNO District, *Lasallian Catholic Characteristics & Practices*, 2016-2017, 3.

[34] Miller, *Holy See's Teaching*, 28

The Lasallian core principle of *Inclusive Community* includes in its 1993 descriptor, "A united community where diversity is respected, where no one is left out, and where everyone finds a place."[35] The Lasallian tradition of being "Brothers" to one another, and older Brothers to their students is extended today to all Lasallian educators, older brothers and sisters to their students, and associated together in relationships nourished by mutual esteem, trust, respect and friendliness.[36] Communion and community animate education in a Lasallian school. Individual diversities are considered an opportunity and a gift, and therefore are recognized and embraced.[37]

<u>Imbued with a Catholic Worldview Throughout Its Curriculum</u>
This essential Catholic school mark appears to align with the Lasallian core principle of *Quality Education.*

The Church highlights that an integral Catholic education aims to develop gradually "every capability of every student: his or her intellectual, physical, psychological, moral, and religious capacities."[38] A Catholic school must be constantly inspired and guided by the gospel and the person and teaching of Jesus Christ, deriving "all the energy necessary for its educational work from him."[39] "Catholicism is 'a comprehensive way of life' that should animate every aspect of its activities and curriculum."[40] It must foster a love for wisdom and truth, and it must prepare students to relate their faith to their particular culture and live it in practice.

The Lasallian core principle of *Quality Education* includes in its 1993 descriptor, "An education is provided that prepares students not only for a job and college, but for life. This education advances the students' abilities to use their talents to critically examine the world, contemporary culture, etc., in light of the message of the Gospels,

---

[35] 1993 Handout at the Student Leadership Workshop of the District of San Francisco. Available at the Archives of the District of San Francisco New Orleans, Napa, CA.
[36] Congregation for Catholic Education. (2014) Educating today and tomorrow: A renewing passion. Vatican City: CCE.
[37] Ibid
[38] Miller, *Holy See's Teaching*, 42.
[39] Ibid, 43.
[40] Ibid, 44.

and to take greater responsibility for their own education."[41] Lasallian educators manifest this, adapted to the needs of their students, through the curriculum (both human and Christian, as described in the Brothers' Rule), pedagogical methods, professional development and formation of educators, school environment, policy, and attention to the whole person.[42]

<u>Sustained by Gospel Witness</u> This essential Catholic school mark appears to align with the Lasallian core principle of *Concern for the Poor and Social Justice.*

The Church highlights the critical and vital witness of a Catholic school's teachers and administrators, since they "reveal the Christian message not only by word but also by every gesture of their behavior."[43] "Catholic educators are expected to be models for their students by bearing transparent witness to Christ and to the beauty of the gospel."[44] Church documents "pay a great deal of attention to the vocation of teachers and their participation in the Church's evangelizing mission."[45]

The Lasallian core principle of *Concern for the Poor and Social Justice* is not as focused on the witness of school administrators and teachers, but rather on the witness of administrators, teachers, and students outwards, "a sensitivity toward the poor and those suffering injustices."[46] As the Congregation for Catholic Education notes, "In particular, schools would not be a complete learning environment if, what pupils learnt, did not also become an occasion to serve the local community."[47] Lasallian Catholic schools were founded to provide a transformative education, informed by Jesus Christ, the

---

[41] 1993 Handout at the Student Leadership Workshop of the District of San Francisco. Available at the Archives of the District of San Francisco New Orleans, Napa, CA.

[42] SFNO District, *Lasallian Catholic Characteristics & Practices,* 2016-2017, 4.

[43] The Catholic School, 43. As cited in Miller, op cit, pg. 53.

[44] Miller, *Holy See's Teaching,* 59.

[45] Ibid, 53.

[46] 1993 Handout at the Student Leadership Workshop of the District of San Francisco. Available at the Archives of the District of San Francisco New Orleans, Napa, CA.

[47] Congregation for Catholic Education. (2014) Educating today and tomorrow: A renewing passion. Vatican City: CCE

Gospel, and the teachings of the Church. This includes educating them to their Christian responsibility of care and concern for others in need. Such Gospel witness informs and sustains Lasallian education, lived out in terms of those admitted to the school or in terms of the developed sensitivity of students toward the marginalized.[48]

The Five Lasallian Core Principles Today

Over the course of the last fifteen years, these *Five Lasallian Core Principles* have gradually become more embedded within the wider operational framework of the District of San Francisco New Orleans.

In or around 2003, Carole Swain, Vice-President for Mission at Saint Mary's College of California, edited the descriptions for the five core principles to a sentence descriptor for each core principle. That edited version was subsequently disseminated within the college community on posters, cards, and other means. These have been shared with students, parents, teachers, staff, and the public. There is also a Spanish translation that is used at parent orientations.

At the District of San Francisco's Mission Assembly in 2006, consisting of some 150 Brothers and Lasallian Partners, one of the approved priority statements formalized the adoption of these principles for the purpose of enhancing the schools' Lasallian climate and culture. It read:

- To enhance the Catholic Lasallian culture and climate of the apostolate, each local institution, with the support of the District Office of Education, will advance our mission among all its students through the intentional use of the Core Principles so that all students can articulate and actively live the mission.

The result of this Mission Assembly priority statement was that a much wider group of Lasallian leaders and teachers began to pay attention to these specific Lasallian core principles and to find ways of integrating their incorporation within their institutions.

---

[48] SFNO District, *Lasallian Catholic Characteristics & Practices*, 2016-2017, 7-8.

Subsequently, in the 2007-2011 Action Plan for the District of San Francisco, one of the priorities is to "Make intentional use of Lasallian core principles among students, helping students know, articulate, and live the mission."[49]

The 2011-2014 District of New Orleans-Santa Fe's Strategic Plan encouraged others to "build on the successes of spreading the Five Core Principles" and also articulated a "Five core rubric for personnel evaluation and curriculum choices."[50] When these two districts combined in 2014 into the District of San Francisco New Orleans, they already shared the common adoption of this set of identity statements.

The most significant recent development of these five Lasallian core principles has been the work involved in creating the latest iteration of an assessment instrument for Lasallian schools in the San Francisco New Orleans District, called the Lasallian Catholic Assessment Process (LCAP). This assessment tool was created in 2002, based on "a vision of the Catholic and Lasallian character of the school within an assessment and review process designed to identify strengths and target areas for growth. The focus of the assessment process is to build on the strengths within the school, affirming and encouraging efforts to live out the Catholic and Lasallian character in all aspects of the school's life."[51] It incorporated six "qualities" that were derived from the five Lasallian core principles which had by then become more generally known and applied among a variety of the schools.

In 2006-2007, this Lasallian school assessment process was thoroughly reviewed and revised, and in 2008 a new version was introduced. The updated second version was "designed to build on the strengths of the first process while expanding and deepening the scope of inquiry to the entire culture of the school: How does the

---

[49] District of San Francisco Action Plan, 2007-2011. Priority C. Available at the Archives of the San Francisco New Orleans District, Napa, CA.

[50] District of New Orleans-Santa Fe Strategic Plan, 2011-2014. Available at the Archives of the San Francisco New Orleans District, Napa, CA.

[51] Catholic Lasallian Assessment Process – 2002-2004 Facilitator Guide (2002), 2. Available at the Archives of the San Francisco New Orleans District, Napa, CA.

Catholic Lasallian spirit and mission permeate all aspects of the school and create a distinctive identity within the school community?"[52] It was at this point that the five core principles were formally incorporated directly into the assessment process. The process was "developed around five Lasallian Core Principles and twenty criteria statements that give specificity to the Core Principles. CLASP [the acronym used at the time] will help the school examine how the five Core Principles permeate the entire life (culture) of the school."[53] Thus the core principles from the 1993 student leadership retreat document became a central, measurable element in the district-wide assessment process.

In 2016, through the efforts of the District Office of Education, the process was again thoroughly evaluated and revised. The broader description for each core principle now came to include statements about our Lasallian heritage and about our Catholic faith tradition, with specific references to that core principle's connection to core Catholic beliefs and commitments. Articulated indicators were described for each core principle, with identifiable evidence areas specified. This latest iteration includes nineteen very specific indicators for the five Lasallian core principles. These indicators are further broken down into specific, measurable or observable evidence areas, providing examples of how that indicator may be observed in particular school contexts.

Here is an example from the LCAP document, illustrating the indicators of the first Lasallian core principle, along with an example of the specific observable evidence for just one of those indicators.

1. Faith in the Presence of God: *We believe in the living presence of God in our students, our community, and our world.*
    Our Lasallian Heritage: Lasallian spirituality finds God in the midst of everyday life, especially in our encounters with students in great need. This Lasallian core principle is embodied in the invocation "Let us remember that we are in the Holy Presence of God." Since the time of St. John Baptist de La Salle and

---

[52] Proposal – Catholic Lasallian Assessment Process – Version 2 (2006), 1. Available at the Archives of the San Francisco New Orleans District, Napa, CA.

[53] CLASP 2008 School Preparation Information (2008), 5. Available at the Archives of the San Francisco New Orleans District, Napa, CA.

the first Brothers, this has served as an invitation to see all things with the eyes of faith, putting Jesus Christ at the center of our ministry. "All things" includes what we teach, how we teach, how we interact with each other and with our students, the environment we create in our schools, and the ways we attend to the religious and spiritual lives of our colleagues and students.

Informed by Our Catholic Faith Tradition: This core principle is rooted in a deeply-held Catholic Christian believe in sacramentality: "The sacramental principle means that god is present to humankind and we respond to God's grace through the ordinary and everyday of life in the world."[54] This invites us – requires us – to "provide the opportunity to open students' hearts and minds to the mystery and wonder of the world and nature, to self-consciousness and awareness, to responsibility towards creation, to the Creator's immensity."[55]

a. A Lasallian Catholic school promotes Catholic identity by presenting and embodying the Gospel of Jesus Christ and the Catholic faith, tradition, and teachings in everything it does.

b. A Lasallian Catholic school has a clear and visible affiliation with its Lasallian heritage and demonstrates a consistent practice of Lasallian principles.

c. Educators in Lasallian Catholic schools see their work as a vocation, animated by the Holy Spirit. They demonstrate a spirit of faith and zeal as they give witness to the Gospel of Jesus Christ through their words and actions.

i. Vocation programs and leadership formation in the school and the District guide students in discerning their God-given vocation in life.

ii. Retreats, service and immersion programs, career programs, and other experiences—provide students with the

---

[54] Groome, Thomas H. *What Makes Us Catholic: Eight Gifts for Life.* New York: HarperCollins World, 2003.

[55] Congregation for Catholic Education. (2014) Educating today and tomorrow: A renewing passion. Vatican City: CCE.

opportunity to discover their gifts and talents and how they can be used to respond to the needs of the world.

iii. Students have the opportunity to hear and reflect on individual vocation stories, especially from faculty, staff, administrators, and the De La Salle Christian Brothers.

d. All Lasallian Catholic schools are united by a common mission and vision, rooted in the heritage of St. John Baptist de La Salle, that is accomplished by working together and by association. All members of the school community see themselves as part of the larger Lasallian Family.

e. A Lasallian Catholic school recognizes its responsibility to work with the diocese and local parishes to deepen the religious participation and commitment of those in the school.

This is a structure that is familiar to anyone who has ever gone through a school accreditation process. Currently, the LCAP document is one of the most thorough expressions of the Five Core Principles to date and a good example of how their original appeal has grown and developed over the years.

Recall that it was an interest in the elements of Lasallian identity—one of those "deep simplicities" Herbert McCabe wrote about which defy easy definition—that led to the 1992 and 1993 lists of Lasallian characteristics. Those characteristics, during the course of twenty-five years, became more and more adopted by students and administrators as their meaning and application came to be experienced in the schools and talked about more widely. These various movements are what led to this LCAP document, one that both describes more fully, and represents more deeply, the Lasallian identity that was the elusive object of the original effort to speak more clearly about the nature of that identity. We had to take our time and be complicated about bringing Lasallian identity to the surface, and now we have something that is much more than mere slogans. We have the real beginnings of a true and reliable definition of "Lasallian Identity" for our contemporary context, and one that will undoubtedly evolve further in the future.

Observations and Questions

<u>Three Key Observations</u>

A. It is important to realize that District administrators involved in this entire process believe that these Lasallian Core Principles are neither definitive nor timeless. Gery Short, who has witnessed their development since the beginning, writes, "they evolved or developed organically. Over a few years we settled in on the set we have today. . . . there was a certain trust and openness to naming these characteristics. If they proved helpful and could be seen as legitimate than we went with them. Other lists were valid, ours seem to connect and persist. . . . [and] if longevity and use are any indicators of validity, the five we landed on must be recognized as such."

B. Greg Kopra, Director of Formation for Mission of the District of San Francisco New Orleans, writes, "it has become clear that these five core principles are in synch with core Catholic beliefs and commitments – what Thomas Groome refers to as "Catholic depth structures. I am not of the opinion that these five 'core principles' <u>define</u> us or even <u>distinguish</u> us – rather, they help to <u>describe</u> what we do and why we do it. Other articulations of core commitments . . . add to the conversation and enrich it. These five 'core principles' have found their way into mainstream formation work with students, teachers, staff, administrators, parents, entire school communities, in CLASP and then LCAP, etc. As such, they give us important, helpful common language that helps to focus our efforts and challenge us as we move forward."

C. These five Lasallian core principles were clearly based on that pivotal Lasallian document *The Brother of the Christian Schools in the World Today: A Declaration*. This gave them a solid provenance and credibility from the start. The roots were deep and sturdy, and so it shouldn't be a surprise that they have persisted as long as they have.

Two Questions

A. Would it be helpful to include a reference to Jesus Christ or the Church in at least one of the core principle labels?

    a. This concern was expressed in 2007 when I was a member of the San Francisco District's Mission Council because I had helped to develop the 2005 Regional *Goals for Lasallian Ministries* document. One of those goals was that "We instill Gospel values." But in terms of Lasallian Catholic characteristics, I have come to understand that as a Catholic school and charism, Jesus Christ undergirds, permeates, and inspires the entire spectrum of concerns and activities in a Lasallian school. Christ is at the center of any cluster of core principles, indicators, and evidence as seen in the LCAP document. It appears to me more appropriate to speak of Christ and the gospel as something that is not a characteristic <u>among others</u>, but is rather as breath is to the body – central and essential to its life. As Br. John Johnston wrote in 1994, "The Christian dimension permeates and shapes every aspect of school life: tone, atmosphere, spirit, signs, symbols, relationships, curriculum, requirements, policies, regulations."[56]

    b. A very interesting and compelling application of these same five core principles may be found in the book "Schools of Character"[57] by Br. Michael Fehrenbach, FSC. In this book, written about and for the Lasallian charter schools in Chicago called Catalyst Schools, the five Lasallian core principles are expressed through intentionally non-sectarian language and interpreted exclusively for educational contexts in which religious language is not permitted.

---

[56] Johnston, John, FSC. "Lasallian Schools Today." 1994. MS. Address at the Lasallian European Congress in Strasbourg, Germany.

[57] Fehrenbach, Michael, FSC. *Schools of Character: Faith-inspired Public Schools in the Catholic Lasallian Tradition*. Winona, MN: Saint Marys Press, 2016.

B. Has our emphasis on the Five Core Lasallian Principles in this age of secularization and disaffiliation actually encouraged our students to move in the direction of secularization?

a. This question came from Charlie Legendre, Director of Evangelization & Catechesis for the District of San Francisco New Orleans, who at this time is attending a 3-week session at the Catholic University in Leuven, Belgium, exploring the study of and approach to faith formation in the 21st century. The question is based on the presentation by one professor, Didier Pollefeyt, who focused on the Melbourne scale of five kinds of Catholic school identities (Cf. a video explanation of "The Melbourne Scale" on YouTube). The first of these identities is "Christian Values Education" in which efforts are made to create a link between generally accepted values and Christianity. Didier's prevailing message "was that Christian values education does not impede secularization. In fact, depending upon the circumstances, Christian values education may actually support movement toward secularization. Christian values education is that type where a particular value is focused upon and an attempt is made to connect that value with the Christian tradition thereby trying to bridge the gap between Christianity and culture. The data indicate that, where students have a strong faith and practice, connecting the value to Christianity is possible. However, where there is a diminished confessional identity, the student is not able to connect the value with the Catholic faith. The students take away the value but not the faith. Christian values education is popular because, many times, the values present an easy, inviting common denominator to which students (and faculty) can easily relate. Christian values education does not, however, present the particulars of the Christian tradition."[58]

---

[58] Charles Legendre to Br. George Van Grieken, FSC. September 6, 2018. De La Salle Institute, Napa, CA.

b. One response to the question is from Greg Kopra, who writes that perhaps "the answer lies in our responsibility to concretely and intentionally 'connect the dots' between each core principle and core Catholic beliefs and commitments. To state such connections accomplishes at least two things: 1) it broadens and deepens one's understanding of the Lasallian core principle; and 2) it catechizes students and adults with regard to some core Catholic beliefs and commitments."[59]

c. A similar perspective would say that the Lasallian core principles, which clearly resonate with student experience and are much more accessible to them than doctrinal statements, simple as they may look initially, are an invitation and an opportunity to engage students in meaningful dialogue, building on their own experience and insights towards a broader and deeper understanding of what Jesus Christ, the Church, and Catholicism are about. We believe that grace builds on nature. We start with where people are, because that is where and how God is present to us in the educational encounter. The model for us is one of accompaniment: Christ on the road to Emmaus. It is finally the character and substance of our communities, our relationships, and our conversations that bring education to life, especially faith-related education.

Conclusion

Vatican II asked religious congregations in 1965 to return to the original spirit of their institutes and adapt them to the changed conditions of the times.[60] In the Lasallian world, this led to the 1967 document *The Brother of the Christian Schools in the World Today: A Declaration*, a document that has remained insightful, visionary, and surprisingly relevant even today. It was the source and basis for the development of the *Five Lasallian Core Principles* in 1992-1993 and evidently continues to shape the substance of what we mean by

---

[59] Greg Kopra to Br. George Van Grieken, FSC. September 13, 2018. De La Salle Institute, Napa, CA.

[60] *Perfectae Caritatis*, 2.

contemporary Lasallian Catholic educational ministry, given the way in which those core principles have come to provide a common language and touchstones for what we mean by being Lasallian today.

Br. John Johnston said in his 1994 talk in Strasbourg, "We must never forget that a Lasallian school – whatever its nature or level – is essentially a Christian school, but a Christian school in which a certain number of clearly defined characteristics are given prominence."[61] Over the years, there have been many articulations of such characteristics, or goals, or operative commitments. The one group of statements that appears to have gained general credibility through longevity and wide use are the *Five Lasallian Core Principles*. These principles do not describe the experience of Lasallian ministry entirely, but they seem to lead others into the most fruitful conversations about that ministry. They do not exhaust the possible ways that one might have conversations about Lasallian ministry and its future, but they seem to focus on the relevant areas that invite ongoing attention. And their language does not at first appear to address the essentially Catholic character of Lasallian schools, but their conscientious engagement within Lasallian schools quickly leads to all those central elements of Catholic education that the Church cherishes and proclaims in its own documents.

As with the gospel itself, the Holy Spirit is present in the human encounter with the text, with words that often speak about the same event or reality from different perspectives or with different languages. This is as true of the resurrection narratives as it is of identity descriptions. It is a dynamic has also been part of the history of the *Five Lasallian Core Principles*. We can be thankful that the richness of that history can continue to provide an accessible way to focus our efforts and to challenge us as we move forward.

---

[61] Johnston, op cit, pg. 4

TECHNOLOGY AND LASALLIAN EDUCATION
SOME ESSENTIAL PERSPECTIVES

This short essay is concerned with 21st-century Lasallian education – primary, secondary, and tertiary – and with its responsible engagement as part of a techno-savvy, even techno-obsessed society. In order to do that, there are some things that we don't need to consider here, and some things that we do need to consider.

We don't need to consider how quickly technology has transformed our personal and professional worlds. We don't need to consider how technology has been embedded in our daily habits, shaped our locus of preferences, and hijacked our eyes, our face-time, and our peripheral vision. But in order to become effective 21st-century educators, we can and should consider here three things when it comes to technology:

1. *Today's Context*: These include some of the observations of contemporary writers about technology's impact on life, on relationships, on society.

2. *Today's Perspective*: These today will primarily be insights from a philosopher who specializes in the topic of technology and today's society.

3. *Today's Practices*: These are some things that come out of our own deeply rooted Lasallian educational tradition, things that have stood the test of time and will do so well into the 21st century and beyond.

Today's Context

While we reap amazing benefits from technology in terms of connection, efficiency, and information, we are also in a situation similar to the famous frog in a pan of water on an active stove-burner. Contemporary technology carries with it an ever-warmer daze that may easily make us blissfully unaware of its potential to boil away relationships, empathy, and genuine human formation. Our digital paradigm "… is so pervasive that we are largely blind to the ways that it influences the way we experience our world."[1]

But such apparent blindness is actually something that not's altogether opaque to our sensibilities. People around us are beginning to articulate the slightly worrying notion that something isn't right with how technology seems to be creeping into all the places and spaces of our lives, like some questionable chemical soaking into the sponge of our lives. As David Brooks, *The New York Times* columnist has written, with today's social media, "You can have a day of happy touch points without any of the scary revelations, or the boring, awkward or uncontrollable moments that constitute actual intimacy… Being online isn't just something we do. It has become who we are, transforming the very nature of the self."[2]

An essay by Andrew Sullivan with the title "I Used to Be a Human Being" summarizes the experience well. This is what he writes:

> "By rapidly substituting virtual reality for reality, we are diminishing the scope of [intimate] interaction even as we multiply the number of people with whom we interact. We remove or drastically filter all the information we might get by [actually] being with another person. We reduce them to some outlines – a Facebook "friend," an Instagram photo, a text message – in a controlled and sequestered world that exists largely free of the sudden eruptions or encumbrances of actual human interaction. We become… efficient shadows of ourselves."[3]

David Brooks says in his commentary that social media encourages social multitasking. "You're with the people you're with, but you're also monitoring the six billion people who might be communicating something more interesting from far away. It flattens the range of emotional experiences." Social media cannot make that same claim – yet. He concludes that online, "every moment is fun and

---

[1] Richard Gaillardetz, *Transforming Our Days: Finding God Amid the Noise of Modern Life* (Ligouri Publications, 2007), pages 6ff.

[2] David Brooks, "Intimacy for the Avoidant" in *The New York Times*, 7 October 2016. [Retrieved from https://nyti.ms/2JZ69Zv]

[3] Andrew Sullivan, "I Used to Be a Human Being" in *New York Magazine*, 19 September 2016. [Retrieved from https://slct.al/2JcNvMK]

diverting, but the whole thing is profoundly unsatisfying. I guess [he says] a modern version of heroism is . . . regaining control of social impulses, saying no to a thousand shallow contacts for the sake of a few daring plunges."[4]

Lasallian Partners, Brothers, students, and parents all swim in the waters of technology, just like billions of people around the world. The way that they use those technologies, and the way those technologies shape or structure their attention, are as varied as the backgrounds, habits, priorities, and friends or acquaintances that each of them has. The technological component is now an irreversible, irresistible, constituent aspect of any education or formation context, whether Lasallian or otherwise.

Mary Hess, a Catholic theologian whose specialty is technology, points out two helpful things. "[P]opular media structure[s] most of our forms of attention in ways that we barely even notice anymore." And "Digital technologies can certainly be extraordinarily useful in expanding access to our learning programs, but only if we implement them in ways that follow from our goals, not that drive them."[5]

I find these insights to be very important. This is because digital technologies are not fully benign. Just like the invention of the light bulb, or solar-powered lights, the item itself may be inert, but its effect is socially and personally transformative, in either positive or negative ways. These inventions may have allowed people to read longer, speak to one another longer, feel more safe, and provide for more flexible work hours; but they also enabled employers to demand longer work times, led to a lack of sufficient sleep, and introduced new night-time entertainments of questionable value. If such technological innovations are not directly attached to clear, limited goals, then anything can happen, and usually does happen.

When applied to an educational context, especially a Lasallian Catholic educational context, an awareness and an integration of those "goals" are even more essential, because some of these goals

---

4 Brooks, "Intimacy for the Avoidant."
5 Mary E. Hess, "Engaging Technology" in *Theological Education: All That We Can't Leave Behind* (Lanham, MD: Rowman & Littlefield, 2005).

necessarily deal with a unique kind of knowledge, that of the Gospel, which sociologist Peter Berger has called a "cosmic redefinition of reality." Another sociologist, Parker Palmer helps us situate the unique kind of knowledge that deals with faith traditions, specifically the faith of Christianity. Transcendence is not an exclusively objective form of knowledge.

Palmer writes that in Jesus, God ". . . was announcing and incarnating a new understanding of reality and our relation to it. Truth . . . is personal, to be known in personal relationships" and we must ". . . allow love to inform the relations that our knowledge creates . . . ."[6] "Truth is not a statement about reality but a living relationship between ourselves and the world" and teaching is "an invitation into personal relationship with reality."[7] Adopting such a viewpoint would radically alter the way in which we teach, because, as he says elsewhere, what happens is that ". . . our epistemology is quietly transformed into our ethic."[8] In other words, what we believe becomes what we do.

This echoes something that Jordan Peterson, a popular modern philosopher, says: ". . . the great myths and religious stories of the past, particularly those derived from an earlier, oral tradition, were moral in their intent, rather than descriptive . . . [They concern themselves] with how a human being should act."[9]

And so a pervasive technological environment brings implications for how we understand, or come to understand, knowledge, learning, and teaching, and subsequently how we do all that. Therefore, this deserves careful initial attention and ongoing vigilance, especially if we intend to pursue specific goals and not have such goals driven for us by the sheer weight and momentum of technology's reach; to allow technology to hijack our attention, our epistemology (how we think), and our ethic (how we act).

------

[6] Parker Palmer, *To Know As We Are Known* (San Francisco: Harper & Row, 1983), page 49.

[7] Palmer, *To Know As We Are Known*, page 47.

[8] Palmer, *To Know As We Are Known*, page 21.

[9] Jordan Peterson, *12 Rules for Life* (Canada: Random House, 2018), page xxvii.

As Lasallian educators, we bring Gospel value to our relationships with our students. The truth of Jesus Christ is personal and known in personal relationships and in community. In the words of Anthony Spadaro, Christianity is fundamentally a communicative event. The Church both *announces a message* and *engages in relationships of communion*. Therefore, the internet "is not a new means of evangelization but is, above all, a context to which the faith is called to express itself . . . [within] . . . the lives of human beings."[10]

However (and it's a big however), the sacred is not an online search away. Google's search algorithm does not include transcendent realities. And the Gospel is not simply one piece of news among many. It attempts to answer humanity's questions by the message of the death and resurrection of Jesus Christ. The Gospel is *meant to be* countercultural on many levels, including the culture of technology. Pope Francis put it into a nutshell: "There are no sacraments on the internet."

And so the goals that we pursue as 21st-century educators, and the way that today's technology supports, serves, or subverts those goals, all come from a very specific understanding of what we are all about. This is our context.

Today's Perspective

One of the most articulate voices on the topic of technology and society is Albert Borgmann, a philosopher professor at the University of Montana. I was exposed to his writings through Richard Gaillardetz, a systematic theologian at Boston College, who wrote a thought-provoking small book called *Transforming Our Days*. In that book, he shows how technology can and does make it difficult to cultivate an authentic Christian spirituality. He wrote the book because he noticed that each of his four sons had a different "take" on technology, depending on their age, with resulting different perspectives on things. And, being a systematic theologian, he wanted to know what was going on here. He found Albert Borgmann, who already back in 1987 had written a book called *Technology and the*

---

[10] Anthony Spadaro & Maria Way, *Cybertheology: Thinking Christianity in the Era of the Internet* (New York: Fordham University Press, 2014), pages 7-8.

Character of Contemporary Life.[11] Among writers on the topic, Borgmann was among the best. For me also, he has provided a perspective that I find very compelling, and more importantly, profoundly accurate.

Borgmann says that for us today, technology operates as a pervasive set of influences about which we are largely blind. It is a largely unrecognized paradigm, which he defines as "a consistent and patterned framework in and through which people encounter their world."[12]

The best way to get a handle on how this paradigm operates among us is to look at specific kinds of experiences and the radically different ways that they are an experience. One set of experiences he calls "focal things," ones that involve "focal practices"; and the other set of experiences he centers around the word "devices." These involve little or absolutely no "focal practices" and are encountered more like commodities – specific results or goods that simply are what they are. The best way to get a sense of each is to look at a couple of examples.

Think of what a fire or wood-burning stove was all about in a premodern home. It was a place for heat, certainly. But it was also a gathering place for the family, for stories and conversation, for companionship and relaxation. In most houses, the kitchen – where the fire was – was the place where the family gathered the most; where they relaxed and talked and ate. But you needed somebody who knew how to build the fire, who went out to cut the wood, who kept it going, who became the family expert. And the fire determined rhythms of life; who did what chores, when to eat, when to come together. People were tutored about fires, about wood; and all sorts of relationships were fostered around that one fire. Here, the fire was a "focal thing." It's much more than simply heat. It's the kind of thing where the context and the good that is sought and produced, directly and implicitly, are inseparable.

---

[11] Albert Borgmann, *Technology and the Character of Contemporary Life: A Philosophical Inquiry* (University of Chicago Press, 1987).
[12] Gaillardetz, *Transforming Our Days*, page 6.

This is an important point so I'll say it again. A "focal thing" is the kind of thing where the context and the good that is sought and produced are inseparable. There are all sorts of other very subtle "goods" and benefits that go way beyond simply the heat that is produced by the fire. There is a whole complex world of what he calls "manifold engagement," a multi-textured, multilayered web of relationships within the much larger world than simply a person and a fire. A focal thing, such as the fire in this case, demands engagement with others on all sorts of levels; and the richness of the whole experience makes it a much more "eloquent reality" than is achieved by the simple production of heat.

Another example is food and the preparation of a meal. Whether large or small, a meal requires going out to shop; knowing how to pick out the best fish or veggies or fruit; gathering the pots and pans and tools and spices called for by the recipe; spending the time cutting, chopping, marinating, kneading, or waiting; getting the dishes and setting up the table; thinking about the environment or context; and cleaning up afterwards. Everyone in the family or group may be involved in any of those activities. Lots of time and energy are invested for the relatively short time of leisurely family enjoyment and conversation that is the dinner itself. And the whole thing is certainly not only about the food, about getting fed. In Gailardetz's words,

> "Meals such as these are "focal" because in diverse ways they gather our attention and hold us in patterns of meaningful engagement with others and with the fruit of the earth."[13]

Specific skills are involved, limits are encountered – even problems, and the world outside is engaged in many different ways – some obvious, some subtle.

The web of interactions, relationships, and requirements that are part of a focal thing are inseparable from its value. Focal things call for, and come about, because of focal practices, a wide range of activities that we must engage in in order to obtain a desired good. With focal practices, which lead to the eloquent realities that are

---

[13] Gaillardetz, *Transforming Our Days*, page 4.

focal things, the goods, the benefits, the results that we desire are *internal to the practice.* They cannot be separated from it. If you take out the practices, the desired goods – especially the ones that we don't readily recognize – disappear. The center cannot hold. It's no longer a "focal thing"; and something else takes its place, something that is more like a commodity than a rich experience.

With the rise of technology, we have developed things that may have formerly been a focal thing but today have been experientially flattened out into single, one-dimensional, strictly functional reality. They are sought and obtained simply, directly, and without human texture or depth, usually comes through a device, and may themselves be thought of more as a device, rather than a focal thing, an eloquent reality. They function more as commodities, coming from something that has no other relationship with the good or service beyond efficiently producing it. Following our examples, a "device" that takes the place of a fire is the wall thermostat; and a "device" that takes the place of a prepared meal is a microwaved dish. Each requires little skill to get the immediately desired results (heat in the one case, food in the other), involves no web of relationships, no learned talents, minimal time engagement, and no other people.

The microwave achieves a proximate good that has a single purpose (efficient heating) and does that very well and quickly. We don't know how a microwave works, and we don't care. Just do the job and give me warm food. If it breaks, I'll just get another one. It works in the background. It's well concealed. Borgmann says that something that is a "device" actually functions best when it's completely unnoticed. It "disburdens" us; no longer intrudes on our lives like creating a meal from scratch might intrude on our lives.

Focal practices require maintenance, while devices discourage maintenance. Focal practices are time-consuming, could actually be boring, and involve a lot of different sorts of engagements, while devices are fast, somewhat flashy, and do one thing really well. Focal practices involve a web of relationships and activities, while devices generally are single-person centered and involve just one actual, real activity (usually involving just the eyes and the fingers).

There is not enough time to pursue the realities surrounding today's social media: internet addictions, and screen-dominance in people's lives, along with their implications for social interaction, relationship-building, empathy development, and personal maturity. I'll end this section with the concluding statement that Gaillardetz makes in his book about focal practices and device practices. His analysis

> "… suggests the importance of preserving practices of human engagement with one another and with the larger world. When goods are reduced to commodities and procured for enjoyment in ways that do not demand or even allow for real engagement with our world, the paradoxical result is a decreased capacity for enjoyment."[14]

Before leaving this section, however, it's important to point out that technology can and does provide a huge amount of benefits for the world and for ourselves. Who wants to go back to the time before washing machines, for example? And there's nothing sinful about having microwaved popcorn, is there? There are also real indications that younger people today are quite aware of the limits of technology; and they actively seek focal practices, eloquent realities, multi-faceted interpersonal experiences. Just recently, I saw this story in *Popular Mechanics*[15] about the growth of new craftsman (creating furniture, boats, bike-frames, etc.). One story was about people interested in spending two days with others in a Brooklyn smithy in order to learn how to make a really good knife.[16] People are seeking out and paying for focal experiences that once might have been part of the normal course of daily life. We hunger for something that seems to be missing.

Today's Practices

So what could Saint John Baptist de La Salle and the educational movement he founded contribute to this conversation? Why should anything Lasallian make a difference for the 21st-century educator?

A story was told about Anna, an elderly lady in San Francisco, who as a little girl had experienced the 1906 earthquake there. When she came to a third grade class to speak about her recollections, there was a time for questions afterwards. But whatever she was asked

---

[14] Gaillardetz, *Transforming Our Days*, page 8.
[15] A focal-practices-based magazine, in my opinion.
[16] Cf. *Popular Mechanics*, April 2018.

about –her early traveling, entertainment, toys – she had to answer that there were no cars, radios, televisions, electronic toys, etc. when she was a little girl. Finally, one little boy asked, "Anna, is there anything the same now as it was when you were our age?" She looked around, thought a little, and said, "Well, the classroom is still pretty much the same."

John Baptist de La Salle may not be around today; but his writings and living charism carry forward the core educational convictions, perceptions, and practices that animate all Lasallian institutions. The Lasallian teaching encounter today is, also, still pretty much the same as when he and others developed and applied those elements that came to be consistently considered as essential. How might they be applied anew today?

Five specific elements in De La Salle's approach are worth bringing forward. They are drawn from classroom contexts; but they are applicable to educational situations that all of us encounter on a daily basis, with or without technology.

Individualized Attention

> "In today's Gospel, Jesus Christ compares those who have charge of souls to a good shepherd who has great care for the sheep. One quality he must possess, according to our Savior, is to know each one of them individually. This ought, also, to be one of the main concerns of those who instruct others: to be able to understand their students and to discern the right way to guide them."[17]

De La Salle uses the metaphor of the good shepherd to describe how Lasallian teachers should approach their students, specifically by knowing them individually. Some need more attention, others need patience and encouragement, and so on. In order to do this well, one must pray for the gift of discernment, he says, which takes time, attention, conversations, and collaboration. In an educational environment inundated with technological requirements, requests, and relationships, it is *not only easy* to avoid such individual attention

---

[17] Meditation #33.1 in *Meditations by John Baptist de La Salle*, translated by Richard Arnandez FSC and Augustine Loes FSC and edited by Augustine Loes FSC and Francis Huether FSC (Landover, MD: Lasallian Publications, 1994).

and care, it may *often become the norm* to do so, or to claim that we simply don't have the time to give this kind of individualized attention, by which I mean face-time, not efficient email responses.[18]

> *To Introduce*: In a conversation, obtain a "digital profile" for each person with whom you work – favorite websites, preferred means of interacting online, social media profiles, etc.

> *To Enhance*: Send those with whom you work links to articles, websites, videos, etc. in areas that you know are part of their interest, whether directly related to formation or not.

The Integration of Faith & Zeal

> "The spirit of this Institute is first a spirit of faith which should lead those who belong to it to look upon nothing except with the eyes of faith, to do nothing except in view of God and to attribute all to God ... Secondly, the spirit of this Institute consists in an ardent zeal for the instruction of children and for bringing them up in the fear[19] of God . . . ."[20]

The spirit of faith looks through, within, behind, and around things, seeking their deeper dimensions, evoking wonder, mystery, and new relationships. Faith is lived out, practiced, and realized in our

---

[18] Some deliberate healthy practices coming from this principle might include spending more time conversing with students than emailing them; having genuine and frequent eye contact in classrooms; and noticing which students and friends get lost in technology, or which ones don't get engaged with technology at all. You get the idea.

[19] This word "fear" might be better translated in its original Hebrew meaning of "awe," especially in an educational setting. Abraham Joshua Heschel. "Awe is an intuition for the dignity of all things, a realization that things not only are what they are but also stand, however remotely, for something supreme. Awe is a sense of transcendence, for the mystery beyond all things. It enables us to perceive in world intimations of the divine, to sense the ultimate in the common and the simple: to feel in the rush of the passing the stillness of the eternal. What we cannot comprehend by analysis, we become aware of in awe" [Abraham J. Heschel, *Who is Man* (Stanford University Press, 1965)].

[20] John Baptist de La Salle, *Rule and Foundational Documents*, translated and edited by Augustine Loes FSC and Ronald Isetti (Landover, MD: Lasallian Publications, 2002), pages 16, 18.

expressed zeal for education. This dual spirit of faith and zeal invites us to uncover the depth structures of things, by way of today's technology, enabling students to discover grander and deeper dimensions of what is studied, and facilitating a personally-driven engagement with the subject matter. This is as true of mathematics as it is of Scripture or history, of chemistry or of literature, philosophy, and theology. *In that process of engaging those deeper dimensions*, the capacity for understanding, for wonder, and for the transcendent is widened and stretched. As the Dominican theologian Herbert McCabe once wrote: "As we engage a mystery, it increases our capacity for understanding it." Along the way, there are many opportunities to foster the development of discernment skills and even simple internet politeness skills. The two habitual partners of faith and zeal in the one educational endeavor equip us to also integrate technology opportunities and educational opportunities.

> *To Introduce*: Recommend websites that engage the visitor to enter into and more deeply develop an understanding of specific topics or areas of study. Include verbal reports, discussions, and the sharing of digital resources.

> *To Enhance*: Invite remote individuals or groups to join your discussion via Skype, Zoom, or similar "live" means, providing appropriate prior readings or topic materials.

Personal Example

> "Example makes a much greater impression on the mind and heart than words. This is especially true of children . . . They are led more readily to do what they see done for them than to carry out what they hear told to them, particularly when the words they hear are not in harmony with the actions they see."[21]

Education happens through genuine personal relationships. Technology is indifferent to personal relationships and may seduce us toward seemingly equivalent substitutes. If education and technology are to be integrated, they will do so via the dynamics of personal relationships. And one of the dynamics that is most powerful is that

---

[21] Meditation #202.3 in *Meditations by John Baptist de La Salle* (1994).

of personal example. This means that how teachers and friends *actually use technology*, both personally and professionally, may be teaching more than what they are teaching *through technology* – the teacher who is wedded to his or her cell phone, who spends more time looking at a screen than at the students, who can't wait for class to end so that they can check their social media accounts.

The first question for the use of technology in most settings should be: will this enhance what I'm trying to accomplish, or not? If not, then it may simply be in the way and a stumbling block to the ends that we are called to pursue. All of us should occasionally review how we use technology – a media-use inventory – ideally with the help of others, so that we can be sure we are using it for the benefit of others and not as an excuse to benefit ourselves.[22]

> *To Introduce*: Like De La Salle did, write down "Rules I Have Imposed on Myself"[23] in terms of your personal use of technology.
>
> *To Enhance*: Ask a good friend, relative, or colleague who knows you well to give you some feedback about your use of personal technology, and then decide the better course ahead.

Practical Orientation

"It is, then, not enough to procure for children the Christian spirit and teach them the mysteries and doctrines of our religion. You must also teach them the practical maxims that are found throughout the holy Gospel."[24]

---

[22] There is a story that illustrates the point. A little boy kept bothering his mother, asking her to listen to him while she was perpetually distracted by her smart phone. She would smile and say that she was listening, and she may even have been listening, but she looked mostly at her phone. More was required. Finally, the little boy said, "Mommy, Mommy, please listen to me; but this time with your eyes."

[23] Cf. De La Salle, *Rule and Foundational* Documents (2002), pages 199-202.

[24] Meditation #196.2 in *Meditations by John Baptist de La Salle* (1994).

De La Salle told his Brothers that it wasn't enough to "teach them the mysteries and doctrines of our religion. You must also teach them the practical maxims that are found throughout the holy Gospel."[25]

The practical curricular elements in the schools that he introduced (learning to read in French first, practicing writing by copying contracts, using real-world arithmetic examples, and so on) . . . these have their parallels in the integration of technology in our educational milieu today. Technology is essentially a practical reality; there is no "spirituality of technology" that can stand on its own. Technology is a spirituality sponge, absorbing how and what it does from those whom it touches. The kind of communication involved in education is essentially personal communication, communication that builds from and into relationships. It is those relationships, bringing them into community and finally into communion with Christ, that are our focus and passion. This is who we are and want to be. Technology may be one attractive way of facilitating its development, but it is by no means the only one or the best one. We have a responsibility to help others become aware of technology and its influence, and teach them to develop ways of negotiating its potential and power in their lives.

> *To Introduce*: Search and share apps and online resources that improve positive personal relationships or help develop a better awareness of their potential.

> *To Enhance*: Monitor the use of your smartphone, alone or with others, using an app such as *Moment*; and, then, discuss the results. Include a practical or "practices" component in each formation activity.

Community & Tradition

> "Union in a community is a precious gem, which is why Our Lord so often recommended it to his apostles before he died. If we lose this, we lose everything. Preserve it with care, therefore, if you want your community to survive."[26]

---

[25] Meditation #196.2 in *Meditations by John Baptist de La Salle* (1994).

[26] Meditation #91.2 in *Meditations by John Baptist de La Salle* (1994).

It has been well said by others that the decisive innovation of the Founder is that education is conducted within the context of community. If there is one thing that stands out brightly within our Lasallian tradition, it is the precious gem of community. The kind of community we are defines who we are – whether as Brothers, faculty and staff, coaches, volunteers, parents, and others. It is educational communities that ultimately "shape the practices by which we structure our attention.[27] Community is the engine that powers the charism forward. In order to be sustained, to be maintained like a wood-burning fire, community requires certain "focal practices." The risk with some popular manifestations of technology is that, as a perhaps unintentional side effect, community dissipates through slow attrition. It is gradually transferred to a virtual platform, one that draws its essential life from somewhere else, somewhere less engaged, somewhere less risky or demanding. Just in the Brothers context, and borrowing a thought from Mary Hess, a community with five members and one television will have a different community dynamic than a community with five members and six televisions. Although today, the analogy might be better applied to personal laptops and I-pads.

I hasten to add that we could have a virtual Lasallian community that is positive and helpful, as indeed exists on Facebook and other platforms, one that maintains a welcome form of our Lasallian connections, even if these are weaker and less embodied. The important thing is not to mistake the benefits of a virtual community with the dynamic immediacy of a real one. Our Lasallian community is the carrier for our Lasallian tradition. If others are to grow into what they learn from our tradition, there must be occasions when that form of enfleshed community exists on a regular basis. Our individual vocational journeys depend on it. Technology's benefits may be in service to that goal, but it will never be a substitute for it.

> *To Introduce*: Demonstrate the diversity of the Lasallian world online, plus the variety of resources that are available via Institute, Regional, and District websites.

---

[27] Mary E. Hess, "Engaging Technology," page 17.

To Enhance: Brainstorm with a Lasallian group the various ways that technology might be used to build and support this particular community, and monitor its progress as different means are pursued.

Sensible Cautions & Suggestions

Here are some cautions, skills and recommended practices in the area of education and today's technologies. The caution centers around internet addictions, and the suggestions around conversation, discernment, awareness, silence, and hobbies.

The major area of caution will be very familiar to everyone. Adam Alter, who has studied internet use extensively, writes in a recent book that "the environment and circumstance of the digital age are far more conducive to addiction than anything humans have experienced in history."[28]

That's a big claim. But it is supported by the simple example of Facebook, which currently has 1.86 billion active users who spend an average of twenty minutes for each visit, scrolling through posts that *are designed* to keep you hungry for the next entry, the next person, the next click-through. While appreciated by those who use the service to stay in touch with family and close friends, for those who make as many as possible so-called "friends" (a misnomer if ever there was one), it is a bottomless well of essentially weak relationality. For some people, Facebook or Snapchat may easily become a habit that perfectly fits the definition of an addiction. Likewise, the virtual game called *World of Warcraft* may be one of the most addictive behavioral experiences on the planet, with one hundred million subscribers around the world. Along with email addiction and pornography addiction, "one recent study suggested that up to 40 percent of the population suffers from some form of internet-based addiction."[29]

---

[28] Adam L. Alter, *Irresistible: The Rise of Addictive Technology and the Business of Keeping Us Hooked* (New York: Penguin Press, 2017), page 4.

[29] Alter, 2017, *Irresistible*, page 26.

I am assuming that this forty percent refers to the group of all those who have internet access. Whatever the numbers, we do not need to let those facts prevent us from engaging technology for positive purposes. It is all the more reason to provide our students, and others, with the tools that will help them understand, discern, and cultivate practices with new technologies that promote and support positive Lasallian goals. A caution may be given when positive results are desired and possible, and that is the case here.

There are also developed skills and habits that actively resist the possible negative influences of new technologies. They are "live" sorts of ongoing focal practices.

CONVERSATION

One of the essential skills that deserves to be promoted is the simple practice of conversation. Shery Turkle points out that conversation cures. It reclaims our attention. Conversations become graced opportunities for growing genuine relationships. She writes,

> "Conversation implies something kinetic . . . To converse, you don't just have to perform turn taking, you have to listen to someone else, to read their body, their voice, their tone, and their silences. You bring your concern and experience to bear, and you expect the same from the other."[30]

Such conversations in educational contexts may be deliberate, circumstantial, casual, or pre-planned. But they are where God's providence becomes immediate and real. If De La Salle's life was profoundly shaped by the conversations that he had, we could hardly object to doing the same ourselves.

DISCERNMENT

Another essential skill has been mentioned already. It is the skill of discernment, the ability to tell the differences between people, perspectives, influences, situations, and the like. In the present context, it is the ability to tell the difference between various technologies and media, which ones are more or less likely to be helpful, healthy,

---

[30] Sherry Turkle, *Reclaiming Conversation: The Power of Talk in a Digital Age* (New York: Penguin Press, 2015), page 45.

or positive, and why. This skill requires both training and monitoring. It is a topic that should be a key element in any education program. Without such discernment skills, the steering wheel for making good choices is untouched, and we go wherever the road might lead.

AWARENESS

Then there is simply the responsibility to remain aware of what new technologies are being developed or are popular. Reading articles and stories about new technologies is a prerequisite for being informed and able to make good choices and good education programs.

SILENCE

The cultivation of silence is something with which most of us are already very familiar. However, it is less common to find an appreciation for silence in technologically-rich settings. About ten years ago, I was in Rome and had a chance to briefly speak with Cardinal Carlo Martini, an elderly archbishop best known for how well he connected with young people all of his life. I asked him how best to help young people discover their vocation in life. He thought for a minute and said, "Brother, two things. Give them an experience of silence and help them open up Scripture for themselves. The Holy Spirit will take care of the rest."

Wise words that I have reflected on frequently. God's presence will become all the more accessible as silence becomes the foundation for our conversations. With today's technology, it is very difficult to mistake noise for something else when coming from a place of silence.

HOBBIES

Lastly, one suggestion is simply the pursuit of a non-technology-related hobby or interest. Taking on a hobby or interest that is personally rewarding reorients a person's perspective, especially if it is something that must be done slowly, at its own pace, that is difficult but manageable, and that is personally rewarding. It slows down our attention, counterbalances the ease of finding solutions to things online – whether informational or emotionally satisfying – and draws us out from our deeper selves and into the community of interest in which we partake. Such practices also introduce us to other dimensions of life, other people, and other realities where God yet dwells.

Conclusion

So, finally, we reach the conclusion. I hope that you will have come to realize that when we are dealing with the 21st-century Lasallian educator and new information and communication technologies, the operative word is "may." All these new technologies, which will certainly become more compelling, inviting, and even helpful during the years ahead, *may* support, enhance, and carry forward education . . . or they *may not*. We need to pay attention when Silicon Valley executives send their kids to Waldorf schools, where they use zero technology,[31] when articles regularly appear that feature young people dealing with their technology addictions,[32] when top researchers and writers question the future of college education.[33] We can only benefit from the input of both philosophers like Albert Borgmann and visionary educators like De La Salle, because they will inform our decisions and structure our habits, our priorities, and our attention.

I have always liked the way that Brother John Johnston[34] described the Lasallian vocation. He said that the Lasallian vocation was "to make the loving and saving presence of Christ a visible and effective reality in the world of education and among the young."[35]

This is a vocation that deserves our best efforts, using whatever resources and methodologies are available to us.[36] New

---

[31] Matt Richtel, "A Silicon Valley School That Doesn't Compute" in *The New York Times*, 2 October 2011.

[32] Bianca Bosker, "The Binge Breaker" in *The Atlantic Monthly*, November 2016 [Retrieved from https://theatln.tc/2HxJyVt]

[33] Kevin Carey, *The End of College: Creating the Future of Learning and the University of Everywhere* (New York: Riverhead Books, 2015).

[34] The late Brother John Johnston was for some time superior general (1986-2000) and vicar general (1976-1986) of the Brothers of the Christian Schools.

[35] Cf. John Johnston FSC, *Pastoral Letter: Representing Jesus Christ Himself* (Rome, 1990).

[36] A few other resources that influenced the articulation of ideas shared in this essay are the following: Ross Douthat, "Resist the Internet" in *The New York Times*, 11 March 2017 [Retrieved from https://nyti.ms/2JZ69Zv]; Claudia Dreifus, "Why We Can't Look Away from Our Screens" in *The New York Times*,

technologies are a potentially powerful asset in facilitating genuine conversations with the Lasallian tradition and with the larger Church.

The practices that emerge from our best appropriation of our own tradition structure the boundaries within which education takes place. Technology may be a flashy, popular, and demanding voice for our attention today, but it is by no means the most important or finally the most attractive. For Christians and Lasallians, Jesus Christ and the student deserve more attention than the voices of technology should ever demand. We must shape that attention intentionally rather than have it shaped for us unintentionally.

Genuine Lasallian education emerges through relationships, through conversations, and through community experiences that grow out of what we have learned from our Lasallian Catholic tradition. If we do so with well-informed discernment and with courageous decisions in favor of our students, then we may confidently send out the following piece of De La Salle's advice as a tweet or a text message today:

"Be satisfied with what you can do, since this satisfied God. But do not spare yourself in what you can accomplish with the help of grace. Be convinced that, provided you are willing, you can do more with the help of God's grace than you imagine."[37]

---

6 March 2017 [Retrieved from https://nyti.ms/2HdnGzr]; Elizabeth Drescher, *Choosing Our Religion: The Spiritual Lives of America's Nones* (New York: Oxford University Press. 2016); Charles Duhigg, *The Power of Habit: Why We Do What We Do in Life and Business* (New York, NY: Random House, 2012); Vigen Guroian, "Restoring the Senses: Gardening and Orthodox Easter," taken from Krista Tippett's *On Being* podcast [Retrieved from http://bit.ly/2qJOuNq]; James Nuechterlein, "Remembering Peter Berger" in *First Things*, October 2017 [Retrieved from http://bit.ly/2HKC5A8]; Christian Smith and Melinda Lundquist, *Soul Searching: The Religious and Spiritual Lives of American Teenagers* (New York: Oxford University Press, 2005); Allen St. John, "DIY Underground: America's Hidden Communities of Craftsmen" in *Popular Mechanics*, 19 May 2011 [Retrieved from http://bit.ly/2F0ofqt]; and Daniella Zsupan-Jerome, *Connected toward Communion: The Church and Social Communication in the Digital Age* (Collegeville, MN : Liturgical Press, 2014).

[37] De La Salle, John Baptist. *Reflections on Their State and Employment That the Brothers Should Make from Time to Time, Especially During Retreat*, "Regarding the Use of Time," # 10, in *Collection of Various Short Treatises*.

Mervyn Soares (The LMent, Sydney, Australia, 2015), after Cesare Mariani, La Scuola de s. Giovanni Battista de La Salle, 1887-1888.

Our Lasallian Vocation
& The Theology of Vocation

Understanding our Lasallian vocation within, or in relationship to, a theology of vocation, is a daunting, difficult, and dense topic. But what I may be able to do is provide some sort of framework for thinking about our Lasallian vocation and share some of the pieces that are part of the conversation surrounding a theology of vocation. You will want to reflect about your own Lasallian vocation, since it is really only by engaging in thinking about your own vocation that you're going to learn what might really be going on there.

Let me start with two vocation catalyst stories; stories about how people have found themselves spurred to think seriously about their vocation in life. As you listen to them, think about whether you have had any similar kind of experience in your life; something seen or heard that made you reflect on your vocational journey.

Here is the first one. Nearly twenty years ago, I was in Chicago for the Huether Conference, and as I came to a street corner downtown, there was a corner parking lot across the street. It was surrounded with tall, brick building. Cars stopping for the red light were sure to notice it. When my eye traveled to the top of this tall brick wall, at the very top was a huge painted sign– large white letters against a jet-black background. It said: "If you're waiting for a sign from God, this is it." Underneath in smaller letters it said "Consider the priesthood" along with a website.

Here is the second one. A religious sister said that she seriously only considered her vocation rather later in life, when she was stuck behind a car at an intersection – also in Chicago, as it happened – and waiting for the light to change. Looking around, she noticed the bumper sticker on the car in front of her. The bumper sticker had three words on it. "Don't Die Wondering." That was what jarred her into seriously reflecting on her own life's trajectory and beginning to explore the movements of her heart (in her words).

These two experiences are not all that different from the experience of many who were "called" at some point in their lives, who through some person, experience, or situation found themselves invited and drawn into the consideration of a life that they had not really imagined for themselves before. In this respect, the very "otherness" of some experiences–short as they may be–are the sort of interruption of one's life that demands attention. It's not a breakdown of things, it's a breaking in of something rather profound, something that plunges into the soul like a silent laser beam. As one author wrote, something like this "is transformative–if we are open to it. Our stories go on, but they go on changed."[1]

Each of us has a different story to tell about how we became involved in this Lasallian charism and ministry, and probably a very different story of why we're still in it. Every individual narrative is unique, personal, and if genuine, also dense, difficult, and daunting.

But how is it that theology might be helpful in understanding what vocation is all about, and how to go about discerning where our vocation could be found? In my reading of some of the literature on this topic, the primary thing that stands out is the fact that we're usually looking in the wrong direction when it comes to this "vocation" business, asking questions that arise out of our consumer culture ("I get to choose to be who I am.") or out of a transactional religious perspective ("I will find my one vocation when it's given to me; when I'm ready for it.") or out of a generally individualized, postmodern expectation of self-realization ("I have to express the self that I've constructed throughout my life."). All of these may be genuine expressions of vocational interest, but none of them are statements of genuine vocational discernment. This is where theology – the thinking about God and God's ways with us – could be helpful, because "How we think about things impacts how we do them."[2]

---

[1] Hahnenberg, Edward P. *Awakening Vocation: A Theology of Christian Call* (Collegeville, MN: Liturgical Press, 2010), 177

[2] *Edward Hahnenberg: "A Wider Witness: From 'Lay Vocation' to the Call of* Missionary Discipleship" YouTube video, 49:47, posted by "John S. Marten Program in Homiletics and Liturgics," October 16, 2015, https://youtu.be/NGvJ-GvaADA (14:26–50 for this clip).

First, I'll share some of the theological insights into vocation that have come from Edward Hahnenberg, a lay theologian currently at John Carroll University and an articulate writer on the subject. He wrote both a comprehensive theology (*Awakening Vocation: A Theology of Call*) and a very accessible introduction into the faith that feeds our call, our vocation (*Theology for Ministry: An Introduction for Lay Ministers*). I'm taking a chance that I may not do justice to what he has written. But if just one or two notions stick with you, or make you curious, or mad, or confused, perhaps you will get one of those books and, by reading it, gain further insights into your own vocational journey, as I did.

After the short summary of some of the theology on the topic of vocation, I'll take a look at the vocation of John Baptist de La Salle, and how his story, his narrative, is informative to the kind of Lasallian themes that may also run in our own contemporary stories, our vocation narratives today.

Vocation in the Bible

The word "vocation" originally and essentially meant a call, from the Latin *vocare*, which of course assumes someone who is called and a "caller" who does the calling. It's a notion that has been around for at least as long as scripture has. In the Hebrew scriptures, both the call of Moses and of Jeremiah stand out rather dramatically. In each case there is a definitive call, a commission, followed by an expressed hesitancy and subsequent assurance that is confirmed by a clear sign or verification. Their "call" happened in the midst of ordinary life and required a certain level of trust that God was indeed the one doing the calling. In other cases, such as with Deborah, who was called to be a prophet and judge in Israel, and Esther, who became an agent for saving her people from eradication, the same detailed steps for hearing and responding to their calls are missing from their biblical accounts, but simply the fact that their accounts are included in the writings of a patriarchal, male-dominated Jewish society gives substance to the reality of truly having being called that must have been in play. We just don't have the same details in their cases.

In the New Testament, being called or chosen or sent shows up all over the place. One scripture scholar writes that "vocation refers to individuals whom God authorizes for a specific task and to groups who are gathered and groomed by God. The writers of the New Testament emphatically state that mortals should never presume to take honors for themselves (Hebrews 5:4) but are clients of a generous God who alone can ascribe such honors. The grace to 'call' or 'choose' is God's alone to bestow."[3] (This is an important observation. A vocation isn't simply something you decide to do, and then you go do it. There has to be an invitation of some kind.) While the primary examples in the New Testament had to do with "the fundamental call of Christ to discipleship and salvation,"[4] Jesus himself also certainly had a call, a rather dramatic one, after he had gone with others to hear John the Baptist preaching. It involved deserts, devils, and decisions. Generally, a couple of important things stand out in the vocational calls that are found in the New Testament:

1) <u>No one in the New Testament volunteers</u> —deciding themselves that they have a call. And those who try to volunteer are dismissed, such as the person who wants to join, but Jesus tells him that even <u>he</u> has nowhere to lay his head, and the person who first wants to go bury his father. Volunteering presumes a role or status that doesn't fit with true discipleship. Only God calls. Only Jesus invites his disciples to join him.

2) <u>The "call" cannot compel anyone to respond</u>. Think of the rich young man who was not ready to give up what he had, even after Jesus — in the words of the writer — "looked at him and loved him." If you invite God's call and receive one, make sure that you're ready for the answer. It is invariably challenging, personal, and deep.

3) <u>Most of those called by Jesus in the Gospel are recruited by people who knew them already</u>. And once called, they are separated from their previous place, instructed

---

[3] Neyer, Jerome, SJ. *Call and Commission in the New Testament.* Accessed November 10, 2018. https://nrvc.net/publication/4851/article/4357-call-and-commission-in-the-new-testament.

[4] Hahnenberg, *Awakening Vocation*, 6.

by and about Jesus, and confirmed in responses or statements Jesus makes to them. So "vocation is initiated by persons who are already believers, who inform close associates about Jesus under some title and invite them to 'Come and see.'"[5] The call of a vocation is a very personal and relationship-oriented sort of thing. (As an aside, it is very interesting that the rapidly growing FOCUS movement follows this exact pattern in its evangelization efforts.)

Even the resurrection narratives are "call narratives," ones that include an experience, a reaction followed by an assurance, a commission, and eventually roles in the church. The dynamics of vocation, or a definitive context of being called, reverberate all through the New Testament narratives. An engaged vocational journey pervades scripture and its stories.

Vocation During the Patristic Period

The patristic period saw radical calls and lifestyles introduced, especially among those who went into the desert to pursue lives of hardship, prayer, and laser-focused attention to God. Most experienced the kind of call that only great commitment and interest can engender. It's important at this point to highlight that, for them and within their society's culture, there was no distinction between one's interior life and one's exterior life – no duality of perception or purpose. Belief and daily life were one thing, one reality, one experience. Vocation was life.

As the church moved into the medieval period, the legal dimensions of religious life and any Christian life grew and expanded. And as canon law developed, permanent "states of life" became defined, with certain obligations attached to each. In the 12th century, the nature of vows and the status of those who had vows, prompted by the rise of the mendicant orders (Franciscans, Dominicans, etc.), led to a distinction between those who were in "secular" and those who were in "religious" states of life. And scholastic speculation, headed by Thomas Aquinas, added the categories of Aristotle into Christian thought. In terms of vocation, "for Thomas, the 'states'

---

[5] Ibid.

are those ways of Christian life within which the individual can realize the 'particular perfection' proper to each state."[6] This led to there now being two *calls*. "The external call predisposes the individual to hear Christ's words; but that external call is not efficacious without an internal grace or call."[7] You could have one without the other, but you need both of them together in order to live out one's proper vocation.

Vocation During the 15th – 17th Centuries

A few centuries later, things really started to get interesting, although it does get a little complicated on the theological level. It was really Martin Luther who first upset the apple cart when, as part of his very vocal polemic against monasticism, he not only emphasized that we are not saved by any of our own work, but only by the grace of God, but that as a consequence there were two separate parts to Christian living: God's love is expressed by faith, and the love of neighbor is expressed by one's vocation.[8] We stand before God by faith; we stand before our neighbor by works, by our vocation. As Hahnenberg writes "In the end, it was Luther's distinction between the realm of heaven and the realm of earth that supported his thorough externalized theology of vocation."[9]

> For Luther, every work is a calling from God. . . . As the concept of vocation passes from Luther, through John Calvin, to the English Puritans, you see a noticeable shift. Luther talked about vocation in terms of one's state of life, station in life. John Calvin emphasizes more the idea of productive labor. And the Puritans run crazy with this notion of work. With this, you get a shift in Protestant tradition from thinking about vocation as faithfulness *within* one's work, to faithfulness *through* one's work, to

---

[6] Holland, Paul. *Theology of vocation through the centuries.* Accessed November 10, 2018. https://nrvc.net/publication/4851/article/4359-theology-of-vocation-through-the-centuries)

[7] Ibid.

[8] Hahnenberg, *Awakening Vocation*, 11.

[9] Ibid.

faithfulness *to* one's work. And the protestant work ethic is born.[10]

The great irony is that Luther's attempt to highlight the sacredness of work leads to a secularization of the notion of vocation, and you get to a point where today in America you can quite comfortably talk about vocation – as in vocational counseling, vocational colleges, *Voc Ed* – without ever mentioning God. [11]

Without surprise, given the historical context of the time, this led the Catholic Church in the Counter-reformation to harden the notion of vocation to exclusively being called to be a priest or a vowed religious. This is a notion that has persisted through to the present day, despite the major change of perspective introduced by the Second Vatican Council over fifty years ago. But more about that in a minute.

First it is important to note that there were some hopeful developments during the centuries in between Luther and the 20th century, and not least of these happened in the early part the 17th century, in France, about fifty years before St. John Baptist de La Salle came onto the scene. St. Francis de Sales, Bishop of Geneva and a gifted preacher, writer, and spiritual director, had written two popular works that advocated what he called "devotion"," which was "great ardor and readiness in performing charitable actions." It was love burst into flame. His inclusive vision was grounded in "his unmistakable confidence in human nature as redeemed."[12] For him, God's love cannot be hemmed in. "It spills over, empowering a response in every way and walk of life."[13] Michael Buckley describes it this way: "The whole of the spirituality of Francis falls within … two movements: the surge that is the human being and

---

[10] Dr. *Edward P. Hahnenberg speaks at Catholic Theological Union – Lecture 1"* YouTube video, 53:14, posted by "LearnatCTU," September 27, 2013, https://youtu.be/CvZW8IpP6JY (26:20-27:16 for this clip).

[11] Ibid., (27:20-42 for this clip).

[12] Hahnenberg, *Awakening Vocation*, 30

[13] Ibid., 31

the outpouring that is the divine providence."[14] Notice that these are two integrated movements, qualitatively different from the two defined and definable activities that we saw in Martin Luther's "faith" and "works" or in the two *call* categories of Thomas Aquinas.

The theologian Louis Dupré provided a description of what lay behind the convictions of Francis de Sales, and it has to do with the relationship between nature and grace, a theological relationship that will be seen to be key to the entire discussion of a theology of vocation. He said that for Francis de Sales, "Grace transforms nature from within, resulting in a single reality that is both human and divine."[15]

The other thing that happened in the 17th century, however, was not so very helpful. With the best of intentions and bucket-loads of integrity, a Catholic philosopher introduced a whole new category of meaning. "Descartes' reflection on his own interior life did not lead to a deeper sense of dependence on God [which he had hoped]. Instead, his *Cogito* ["I know, therefore I am."] became the ground for a new self-sufficient certainty."[16] Hahnenberg summarizes the reverberations well, especially in terms of what happened with the relationship between nature and grace. He writes: "[T]he great irony is that Christian theologians of the late medieval and early modern periods actually helped to foster a split between the human subject and its transcendent source that would ultimately push God out of the world. ... Grace became reduced to a kind of 'add-on' to creation, an extrinsic and transient force operating on an independent nature. Within this dualistic understanding of the nature-grace relationship, vocation suffered. For when grace becomes seen as a supernatural gift, an extrinsic power or divine energy transmitted to our soul, then one's vocation becomes detached from one's self. ... Once nature – that is, creation or the world –

---

[14] Buckley, Michael J., "Seventeenth-Century French Spirituality: Three Figures," in Christian Spirituality, ed. Dupré, and Saliers. Quoted in Hahnenberg, *Awakening Vocation*, 40

[15] Dupre, Louis. *"Passage to Modernity: An Essay in the Hermeneutics of Nature and Culture"* (New Haven, CT: Yale University Press, 1993). Quoted in Hahnenberg, *Awakening Vocations*, 227

[16] Hahnenberg, *Awakening Vocation*, 73.

became an independent entity, a closed system functioning on its own and toward its own end, the order of grace could only be seen as a divine addition, an intrusion or supernatural 'add-on' to the order of nature."[17] Just as with what happened between faith and works in Luther's case, or with the separate external and internal calls of Thomas Aquinas, nature and grace became more estranged from one another and less integrated. Why is that important? Because this led to the assumption that "the grace of vocation was an outside force touching the soul of an individual . . . A vocation became some 'thing,' placed in an individual by God, but difficult to determine. Thus from the seventeenth century on, Catholic theologians writing on priestly formation all struggled with the same question: how do we know when someone 'has' a vocation?"[18]

Despite some fine efforts in 17th century France by St. Francis de Sales, Cardinal de Berulle and Jean-Jacques Olier to focus on the importance of the interior life for everyone, it wasn't until Vatican II that the vocation of the laity – of ordinary people – came to be front and center of what the church is and should be about.

Vocation from Vatican II to Today

The Vatican II document, *Lumen Gentium*, the Dogmatic Constitution on the Church, described the laity as "those who must strive after Christian sanctity for the glory of God in their own special way, including secular activity. Actively engaged in the concerns of this world, but led by the spirit of the gospel, they courageously fight the evil of this world and even sanctify the world so to speak from within through their Christian calling."[19] All I can do here is to urge you to re-read that document, especially chapters 4 and 5, because we don't have time to delve any further into its life-affirming, positive statements about the vocation of Christian life in the 20th century. This is especially crucial in terms of the lay nature of our Lasallian vocation.

It is too complicated at this point to look at the influence of St. Ignatius and the how his *Exercises* helped in advancing vocational

---

[17] Ibid., 74

[18] Ibid., 80

[19] Ibid., 39

discernment, or Karl Rahner and his major insights into God's infused presence within us and how that shapes how we are called. But here is a short section from Hahnenberg's work so that you can get a glimpse of their perspective.

> "[V]ocation is not a detailed blueprint imposed on my life from above. It is not a hidden plan silently stored away; shared with some through a secret voice. Rather, my vocation is right there in front of me. It *is* me – <u>my life lived out in harmony with the gift of grace,</u> which is nothing other than God's loving presence within. Thus discernment is a process of reflecting on my fundamental identity before God. Each of us decides what to do by placing particular possibilities for life before this fundamental sense of ourselves, listening for either resonance or dissonance. Harmony between the two helps us know what we are called to do. … According to Rahner, Ignatian discernment "works" because it recognizes that an authentic vocational choice can only be made when an individual is freed (by God's grace) from any particular attachment to the object of that choice and "has thus achieved openness to immediacy to God as the sole focus of his existence." … [W]e slowly come to see that the response we expect from God is the one that God answers through us – through our choices, our lives, our vocation."[20]

---

[20] Ibid., 226, 227, 228. At the same time, Vatican II's perspective did not immediately result in a change of perspective on the part of the rest of the Church. "[M]any of the underlying assumptions remained in place. And today, Catholics continue to talk about vocation in ways that are both overly institutionalized and overly interiorized. . . . We may challenge a theology of supernatural grace that reifies vocation or turns discernment into a pseudo-mystical scavenger hunt. However, within this history of institutionalization and the interiorization of vocation lie, waiting to be recovered, the resources for a broader and more holistic vision. In Francis de Sales' inclusive view of holiness and his graced view of the person, in Ignatius of Loyola's attention to experience and his appreciation for narrative, in Vatican II's world-affirming spirituality and its sensitivity to history, we find the building blocks for a contemporary theology of call. In the last half century, Catholicism has seen a revival, a renewal, even a revolution in its understanding of God and the human person, in its ecclesiology and its ethics, But the greatest theological transformation is the one that runs underneath all of these – a revolution in the theology of grace. If we are still struggling to talk about the

When we come to know and rest in ourselves – in the presence of God known, aware, and engaged – and look at our life choices from that quiet place, God's call, God's vocation for us, is not the discovery of some hidden plan – some pseudo-mystical scavenger hunt[21] – but rather is found by following that profound resonance emerging between our deepest sense of ourselves before God and a particular path that lies before us.

And there's that something more, although it is difficult to nail down.

Discerning a particular path in resonance with our deepest sense of ourselves before God may be confirmed, or validated, or solidified by what Ignatius called a "consolation without a preceding cause."[22] If at that deepest part of yourself, aware and in touch with the transcendent, you contemplate a choice that brings what Ignatius calls "consolation" (peace, tranquility, clarity, balance, etc.) for no discernible reason whatsoever, this pierces through any self-deception and the idolatry of ideas, and can only come from God. (So say Ignatius and Rahner.) The reason for the "rightness" of the choice is completely unidentifiable, but irresistible. The examples that come to mind are C.S. Lewis's story of his conversion, or the growth of Dorothy Day's and Thomas Merton's vocations, or Rilke's letter to a young artist telling him to live into the questions, or the transformation in the vocational journey of Oscar Romero, or Jonathan Sacks describing how he came to embrace his Jewish roots; and those are just some of the published ones. Each had never anticipated or planned for their eventual vocation; each was surprised by joy, as it were – which is the title of C.S. Lewis's book about his road to Christianity. But you have to take the time, you have to make the effort, you have to do the boring bits. God only works in and through the real world, via real circumstances, events,

---

breadth and depth of God's call in ways that are intellectually cogent, spiritually meaningful, and pastorally relevant, it is because we have not yet thought through vocation in life of this grace revolution." Ibid., 90

[21] Ibid., 90

[22] Ibid., 144

and people. As Lasallians, we should know that from De La Salle's own story, which we'll get to in a minute.

I'll finish up this section with an example of this deep experience of transcendence; an unanticipated encounter with deep grace, with God's presence, that led to life-changing consequences. Anthony Bloom was born and raised in Russia but moved to Paris after the Russian revolution and became a surgeon in the French army and the French underground during WWII. This is what he wrote later in his life:

> "I met Christ as a Person at a moment when I needed him in order to live, and at a moment when I was not in search of him. I was found; I did not find him. I was a teenager then. Life had been difficult in the early years and now it had all of a sudden become easier. All the years when life had been hard I <u>had</u> found it natural, if not easy, to fight; but when life became easy and happy I was faced quite un-expectedly with a problem: I could not accept aimless hap-piness. ... Happiness seemed to be stale if it had no further meaning. As it often happens when you are young and when you act with passion, bent to possess either everything or nothing, I decided that I would give myself a year to see whether life had a meaning, and if I discovered it had none I would not live beyond the year.
>
> Months passed and no meaning appeared on the hori-zon. One day, it was during Lent, and I was then a member of one of the Russian youth organizations in Paris, one of our leaders came up to me and said, 'We have invited a priest to talk to us, come'. I answered with violent indigna-tion that I would not. I had no use for Church. I did not believe in God. I did not want to waste any of my time. Then my leader explained to me that everyone who be-longed to my group had reacted in exactly the same way, and if no one came we would all be put to shame because the priest had come and we would be disgraced if no one attended his talk. My leader was a wise man. He did not try to convince me that I should listen attentively to his words so that I might perhaps find truth in them: 'Don't listen,' he said. 'I don't care, but sit and be a physical presence'. That

much loyalty I was prepared to give to my youth organization, and that much indifference I was prepared to offer to God and to his minister. So I sat through the lecture, but it was with increasing indignation and distaste. The man who spoke to us, as I discovered later, was a great man, but I was then not capable of perceiving his greatness. I saw only a vision of Christ and of Christianity that was profoundly repulsive to me. When the lecture was over I hurried home in order to check the truth of what he had been saying. I asked my mother whether she had a book of the Gospel, because I wanted to know whether the Gospel would support the monstrous impression I had derived from this talk. I expected nothing good from my reading, so I counted the chapters of the four Gospels to be sure that I read the shortest, not to waste time unnecessarily. And thus it was the Gospel according to St Mark which I began to read.

I do not know how to tell you of what happened. I will put it quite simply and those of you who have gone through a similar experience will know what came to pass. While I was reading the beginning of St Mark's gospel, before I reached the third chapter, I became aware of a presence. I saw nothing. I heard nothing. It was no hallucination. It was a simple certainty that the Lord was standing there and that I was in the presence of him whose life I had begun to read with such revulsion and such ill-will.

This was my basic and essential meeting with the Lord. From then I knew that Christ did exist. I knew that he was *thou*, in other words that he was the Risen Christ."[23]

Anthony Bloom subsequently joined the Orthodox Church, became a priest, and eventually was archbishop of the Russian Orthodox Church in Great Britain, becoming a compelling speaker and writer, especially among young people. The key to his conversion involved two integrated things: an interior movement brought on my by circumstances, events, and people; and God's felt presence, the perceived touch of God's grace.

---

[23] http://www.mitras.ru/eng/eng_biog.htm

Vocation and De La Salle

This is a good segue to the story of St. John Baptist de La Salle, because I firmly believe that his vocation journey, in fact, is also an example of someone who found his life radically changed by the providential guidance of God through events, circumstances, and other people, paying close and deliberate attention to both God and to his own inner spiritual journey, and then making real and practical choices on that basis.

Br. Gerard Rummery, FSC, in a video that was recorded some years ago, provided an overview of why he thinks De La Salle was such a great man and inspiration for so many others up to the present day.[24] What the video highlights is the amazing thing that happens when, in Br. Gerard's words, you see God working through the events of your life – when you see those events as calls from God. In a very short period, one trajectory became an entirely different one for De La Salle. In fact, the new trajectory was NOT the one that he had anticipated, that he had wanted, or that even had any particular appeal to him. It was solely his conviction that God was calling him in that direction that made him get involved, one decision leading to another until he found himself doing something he had never foreseen for himself.[25]

Here is a quick summary of some of those major decision:

---

[24] https://youtu.be/rmIOfmZ91G8

[25] "I had imagined that the care which I assumed of the schools and the masters would amount only to a marginal involvement committing me to no more than providing for the subsistence of the masters and assuring that they acquitted themselves of their tasks with piety and devotedness. . . . Indeed, if I had ever thought that the care I was taking of the schoolmasters out of pure charity would ever have made it my duty to live with them, I would have dropped the whole project. . . . Indeed, I experienced a great deal of unpleasantness when I first had them come to my house. This lasted two years. It was undoubtedly for this reason that God, Who guides all things with wisdom and serenity, Whose way it is not to force the inclinations of persons, willed to commit me entirely to the development of the schools. He did this in an imperceptible way and over a long period of time so that one commitment led to another in a way that I did not foresee in the beginning." Blain, Jean-Baptiste. The Life of John Baptist de La Salle, Founder of the Brothers of the Christian Schools. Translated by Richard Arnandez. Romeoville, IL: Christian Brothers Conference, 1983. Vol. 1, Bk. 1: 60 - 61.

- Age 19 – (October 18, 1670) He starts at St. Sulpice Seminary.
- July 19, 1671: His mother dies / April 9, 1672: father dies.
- June 24, 1672: His family members move to different places.
- April 9, 1678: He is ordained.
- April 17, 1678: Nicholas Roland dies.
- March 15, 1679: He meets Adrian Nyel.
- April 15, 1679: The first school opens.
- Christmas, 1679: The teachers move to house rented by DLS.
- Easter, 1680: The teachers experience week of living at DLS's house from morning to evening. (During this time period, DLS also receives his PhD.)
- June 24, 1680: He invites Nyel and teachers to share a table at his house.
- Christmas, 1680: He goes to Paris to consult with Fr. Barre
- April 2-9, 1681: he conducts retreat for teachers.
- June 24, 1681: He brings teachers to live with him.
- June 24, 1682: They move to a rented house on Rue Nueve.
- July 30, 1682: The De La Salle family home is sold.
- August 16, 1683: De La Salle resigns as canon of cathedral,
- Winter 1683: DLS distributes his wealth to the poor.

Many of those in the Lasallian world are somewhat familiar with the details of De La Salle's life story. It has shaped the charism that we all share, providing touchpoints that continue to give life to how we do what we do in our institutions. So what are some of the key concepts that situate our call as Lasallians in a broader context.? Let me offer just three of them. You will find other points of alignment or resonance when you next read a biography of De La Salle – that's part of YOUR vocational journey.

1) <u>De La Salle was really stubborn</u> when it came to following what he thought was right, especially when it came to something he felt sure he had to do based on his religious convictions. The obvious example is bringing the teachers into his own house and living with them. But that's only one

dramatic illustration of a life-long commitment to this sort of integrity. The former chief editor of the monumental *Dictionnaire de Spiritualité*, André Rayez, became convinced that historians have not given De La Salle due credit for the innovations he introduced through the various courageous responses he made to situations as they arose. He writes, "That 'unruffled boldness' of the Founder's can be explained in the last analysis, only by the spiritual quality and the genuine holiness of his life, for his only ambition was at all times and despite all obstacles to adhere, in a view of faith, to God's will clearly known, and to the designs of Providence."[26]

2) <u>De La Salle listened well</u> and believed in paying attention to others and integrating their narratives, their input, their experiences, into the development of this educational movement and his own involvement in it. When he was first working with the early teachers, both as the group's leader and, at their request, the group's spiritual director, one of his biographers, who knew and lived with De La Salle, says that nothing was introduced by authority. Instead "he flattered them by giving them the satisfaction of being themselves the creators of their own vision and their own plans for making it a reality. In this way they became, in effect, their own legislators."[27] And toward the end his life, in 1714, when the Brothers ordered him back to Paris from Grenoble, under the vow of obedience that he had taken with them some twenty years earlier, and take up the government of the Institute once more, despite his genuine reluctance to do so, he returned and did as he had been requested. The voice of the others was also the voice of God for him.

---

[26] Rayez, S.J., André. "Etudes lasalliennes." *Revue d'Ascétique et de Mystique* 28 Jan-March (1952) and *Lasallian Studies*, 4

[27] Quoted in Aroz, Leon, Yves Poutet, and Jean Pungier. Beginnings: De La Salle and his Brothers. Translated by Luke Salm. Romeoville, IL: Christian Brothers Conference, 1980. 23

3) <u>For De La Salle, interiority, prayer, and the spiritual life was never an add-on</u> or an extra nice-to-have thing. These were essential, life-giving and action-shaping dimensions of all that he did and all that he expected of his teachers. Interiority, prayers, and the spiritual life was how the Lasallian charism was brought to life; it was how his unique *pedagogy of fraternity*[28] was shaped. The vocation of a teacher and the vocation of attaining salvation were not two different separated things. He writes, "Do not distinguish between the duties of your state and what pertains to your salvation and perfection. Rest assured that you will never effect your salvation more certainly and that you will never acquire greater perfection than by fulfilling well the duties of your state, provided you do so with a view to accomplishing the will of God."[29] Similarly, the *Rule* for the Brothers that De La Salle wrote with them includes this statement: "The Spirit of this Institute is first a Spirit of faith which should lead those who belong to it to <u>look upon</u> nothing except with the eyes of faith, to <u>do</u> nothing except in view of God and to <u>attribute</u> all to God ... Secondly, the Spirit of this Institute consists in an ardent zeal for the instruction of children ..."[30] Later on he said that those who do not have this spirit should be considered "dead members." Pretty strong language! He really believed this.

So I don't think it's a stretch to say that De La Salle's vocational journey emerged and evolved with just the kind of focused, deep attention to the movement of both his interior life and the needs of those around him that the theology of vocation talks about in contemporary times, even though his 17th century language and perspective may have been expressed differently. And the fact that he was able to reflect in 1694 that he was led, one decision after

---

[28] Lauraire, Leon, FSC. "A Pedagogy of Fraternity" AXIS: Journal of Lasallian Higher Education 7, no. 3 (2016). Presentation at the FSC Casa Generalizia on May 12, 2015. 31.

[29] De La Salle, *Collection of Various Short Treatises*. Translated by W. J. Battersby. Edited by Daniel Burke. Romeoville, IL: Lasallian Publications, 1993. 78.

[30] De La Salle, John Baptist. *The Rule of 1705: An English Translation*. Translated by O'Gara, Eugene. Moraga, CA: Buttimer Institute, 1989. 1

another, to a place he had not anticipated, confirms for me a recognition of this as a "call," a "vocation," a movement of events and decisions that was cumulative, unpredicted, and highly formative.

In that respect, I think of De La Salle very positively in light of the conclusion that Hahnenberg offers about the theology of vocation: "Thus to discover my vocation is to hear a certain harmony between who I am as a child of God and how I live in the world, with and for others. ... [W]hat faith-filled people are saying when they say that they 'have been called' to this or to that is not that they have found some hidden plan but that they have felt a profound resonance between their deepest sense of themselves before God and a particular path forward. ... Instead of being called out of a sinful world, we are called into a suffering one. Instead of being called to some special state of life, we are called to the other in need. ... [D]iscernment demands nothing less than the long and difficult path of discipleship."[31]

A Closing Story

As a closing story, let me share with you a 10-minute conversation that I had in 2007, and that still sticks with me today because of its simple and profound insight into how a gospel-based vocation perspective might be best facilitated for those young people who are entrusted to our care, and in an age of disaffiliation and church suspicion. This goes back to when I had been invited to help staff the General Chapter of the Brothers at the Motherhouse in Rome; five weeks of work preparing, overseeing, and leading the prayer and liturgy experiences for the assembled delegates. At the time I was the Vocation Director for our District and had also taken on the role of Regional Director of Vocation Ministry, responsible for marketing and promoting the Brothers vocation in North America.

There were several invited speakers that I was able to listen to from the back of the assembly hall. One of them was the 80-year-old retired cardinal archbishop of Milan, Carlo Maria Martini, SJ, whose 22-year stint in that role had especially endeared him to young people. He knew them well, and they loved him well. In the middle of his two-hour talk to the chapter delegates, he had to take a break,

---

[31] Hahnenberg, *Awakening Vocations*, 231, 232, 233

simply to rest in his room for a half hour. But I had a burning question for him, and I knew that if I didn't follow up and do something about it, I wouldn't be able to ask him later and would certainly regret it.

So I built up my courage, snuck down to his room, knocked on his door, and asked if he would have just a few minutes for me. He graciously invited me in, asked me to sit down, and was all attention. As it was, I didn't know him or his background, but I was very impressed with what he'd already said to the delegates. And so this is what I asked him. "Cardinal, I'm involved right now in vocation ministry with young people in the United States. What is the best thing that we can do to help young people find their vocation?"

He was silent for about two minutes, quietly thinking about the question – already a very impressive thing to me, because it meant that he took the question very seriously and would not respond with a prepared kind of answer. He was "in the moment," as they say, and clearly saw each moment of his day in a providential, God-filled light. Then he said, "Brother, two things. First, give them an experience of silence. And second, help them to open up scripture for themselves. The Holy Spirit will take care of the rest." I was silent for some time. Then I thanked him sincerely and left, touched by his words and by the convictions and sentiments behind those words, which have echoed in my mind ever since then. They still do.

Finally, a theology of vocation is only as good as the vocations that it informs, encourages, shapes, and develops. The <u>real</u> vocation journey is essentially a Gospel journey, a journey of faith, not simply a personal quest. Hahnenberg puts it well: "[T]he great good news of the Christian call is that following Jesus frees us. … To live one's life as a response to God's call is a pilgrimage, a shared journey of faith, solidarity, and transformation in the light of Christ – the marks of a very different kind of quest."[32]

---

[32] Ibid., 233

TRANSFORMATIVE LASALLIAN OPERATIONAL DIMENSIONS

One of the outstanding phrases from the Emmaus story is that for those who walked on the road with the resurrected Jesus whom they could see, was that "Their eyes were opened" (Lk 24:31). To talk about having your eyes opened is to highlight the bursting in of a new revelation, a new awareness, a new collation of the facts, a new place from where to see things that we thought we already knew. The facts haven't changed, but we have, and our comprehension in seeing things has. The facts aren't in a new place, but we are. And because of that, how we do what we do in the future must change, because we now see things in a new light.

Look at the piece of artwork by Shigeo Fukuda on this page. It looks to be a rather modernist metal sculpture whose meaning or intent is beyond the comprehension of most. As much as you try, it appears to make little sense on the face of it.

But if it is seen from a different place – a little further away – and with the light shining on it in a particular way – from above in this case – then the whole thing makes much more sense; not because the sculpture has changed, but because where we see it from, and the light's direction changed. Even something that appears to be incomplete, with lots of gaps and not a lot of solid matter, can cast a shadow that is not only substantial, but that conveys a clarity that would not have been seen before.

Given the right light and particular viewpoint, any group of facts that was not comprehensible before may suddenly take on new meaning and cast a shadow or outline a story that is not only very clear, but also compelling and inspiring. This is also the case with the Gospel itself. But here it is a belief based on fact that brings comprehension; i.e., the tremendous fact of the resurrection. The light of this fact alone, as Saint Paul says so well, sheds transformative light on literally everything else.

This same dynamic is part of the experience of hundreds of thousands of Lasallian educators over the last 340 years, both Brothers and a vast number of others – students, teachers, parents, and so on. For reasons that are difficult to nail down, the story of Lasallian education has waxed and waned, grown and diminished, despite all of the historical challenges that happened from the very beginning of the Institute up to the not inconsequential challenges of today. This Lasallian ministry and charism, like and with the Gospel, carries a dynamic that generates its own momentum.

Why is that? What is it about this educational movement that has allowed it, has driven it, to adapt to so many places and contexts, taking on such a variety of education-related works, and persisting through so many challenges and difficulties?

Let me offer for our consideration what might be called five transformative operational dimensions of the Lasallian network and charism. Others exist as well, as with any living, dynamic social or educational movement. And there are those among you who would be happy to put your own list of factors together – and you should. But for me, these, I believe, are some key aspects of our 340-year-history that have helped ensure its ongoing vitality.

After a short description of each transformative operational dimension, I will also provide at least one suggestion as to how that particular key dimension of our ministries might be fed and actualized further today.

De La Salle Himself

John Baptist de La Salle's personality and perspectives shape the DNA of this apostolate, this charism. His spirit and story imbue our educational vision, approach, and execution. When you read his story, you find out that he was a dedicated, hard worker who took his spiritual life very seriously, and who persisted in what he set out to do, relying on a wholly unreasonable trust in God's Providence. He was stubborn, a natural leader – by which I mean one with genuine humility, and he was not afraid of taking on more than others might think wise or feasible. If it had to do with addressing an educational need, he stepped up and looked at what could be done to address that need. He took that first step and then allowed lived experience to inform the process.

He also led by example and with a deep respect for God's movement in the lives of those who were with him; God's dynamic presence within his own circumstances and within those around him. One of his very early biographers, who lived with him, describes that leadership, saying that he "was content to lead the teachers by the hand, so to speak, to let them see from their own experience and from his exhortations and example what was the best course to follow." Nothing was introduced by authority. Instead, "he flattered them by giving them the satisfaction of being themselves the creators of their own vision and their own plans for making it a reality." In other words, he allowed his trust in God's presence in and through others guide the future of the work that they shared. Many examples today, in this region and others, attest to the success that this kind of leadership enables.

By his own example and leadership, De La Salle single-handedly lifted teaching up to be a genuine vocation, a ministry, a way of following the Gospel and Jesus Christ.

How might this key dimension become a more engaged reality today? Perhaps one specific way is for Lasallian ministries to sponsor, individually or with others, an annual student essay, video, or public-speaking contest around a key aspect of De La Salle's life or educational approach, with the question or theme changing yearly. Given significant enough prizes, such contests generate interest, research, conversation, and greater awareness. And doing so among a set of Lasallian ministries creates subject matter for classes, staff discussions, parent newsletters, integrating conversations about this pivotal figure within the community that he founded.

Focus on Education

We do one thing, and we work very hard to do it well. The focus of those in the Lasallian world is on education, writ large. This is meant both literally and figuratively. Our apostolate is education, education, and education. AND such education is not confined to the classroom, to lessons and tests, or only to knowledge and skills. A Lasallian education deals primarily with young people and their learning needs, and it embraces the building up of character, relationships, community, leadership, and all those things that lead to living life to the full.

Education for us is a sacred project, a holy endeavor, a privileged encounter. For me, this was well articulated in a document from over fifty years ago, called the *Declaration of the Brother in the World Today*, a post-Vatican II document that remains extremely readable and relevant. With some minor edits towards making the passage a bit more inclusive, this is what one section said about the apostolate of teaching:

> "It is apostolic to awaken in students a serious attitude towards life and the conviction of the greatness of human destiny; it is apostolic to make it possible for them, with intellectual honesty and responsibility, to experience the autonomy of personal thought; it is apostolic to help the students to use their liberty to overcome their own prejudices,

> preconceived ideas, social pressures, as well as the pressures that come from disintegration within the human person; it is apostolic to dispose students to use their intelligence and their training in the service of others, to open them to others: to teach them how to listen and to try to understand, to trust and love; it is apostolic to instill in students a sense of trustworthiness, brotherhood, sisterhood, and justice."[1]

What we do in our schools, classrooms, offices, youth ministries, etc., is live out the Gospel in the educational world. We evangelize through education.

We are the ones whose ears perk up when we hear someone nearby talk about schools, or about working with difficult kids, or the latest government educational scheme, or simply about their own educational experience. If it deals with teaching and learning, education, schools and services for kids and families, we want to be part of the conversation. And it's darn sure that most of us will have an opinion or an experience to share. Education is our passion and our focus; it is what we love, and it is what we do.

One of De La Salle's insights was that students need and deserve fully committed, focused, dedicated, and well-trained teachers, and not just those who happen to do some teaching on the side, or who are teachers until something better comes along. Nothing should get in the way of the ministry of teaching. It is one reason why, for us and within our charism, ordained ministry did not become an option. Our vocation was education and education alone. Education is our primary vocation, and we are more than content with that reality.

So how might this key dimension become a more engaged reality today? One specific way might be for teachers to share their own vocation stories. In one of our schools in the U.S., one Friday a month is vocation Friday, and all the teachers are invited, at the beginning of their classes, to share a bit (about 3-5 minutes) about their own vocation story, how they became a teacher. Those who prefer not to do so can cede their time to administrators, coaches,

---

[1] Brothers of the Christian Schools. *The Brother of the Christian Schools in the World Today: A Declaration.* Rome: 1997. (40.2)

or others in the school community who would like to do so but don't have classes themselves. This has proven to be very effective among the students. Not only do they develop an appreciation of the teaching vocation, but they also begin to think about their own vocation in life. In fact, it became so engrained in the school that the standard question to try to distract a substitute teacher in class was to ask, "Could you tell us something about your vocation story, how you became involved in education?"

Self-Adjusting, Adaptable, & Relevant

Because of these two first things — the way that De La Salle shaped those first schools and those first teachers and their common growing passion for doing education well — Lasallian education became one that is essentially experience-driven, using what might be called a "monitor and adjust" process for ensuring successful pedagogy.

The Brothers worked together to make sure that the best methodologies for the time were being used. They paid attention to what the students really needed in their particular context and worked hard to provide it. In the coastal town of Calais, for example, where maritime jobs were uppermost, classes included navigation, geometry, and all that was needed for good seamanship. In large cities, the math courses worked with ledgers, bills, invoices, and the handling of money. At Saint Yon in Rouen, where there were older students, what is arguably the first secondary school curriculum was devised and implemented. And a school that was started on Sundays for those older students who worked during the week made sure that the courses offered were those that they needed and wanted.

Certain more senior Brothers would also be allowed to try new methodologies or new courses, and those courses would be evaluated and changed as needed; sort of like a Research & Development arm of the Brothers. Eventually, if they proved effective, they would be adopted by other Lasallian schools and thereby benefit the wider student population.

The project in which this collaborative, experience-driven, monitor-and-adjust methodology was made most abundantly clear was in the development of what might be called the early operational handbook of the Lasallian Schools. (I sometimes call it the "franchise binder" for the Lasallian schools.) Called the *Conduct of Christian Schools* and first published in 1720, the book represented forty years of in-the-classroom experience, of trial and error, of conversation and development, of drafts and rewrites. What was the result? A text that was clearly and obviously written by teachers for teachers. Here are some random samples:

> *The teacher will take great care to see that all read quietly what the reader is reading along. From time to time, the teacher will make some of them read a few words in passing, surprising them and finding out if they are following…* It's clearly a teacher who wrote that.

> *When the students begin to write, it will be useful to give them a stick of the thickness of a pen to hold. On the sticks, there will be grooves to indicate where the fingers should be placed. This teaches the students to hold the pen properly…* This is also something that only a teacher would devise.

> *At each hour of the day, some short prayers will be said. These will help the teachers to recollect themselves and recall the presence of God; it will serve to accustom the students to think of God from time to time and to offer God all their actions.* We all know the value of doing this.

This particular text was never static during the subsequent 250 years that it was published. We know of at least 23 different editions, some completely revised, and reaching up to the middle of the last century.

From the *Conduct* to a book on politeness (geared for inner city boys and including a chapters on spitting, coughing, and what to do with your nose), to a set of fifty songs, with pious texts set to popular tunes of the time that were sung at the end of the school day, to sets of prayers for use during Mass or Confession or other times in church; whatever the students needed or whatever would benefit them was created and constantly adapted and revised to keep them relevant to the needs of the time. It was the way that Lasallian education remained living, active, and engaged.

How might <u>this</u> key dimension become a more engaged reality today? One way is by intentionally supporting teachers who wish to develop new courses or teaching methodologies, seeing such innovation and interest not as exceptional but as simple part of being a Lasallian institution. Disciplined creativity in pedagogy is a norm for us. In some schools, budgets specifically include funds available for supporting new pedagogical trends, leading individuals to apply for the funds to a school committee created for the purpose, and thereby pursuing their own interests while also benefiting the whole school community.

Community & Association

A few years ago, I ran into a quotation that was attributed to Br. Robert Schieler, our Superior General, and it struck me as very insightful and completely true. He said: "The decisive innovation of the Founder is that education is conducted within the context of community."[2]

This commitment to community rings true on so many levels. De La Salle already appreciated the strength that a religious community brings to a challenging ministry. His work with the Sisters of the Child Jesus showed him that. Then when Adrien Nyel got him involved with this new project of providing an education for the poor boys of Reims, he came to see over a number of years that this whole thing would only work if it was based on a committed set of teachers who would see their work as a ministry and who would work together to ensure its success.

Those early teachers saw it themselves. When it came to naming themselves as a group, they chose the name of "Brothers," proclaiming to the public that they were "brothers to one another" in their educational ministry (a community of educators rather than a collection of independent contractors) and also "older brothers to those God had entrusted to their care," part of a broader educational community that included the students.[3] At that time, a committed spiritual life and a life of singular dedication meant a religious community of some sort, although you will remember that De La

---

[2] Some time later, when I had a chance to ask him about this quote, he said, "I never said that." I told him that he probably didn't remember saying it, but that it was a great quote, and that I was going to use it nevertheless

[3] Canon Blain, Book 2, Chapter III, "A Distinctive Garb," subsection "A new name: Brothers of the Christian Schools." P. 186.

Salle had an abiding interest in training country schoolmasters who worked by themselves in the villages.

The engine for effective Lasallian education, from the very beginning, was a genuine, living community. Lasallian education is one that revolves around what Lasallian scholar, Leon Lauraire, calls a "pedagogy of fraternity." [4]

Such united dedication came to be seen as crucial when everything seemed to be falling apart about ten years after our sporadic beginnings – people were leaving and dying, lawsuits were piling up, plans for the future fell apart, and the mood was pretty grim.

And so De La Salle and two others made a private vow, secret at the time and for many years after, probably in some room at Saint Yon in Rouen. And what was that vow? Was it a vow of poverty, chastity, and obedience? No. Was it a vow of service to the poor through the schools? No.

They decided to "…make a vow of association and union to bring about and maintain the said establishment…" meaning the Christian Schools, even if only the three of them remained. That's putting a stake in the ground. That's saying that community – called association here – is the foundation for ensuring the success of these schools.

Three years later, after the society stabilized and 12 Brothers for the first time made perpetual vows, the vow formula similarly said ". . . promise and vow to unite myself and to remain in Society with Brothers Nicolas Vuyart, Gabriel Drolin, and . . . to keep together and by association gratuitous schools wherever they may be, even if I were obliged to live on bread alone, or to do anything in the said Society at which I shall be employed . . ."

I highlight this in order to stress the fact that this community thing is not just a nice-to-have for us. Association, which underlies what community is all about for us, and which is manifested in and through genuine community, requires commitment. For the Brothers, it is a commitment by practice, disposition, and a public vow –

---

[4] Lauraire, Leon, FSC. "A Pedagogy of Fraternity" AXIS: Journal of Lasallian Higher Education 7, no. 3 (2016). Presentation at the FSC Casa Generalizia on May 12, 2015. Pg. 31.

although we certainly don't exercise it all perfectly. For other Lasallian educators or ministers, it must be a commitment by practice, disposition, and presently a sort of private vow or private decision, the kind of decision you make when something really important happens in your life – like falling in love with someone, having a baby, or burying a parent or student. It is a resolution to set out in a certain direction, do things in a certain way.

De La Salle recognized that community might not be perfect, but it was central. He said that "union in community is a precious gem, [and] if we lose this, we lose everything." For a saint not usually given to hyperbole, that is a pretty strong statement. We would do well to heed its message.

How might this key dimension become a more engaged reality today? One thought follows from the annual CAP process – Community Annual Program – in Brothers communities, whereby a day or more at the beginning of each school year is spent reviewing and articulating the priorities for the year in a wide variety of areas, usually defined by the District or the Visitor. It puts an intentional focus on the actual ways the community operationalizes its life for the year.

Perhaps schools might pursue an annual SCAP process, or a School Community Annual Program, one that would address areas of faculty engagement, social outreach, vocation ministry, school prayer life or spirituality support; anything that touches the school community, engages the school community, and directly or indirectly builds the school community towards intentional ends. Community takes work to do well.

A Spirit of Faith & Zeal

There is a second part to the verse from the Gospel of Luke that is the focus of today: "Their eyes were opened **and they recognized him**." It's one thing for our eyes to be opened. But the next question is, "Opened to what?"

A school in the Lasallian tradition cannot be separated from a school in the Christian tradition, specifically the Catholic Christian tradition. The kind of educational community that characterizes a Lasallian school emerges solely with reference to the kind of faith community that characterizes the Body of Christ. Both the context and the substance of what occurs in a Lasallian school on a daily basis arise out of dynamics and paradigms that have a Christian character, that are part of the world-wide and local Catholic Church community.

De La Salle delved into the work of educating the young in order to make the Gospel and Jesus Christ an effective and living reality in their lives. He came to see that his teachers were to "preach" an alternative way of life, becoming ambassadors for God's incarnated Word and bringing Jesus' spirit, the Holy Spirit, within the lives of their students. By example, vigilance, instruction, care, and a well-organized program of Christian formation, the Gospel would have a chance to take root, and those who were presently "far from salvation" would find it within reach. They would learn to live life to the full.

De La Salle uniquely expressed this by driving home the importance of the Spirit of Faith & Zeal. The language took shape toward very end of his life, when he was asked in 1718 to write up changes to the Rule that the Brothers had approved at their General Chapter — a set of meetings De La Salle had not been part of. In that final document, De La Salle added a short section that has remained in all the subsequent iterations of our Rule.

"That which is of the utmost importance, and to which the greatest attention should be given in an Institute is that all who compose it possess the spirit peculiar to it." This applies today as much as it did back then.

In fact, "those who do not possess it and those who have lost it, should be looked upon as dead members." It applies to teachers old and new, administrators old and new, and anyone else old and new associated with this ministry and charism.

This spirit is, first, a spirit of faith, and second, a spirit of zeal. [*I won't read it all; take a look at it on the screen.*] Another added prescription was that the Brothers should read the New Testament daily, "looking upon it as their first and principal rule." I would suggest that <u>if</u> those two things were done regularly and well – keeping the spirit of the Institute and reading the New Testament regularly –

we would all be well served, because we would be paying attention to that through which our eyes could truly be opened.

And how might this key dimension become a more engaged reality today? Here is a suggestion was offered at last November's Huether Conference in Minneapolis, when Gery Short received the John Johnston Award. Gery had just retired from 30 years with us as one of the first lay Lasallian partners. He was head of our office of education for over twenty years, spearheading new works for the poor and an increase in lay leadership. He also served as chair of the first international mission assembly, among other responsibilities. With his family's support, he stands out as a very credible and impressive figure among Lasallian Partners. Okay, that was the build-up. What stood out in his speech in Minneapolis was when he said that he was going to put "a stake in the ground for the future." It was this:

> "We must commit ourselves to firmly establish the spirit of faith as a foundational and effective reality in each and every one of our works. We must ask, how do we make prayer and spirituality, the spirit of faith, the core of who we are and what we are about? How do we make prayer and spirituality real for ourselves as educators and our students in an authentic, understandable, and deeply significant way."

In terms of the centrality of the Lasallian Spirit of Faith & Zeal, that's about as clear and direct as anything that I might be able to say. And is comes from a lay partner like yourselves who is well aware of the realities of the Lasallian world today.

So these are five transformative operational dimensions of the Lasallian network and charism that I suggest deserve our attention. Without them, mission creep is inevitable. With them, the non-negotiables that have ensured our success in the past will be safeguarded into the future.

Conclusion

We started out with the image of the disciples and Jesus talking on the road to Emmaus. And it will be fitting to close with that same image.

De La Salle's own meditation on that story says this: "[w]e cannot do better than model our conversations on the one that Jesus Christ had with his two disciples who were on their way to Emmaus, and also the ones that the two disciples had with each other <u>before</u> Jesus Christ joined them, and <u>after</u> he left them." (M30.3) De La Salle highlights three conversations – before, during, and after their encounter with Jesus. And he writes that in order "To model your conversation on that of the two disciples and Jesus Christ with them, it is good for you to know . . . that they spoke only of good things." (M30.2)

Such conversations were something that I experienced a few years ago, when I joined 20 Brothers and 240 Lasallian children of God – Lasallian high school students – on an 8-day *Camino de Satiago* pilgrimage walk in Spain.

It was 140 miles, and the first couple of days were rather grueling. But eventually, it became a wonderful and great adventure for everyone. And what began to emerge was the quality of the conversations.

When you spent 3-4 hours walking with someone, there is only so much chitchat you can do before you find yourself beginning to talk about more important things, but doing so in a comfortable and companionable way, listening closely to the other person, and responding genuinely with empathy, kindness, humor, along with some challenges and quiet candor.

And you have all sorts of conversations with people along the way; ones that you could not have anticipated, and some of which were wonderfully rich and sincere. You never knew what lay ahead; but it was good.

At the end of this short pilgrimage, when I was going through my photos, I was suddenly reminded of that famous painting of Jesus on the road to Emmaus, talking with the disciples. And I thought, "So that's how it was! Of course. Jesus spent hours and hours speaking with his disciples on the road. It was through those conversations that the gospel took root in the hearts of his disciples. I had only experienced a tiny bit of that on the Camino walk. But it was enough; enough to realize that De La Salle's observation that they talked about the good things is correct and very insightful.

And it is good advice for us today. 340 years down the line, it is through our conversations – here at the conference, back in our ministries, even at home – that we engage our vocational life, that we engage our role in the Lasallian community, <u>or not</u>. Those five transformative operational dimensions live or die on the conversations that we have, formal and informal, at school or outside of school.

If we make only one private commitment – the commitment and intention to speak only of good things, or at least mostly good things – we would be shining a light on the transformative parts of our living Lasallian tradition, and doing so from above, as it were.

By casting our light on the good of our common Lasallian educational ministry, we come to notice – and others come to notice – the shadows that are cast, what stands out in people or projects that may have been previously unseen or unknown. It shares in God's own kind of light, the living out of God's loving and holy presence. That is how grace comes to life in and through us.

How important is such grace for us? Well, De La Salle puts it best:

> *"Be satisfied with what you can do, since this satisfies God, but do not spare yourself in what you can do with the help of grace. Be convinced that, provided you are willing, you can do more with the help of God's grace than you imagine."*[5]

This invitation to take on God's grace in all that we do is the way of Jesus. And when Jesus thereby lives more and more in our hearts, we more and more live our Lasallian lives – our Lasallian vocations – to the full.

Then indeed we can and should respond "Forever!" to that invitation and live it out with an exclamation mark.

---

[5] De La Salle, John Baptist. *Reflections on Their State and Employment That the Brothers Should Make from Time to Time, Especially During Retreat*, "Regarding the Use of Time," # 10, in *Collection of Various Short Treatises*.

VARIOUS LASALLIAN REFLECTIONS

Soul for Soul

As the school year commences, we might do well to recollect – bring back to our attention – what we are about simply as educators, let alone as Lasallian educators. Our purpose dwells more in the realm of virtue and its emergence than in the realm of utility and its application. Our context is more a web of relationships than an org chart of job descriptions. Our daily world includes both sets of realities perhaps, but our intentional focus habitually differs from that of most organizations. This is as it should be, because we are about the shaping of souls.

De La Salle writes: "You have committed yourselves to God in the place of those whom you instruct. By taking upon yourselves the responsibility for their souls, you have, so to speak, offered to him soul for soul. [Ex. 21:23]" (M 137.3) This is a religiously intimate responsibility.

It is one "that requires you to touch hearts, but this you cannot do except by the Spirit of God." (M 43.3) "You must... imitate God to some extent, for he... loved the souls he created." (M 100.3) The imitation of God becomes incarnated in the teacher's daily relationship with students. "Every day you have poor children to instruct. Love them tenderly... following in this the example of Jesus Christ." (M 166.2) Through such brotherly/sisterly devotion and deep

---

¹ Photo by Justin Luebke on www.unsplash.com

attachment to the good of their students, teachers are able to draw down God's graces upon those entrusted to their care. This is a foundational perspective within our Christian tradition, as expressed through our own Lasallian Catholic lens of over three centuries, and it persists.

Such a foundational perspective on education has been at work throughout human history, lying at the root of multiple valued traditions. It is well described by C.S. Lewis in the little book, *The Abolition of Man*. He says that it is a basic human conviction that truths lie embedded in particular things themselves. Education is an introduction, an initiation, into the engagement with those truths; i.e., it is the cultivation of genuine virtue. Aristotle held that the aim of education is to make the pupil like and dislike what s/he should. Common to Greek philosophy, the Hindu *Rta*, the Oriental *Tao*, the Confucian *Analects*, the Jewish *Law*, etc. "is the doctrine of objective value, the belief that certain attitudes are really true, and others really false, to the kind of things the universe is and the kind of things we are." According to Augustine, virtue is "*ordo amoris*, the ordinate condition of the affections in which every object is accorded that kind and degree of love which is appropriate to it." In Lewis' words, "the task is to train in the pupil those responses which are in themselves appropriate, whether anyone is making them or not, and in making which the very nature of [hu]man consists."

What does this mean for us? "The task of the modern educator is not to cut down jungles but to irrigate deserts." Perhaps one of the sad consequences of today's pervasive paradigm of scientific materialism is an absence of the capacity to see and develop genuine virtue, much less value its often difficult pursuit. Our mission, if we decide to accept it, involves the training of those attitudes, perspectives, and relational experiences by which "emotions [are] organized by trained habit into stable sentiments" so that our students are guided and accompanied into their best and surely most demanding selves, precisely according to how that "best" has been experienced, described, and known throughout the greater part of human history.

This is what the shaping of souls is about, both theirs and ours.

A Few Daring Plunges

The vibrancy and noise of online social connections—today's virtual *bacchanal* for eager minds and silent eyes—reflects a deep human need for, and appreciation of, connection and belonging. But we know, or should know, that such thin connections are no substitute for the unpredictable richness of even the most fleeting of real human encounters. And without realizing the difference between the two, device-based habits may easily turn into an accepted but impoverished normality. David Brooks writes that with today's social media "You can have a day of happy touch points without any of the scary revelations, or the boring, awkward or uncontrollable moments that constitute actual intimacy. ... Being online isn't just something we do. It has become who we are, transforming the very nature of the self."[2]

Are authentic connections becoming passé? Dr. Jean Twenge in her book *iGen* makes a strong case that authentic connections are no longer the norm for adolescents today. "Born after 1995, iGen is the first generation to spend their entire adolescence in the age of the smartphone. With social media and texting replacing other activities, iGen spends less time with their friends in person—perhaps why they are experiencing unprecedented levels of anxiety,

---

[2] Brooks, D. (2016, October 7). *Intimacy for the Avoidant.* The New York Times. Retrieved from https://nyti.ms/2JZ69Zv

depression, and loneliness." The full title of her book is *iGen: Why Today's Super-Connected Kids Are Growing Up Less Rebellious, More Tolerant, Less Happy - and Completely Unprepared for Adulthood - and What That Means for the Rest of Us*. Anyone who works with young people today should read it, not only because of the solid research, but also because it will make you think about what is best for those entrusted to your care. "This ought to be one of the main concerns of those who instruct others: to be able to understand their students and to discern the right way to guide them." (DLS, Med 33.1) This book looks at why, for example, with so many virtual contacts, young people are more lonely than in the past.

A recent CIGNA study showed that over half of Americans view themselves as lonely, and the survey "found that actually the younger generation was lonelier than the older generations."[3] The least lonely were those of *The Greatest Generation* - 72 years old and above. Why is this not such a big surprise to some of us who are older? Perhaps we discovered by long experience that achieving a skill or a goal requires actual time, effort, conversation, and engagement - most of which may be facilitated by devices, but none of which may be substituted for them. Even going to a deli requires time, effort, conversation, and engagement. Silently ordering online - scan menu, make choices, fill in address, pay with card - makes opening the door for the delivery person - brief eye-contact, minimal talk - the most profound human encounter of the whole interaction. And drone-delivery will eventually make even that unnecessary. Is it any wonder that chronic loneliness, serious hole-in-the-soul loneliness, is on the rise?

How then might we as educators make a positive difference and guide young people into a different kind of *Promised Land*? Lots of ways; but here is a simple one. Find a place on the school property where there is student traffic, and stand or sit or wander there every day, making eye contact with as many students as possible. Say hello, smile, whatever; but engage! You will quickly find that it becomes deeply rewarding, and also perhaps challenging (to keep doing). Human nature itself guarantees that even minimal effort in

---

[3] https://www.npr.org/sections/health-shots/2018/05/01/606588504/americans-are-a-lonely-lot-and-young-people-bear-the-heaviest-burden

addressing the deepest of longings of people bears a vastly dispro-portionate, cumulatively positive reward for everyone. Eye contact is the invitation, and then "a smile is a flower is a smile of the heart." (Pope Francis) How hard can it be? And if it is hard, then more time, effort, conversation, and engagement are needed. The more we enter into something new, the greater our capacity becomes for doing it.

Heroic endeavors are called for today, because social media gener-ally "flattens the range of emotional experiences. . . [E]very moment is fun and diverting, but the whole thing is profoundly unsatisfying. I guess a modern version of heroism is ... regaining control of social impulses, saying no to a thousand shallow contacts for the sake of a few daring plunges."[4]

Teachers are at the forefront of what Br. Leon Lauraire calls our uniquely Lasallian *"pedagogy of fraternity."* Daring plunges, even brief ones, are the happy requirement for its realization.

---

[4] Brooks, D., op. cit.

The Joy of Gratitude

"Gratefulness is the inner gesture of *giving* meaning to our life by *receiving* life as gift. The deepest meaning of any given moment lies in the fact that it is given. Gratefulness recognizes, acknowledges, and celebrates this meaning."[6] This quotation is by Br. David Steind-Rast, OSB, one of the most articulate evangelists for gratitude, gratefulness, thanksgiving, and all those words that convey a reaching out into the world with arms wide open.

The spontaneous joy of engaging life's nature as pure gift reminds me of the young two-year-old son of some very good friends of mine, who—years ago now—unselfconsciously brimmed over with life and mischief, climbing onto furniture and ledges with way-too-risky abandon, a smile on his face and giggles as companions, hugging people and things with the kind of joy that only children seem to be able to display with unvarnished transparency. Every moment was precious, was now, was embraced with love and palpable, infectious joy. Jesus' words, "Let the children come to me . . ." suddenly made lots of sense. Children live with raw gratitude even while being significant recipients of the generosity of others. Both are very much alive.

---

[5] Photo from vimeo.com/135308696

[6] Steind-Rast, David, *Gratefulness, the Heart of Prayer*, Paulist Press. 1984. Pg. 207

Gratitude seems to me to be the flip side of generosity. With generosity, we express actions and intentions of unconditional love; with gratitude we receive actions and intentions of unconditional love. The best kinds of generosity are given unasked, unexpected, and previously unknown. The best kinds of gratefulness are received unasked, unexpected, and previously unknown. The most generous people tend to be the most grateful, and *vice versa.* Generosity and gratefulness appear to be two vectors of love's living dynamic.

These same vectors are found in education and teachers. St. John Baptist de La Salle tells his teachers: "Thank God for the grace he has given you . . . and calling you to such a holy work of instructing children and leading them to piety."[7] And "Thank God, who has had the goodness to employ you to procure such an important advantage for children."[8] But this invitation to teachers to be grateful is a notion that is actually quite challenging. Our internal perspective may at times–among other people, of course; not ourselves–run more along the lines of "These kids should be grateful that they have me as a teacher . . . they don't appreciate all the work that I do for them, how much time I put into the classes, and what I've given up to do this job well . . . they really don't have a clue." Such thoughts are based on a transactional approach to teaching; I do this for them, and they should do that for me. The vectors finally point inward.

Of course, most veteran teachers, although unfortunately not all, sloughed off that old cloak years ago and listen to such sentiments with a wry grin on their faces. They walk into most classes with genuine and daily gratitude, because by virtue of their years of experience they have been drawn into the deep generosity of teaching with all of its concomitant joys and blessings. They know that they plant seeds and that the growth comes from elsewhere. (Cf. 1 Cor. 3:6) Most students are never seen again, and so they will never know if those seeds had ever taken root. And if my experience is any indication of the experience of others, the things that did take root

---

[7] De La Salle, John Baptist. *Meditations by St. John Baptist de La Salle.* Landover, MD: Christian Brothers Conference, 1994. (MED 99.1) Pg. 183.
[8] Ibid. (MED 193.1) Pg. 435.

may not even have been the most obvious seeds. (I still wash and dry my hands like my 3rd grade teacher did in the corner of the classroom every morning.) Diving into the kind of arms-wide-open generosity that genuine teaching calls for cannot but coat one's life with the cumulative gratitude that only steady or great love can bring, whether received or given.

Finally, teachers must step out of the way, trusting the generosity of God's movement in the lives of their students. And that is something deserving our gratitude as well. It's not all up to us. "Teaching is cooperative art similar to the nurturing that defines farming; involving watering, pruning where necessary, etc. It consists in developing a respect for mystery, a capacity for trust, and a skill in serious reflection. Through revelations and challenges, experiences and analyses, insights and application, others are led to develop habits of perception; to grind their lenses, as it were, so that the reality of God might be seen in focus and encountered in the full light of truth. Once a path for God is cleared and opened, the teacher steps aside and lets the mystery commence."[9] Stepping aside is a most generous thing, and gratitude for that particular thing may be the last seed dropped into students' lives.

For a gratitude kick start, watch the Louis Schwartzberg video "Gratitude Revealed"[10] and listen to Br. David Steindl-Rast's narration. There is no better invitation to the joy of gratefulness.

---

[9] Nouwen, Henri J.M. *Creative Ministry.* New York, N.Y. Doubleday, 1971. Pg. 11.
[10] https://vimeo.com/135308696

The Gift of Silence

Have you ever been in a place where it is so quiet that the absence of sound begets a unique richness and palpable substance? The anticipated "nothing" turns inside out, and a very much kind of "something" emerges. What comes to mind is my nighttime visit to a mountaintop near Sonoma, CA, where amateur astronomers quietly gather to share their passion under star-filled skies, waving about red night-vision-preserving flashlights and beckoning visitors stumbling around in the dark to come and squint through their telescopes to see this or that galaxy or star cluster millions of light-years away. A similar sense of silence is found by others in the quiet company of loved ones, or in a walk in the woods – perhaps with their dog, or in driving a car with the radio turned off and comfortably settled into a semi-automatic mode, or idly watching children play in a public park. The "something" seems to consist of an inner settledness, an unanticipated resonance with the disposition of redwood trees and evening high-Sierra lakes. Each instance carries a hint of eternity and of grace; this is a "something" that strikes us as timeless and good and simply for us. It's the kind of experience that allows the word "blessed" to make sense.

"A human being is dust called to glory. ... The call directed to us ... is to raise our soul's eyes to glimpse the other side; then, to

---

[11] Luc Olivier Merson (French, 1846-1920) – *Rest on the Flight into Egypt* – Museum of Fine Arts, Boston

realize that, in Christ, a passage exists. The ladder of humility, laid flat, carries across. To own that I am dust is an act of daring. By that admission, I make peace with my poverty. I resolve to dwell within it. … I am taught to let glory, by grace, lay claim to my being even now, to make it resonant with music of eternity. I learn to look towards eternity as home."[12] Such sentiments may be easier to reach towards, or even touch, in a monastery or on top of a mountain late at night than in an airport, a shopping mall, or a busy family or school community. Yet the fact that it is possible is itself an invitation to do so. In that sense, and probably for that reason, Advent speaks of the reaching, and Christmas proclaims the invitation.

St. John Baptist de La Salle knew the value of example, the influence of what is experienced, and the learning potential of what is observed: "Do you wish your disciples to do what is right? Do it yourself. You will persuade them much more readily through your example of wise and prudent behavior than through all the words you could speak to them. Do you want them to keep silence? Keep it yourself." (Med 33.2) The deep-down silence that is the condition for being open to God's presence in our lives is also the substance of how God "teaches" us. "We learn to speak to God only by listening to him; for to know how to speak to God and to converse with him can only come from God." (Med 64.2) Does this mean that we should hide in a cave in order to find God? We could, and people do, but thankfully God is more egalitarian than that. Think of the parable of the prodigal son, or the shepherd and his one lost sheep. If anything, God seems to be more readily found by way of forgiveness and mercy, through the cracks of life, than through any direct, stable, predictable, and definitive path.[13]

Such cracks appear to be much more prevalent in contemporary society, contributing to the age of the "Nones," and yet today's society leaves people bereft of ways to fill them. David Brooks writes,

---

[12] Varden, Eric. *Shattering of Loneliness: On Christian Remembrance*. London: Bloomsbury, 2018. Pg. 21, 32.

[13] Cf. Ralph Waldo Emerson's "There is a crack in every thing God has made." (1841), Hemingway's "The world breaks everyone and afterward many are strong at the broken places" (1929), and Leonard Cohen's now-famous "There is a crack, a crack, in everything. That's how the light gets in." (1992) https://quoteinvestigator.com/2016/11/16/light/

"Sometimes I look at the rising suicide and depression rates, the rising fragility and distrust, and I think it all flows from the fact that we've made our culture a spiritual void. When you privatize morality and denude the public square of spiritual content, you've robbed people of the community resources they need to process moral pain together."[14] So while Santa Claus and Black Friday are hugely successful, their benefits fall through the cracks, as it were, and the substance of things hoped for remains as hidden and ignored by most people as are the stars above. We have lost virtually all of our night vision, and even the tiny clusters of light seem out of reach.

What to do? Wave about red night-vision-preserving flashlights of mercy to help show the way of forgiveness, and beckon visitors stumbling around in the dark to come and squint at what we have been able to see, however far away and indistinct. Because at some point they will step back, take in the whole of it, and be touched by a tiny, silent whisper of presence and love[15] that transforms absence into presence, nothing into something, and Christmas into Christ. And then we can truly say with Tiny Tim, "God bless us, every one!"

---

[14] Brooks, David. *Fighting the Spiritual Void*. New York Times, Nov. 19, 2018. https://www.nytimes.com/2018/11/19/opinion/mental-health-ptsd-community.html

[15] God said, "Go out and stand on the mountain before the Lord, for the Lord is about to pass by." Now there was a great wind… but the Lord was not in the wind; and after the wind an earthquake, but the Lord was not in the earthquake; and after the earthquake a fire, but the Lord was not in the fire; and after the fire a sound of sheer silence. When Elijah heard it, he wrapped his face in his mantle and went out and stood at the entrance of the cave. - 1 Kings 19:11-12 (NRSV)

Where Our Hope Lies

People living in the world think very little about God and have little concern about their salvation. Their sole occupation is usually with their temporal affairs and the needs of the body. It would seem that most have nothing to hope for or to fear beyond this present life.

- St. John Baptist de La Salle[17]

At the end of each calendar year, billions of people around the world "welcome in the new year" with fireworks, parties, and resolutions about personal diet, exercise, and healthy living. This utterly regular change of one day into the next is transformed into a personal hoped-for change of one way of life into another. A focused consciousness of time is suddenly leveraged to pursue our deeper aspirations, and the beginning of a new year becomes a celebration of hope.

People who have no common ties of culture, religion, family, or profession gather in large public spaces to put on funny hats and glasses, create noises of all kinds, and express the happiness of simply being alive. For just a little while, it doesn't matter what you

---

[16] Photo by Kristopher Roller on www.unsplash.com
[17] Meditation 58.3

do, who you are, who you know, or how much you have. All share the aspirational nature of lived humanity, of a consciously shared individuality. It's not so much that we really know what we want more of, beyond simply life; just that there is a certain set of things about which "more" is desirable and worth pursuing. For the vast majority, what we reach for at this time are larger, more comprehensive, and less definitive objectives than those which we have just asked for and received a week ago at Christmas. Where we had so recently asked for a coffee maker or a DVD, we now aspire to world peace, a just society, genuine community, and a happy relationship or family. The transition of time implied by the start of a new calendar year reminds us that our own time is limited, and that we had better start thinking about some of the things that we know, deep down, are finally really important. Thankfully, such hopes are generally positive, informed by our past experiences, priorities, and upbringing. They are indicators of where our attention is drawn in the quiet of our hearts.

While such New Year's aspirations tend to be uniformly positive, the insight from the architect Mies von der Rohe applies: "God is in the details." This is the real challenge. The world in which we live and move and have our being overwhelms - or at least helps to shape - any aspirations that we wish to pursue. The details of contemporary life tend to aggregate around ideals whose gravitational pull is largely determined by the untamed political crowd-sourcing of social media and the "news" it generates. In contrast, religion by its nature comes from different roots and drinks from far more ancient, deeper, and less noisy wells, where details inspire and evoke what is important instead of defining and determining it. They are the source of meaning, of what we come to know as important, of what informs the character of our lives. And as Andrew Sullivan has written, "if your ultimate meaning is derived from religion, you have less need of deriving it from politics or ideology or trusting entirely in a single, secular leader. It's only when your meaning has been secured that you can allow politics to be merely procedural."[18]

---

[18] http://nymag.com/intelligencer/2018/12/andrew-sullivan-americas-new-religions.html

It would be a safe bet to say that the hopes of those whose ultimate meaning is derived from genuine religious sources is qualitatively different from that of those whose ultimate meaning is derived from politics or ideology or a single, secular leader. Therefore, while I am happy that New Year's revelers harbor positive hopes of one kind or another, I pray that they have the wherewithal to bring them into fruition. But I think that those whose positive New Year's hopes emerge from within an engaged, genuine, vibrant, religiously focused community have a much greater chance of actually being enacted, however provisionally and incrementally, because those dwelling in such a community will be familiar with habits of perspective, relationship, and justice that are further realized simply in the pursuit or in the doing of them. "Christ has no body now but yours." (*St. Teresa of Avila*)

For those of us who constantly challenge ourselves to live up to the aspirations of our faith, the sentiments expressed in the New Testament – the details – are more than just nice ideas. They are, or can become, the fireworks of our lives.

Happy New Year! "May the God of hope fill you with all joy and peace as you trust in him, so that you may overflow with hope by the power of the Holy Spirit. (*Romans 15:13*)

A Well-Played Match

It is entirely contrary to decorum to grow overexcited when you play. Still, you should not play in a careless manner nor lose deliberately as a way of flattering your opponent. This would make the person with whom you are playing think that you care little about contributing to his enjoyment in a well-played match.*

- St. John Baptist de La Salle[20]

And so we come to Super Bowl Sunday, the closest thing that we have to a national ritual expression of our deep devotion to sports. Whether football fans or not, there are over 100,000,000 of us who tune in to cheer on our favorite teams, consume our favorite snacks, sit and argue the merits of players and plays with our favorite people, and generally settle into a comfortable afternoon as relaxing as that of the players is intensely active and professionally anxious. (Winners earn over $100K and a $35K ring.)

De La Salle understood the dynamics and positive aspects of sports and games. He wrote about the sorts of games that inner-city boys in 17th century France knew and loved outside of school . . . and sometimes during school. Here are some examples taken from the book he wrote on politeness, a book that was used as a reading

---

[19] Photo by Ben Hershey on www.unsplash.com
[20] *Rules of Christian Decorum and Civility: Amusements* (Pg. 91)

textbook in his schools, so that these 10-to-13-year-old boys would learn something useful along with their reading skill.

- *"You can play many different kinds of games. Some exercise the mind more; others afford more exercise to the body."*
- Games of chance *"are not only forbidden by God's law, but they are not even permitted by the rules of decorum. Consider them unworthy of an educated person."*
- *"It is very impolite for you to make fun of a player who has shown a lack of skill."*
- *"There are two passions that you must particularly guard against, so that you do not yield to them when playing games. The first is avarice, and this is ordinarily the source of the second, impatience and fits of anger."*

As teachers and coaches, we can also learn from De La Salle that who we are and what we do influences others as much as, or even more than, what we say. *"Example makes a much greater impression on the mind and heart than words, especially for children, since they do not yet have minds sufficiently able to reflect, and they ordinarily model themselves on the example of their teachers (coaches). . . . They are led more readily to do what they see done for them than what they hear told to them, above all when the teachers' (coaches') words are not in harmony with their actions."* (Med. 202.3)

A section of the *Conduct of Schools* (1720) lists, with real insight, six ways that a teacher can be unbearable to students.[21] Notice that it talks about <u>teachers</u> being unbearable, not <u>students</u>. With a few slight changes, here is how that section might be applied to coaches and sports.

- *First, the coach's corrections are too rigorous and the yoke which the coach imposes upon the athletes is too heavy. This state of affairs is frequently due to lack of discretion and judgment on the part of the coach. It often happens that athletes do not have enough strength of body or of mind to bear the burdens which many times overwhelm them.*
- *Second, when the coach enjoins, commands, or demands something of the athletes with words too harsh and in a manner too domineering.*

---

[21] There is also a section that lists six ways that a teacher's (coach's) weakness leads to laxity, but there is not enough space in this reflection to list them. Worth looking up, however, in *The Conduct of the Christian Schools* (2007) – Pages 135-137.

Above all, the coach's conduct is unbearable when it arises from unrestrained impatience or anger.

- *Third, when the coach is too insistent in urging upon an athlete some performance which the athlete is not disposed to do, and the coach does not permit the athlete the leisure or the time to reflect.*

- *Fourth, when the coach demands little things and big things alike with the same passion.*

- *Fifth, when the coach immediately rejects the reasons and excuses of athletes and is not willing to listen to them at all.*

- *Sixth, when the coach is not mindful enough of personal faults that he [or she] does not know how to sympathize with the weaknesses of athletes and so exaggerates their faults too much. This is the situation when the coach reprimands them or punishes them and acts as though dealing with an insensible instrument rather than with a creature capable of reason.*

So when you watch the Super Bowl, think on these things, and see whether it might be helpful to text De La Salle's advice to the players and coaches in order to ensure "a well-played match."

From Here to Eternity

22

*You have to suffer a constant martyrdom that is no less violent for the spirit
than Saint Bartholomew's was for his body. You must, so to speak, tear off
your own skin, which Saint Paul calls the old man, in order to be clothed with
the Spirit of Jesus Christ, which is, according to the same Apostle, the new
man. Let this, then, be your effort throughout your life, so that you may truly
become disciples of Jesus Christ.*

- St. John Baptist de La Salle[23]

Lent is just around the corner, and the prospect of "mortification"
and "fasting" and "discipline" is not on the top ten list of anyone I
know. Most of us see this time of preparation for Easter as the "less
fun" season of the liturgical year; no peppy Lent songs like before
Christmas, and less decoration. But Lent has gotten a bad rep. As
Anthony Bloom says so well, "Contrary to what many think or feel,
Lent is a time of joy. It is a time when we come back to life. It is a
time when we shake off what is bad and dead in us in order to

---

[22] Photo by Vidar Nordli-Mathisen on www.unsplash.com

[23] De La Salle, John Baptist, *Meditations by St. John Baptist de La Salle*, trans. Richard Arnandez, and Augustine Loes, eds. Augustine Loes and Francis Huether,
(Landover, MD: Christian Brothers Conference, 1994), 293-4 (Med. 159.3)

become able to live, to live with all the vastness, all the depth, and all the intensity to which we are called. . . . This notion of joy that is connected with effort, with ascetical endeavor, with strenuous effort may indeed seem strange, and yet it runs through the whole of our spiritual life, through the life of the Church and the life of the Gospel."[24] If we are to be like Jesus, if we are to draw out the Reign of God in our midst, then we have to come to the realization that "The Kingdom of God is something to be conquered. It is not simply given to those who leisurely, lazily wait for it to come."

So if we are to take Lent seriously, there is work involved. And as with all spiritual things in our lives, such work is a matter of desire, drive, and discipline. We all need a Lent coach! What would a Lent coach do? The answer depends on the person receiving the coaching. The unique background, interests, talents, habits, and aspirations of each individual are brought into play for any coaching endeavor. But coaches also know that some general things are true pretty much all of the time: i.e., you have to motivate people, you have to show people how to do things right, and you have to get people to practice the basics over and over and over again. The funny thing is that athletes of all stripes are happy to make this effort for sports, but few are willing to make this effort for their spiritual lives. Why is that? And what would it look like if you actually followed the very best Lent coach this year?

John Baptist de La Salle, our Lasallian coach, "puts the emphasis on fidelity to the duties of state, observance of the daily spiritual exercises, attention to little things, in a word, on the mortification of the spirit and mind. . . . De La Salle urges his disciples to accept, and even love, the sufferings of the day in imitation of their teacher, Jesus Christ, and in living the Pascal Mystery, or simply as a condition of the Christian life."[25] He is pointing the way to our very best coach for the Lenten season. Can you guess?

That very best Lent coach is Jesus himself; what he says in the readings during Lent, what he shows us in his actions during Lent, and what he invites us to enter into during the liturgies of Holy Week.

---

[24] Bloom, Anthony - http://mitras.ru/eng/eng_19.htm
[25] Rodrigue, Jean-Guy – Introduction to the *Meditations*, op. cit., 13.

Here is the best coach for our spiritual lives. All we have to do is take his coaching seriously: pay attention to how he motivates us, learn how to do things right, and practice the basics over and over and over again.

What would the result look like? Here is one example: "How often does someone cry for help and we understand nothing? How often has our heart been stirred and our mind begun to understand, but we were not used to compelling ourselves, and our will wavered, and wavers too long, until it is too late. . . . Let us learn first of all to be grateful that God gives us the possibility to do right, instead of preening ourselves and being proud of the fact that for once we have done what should be natural to us always. And then gradually we may . . . learn to be humble in a way in which no one knows, not declaring that we are unworthy, but in adoration of God's greatness, in veneration of other people, in the readiness to forget ourselves completely for the sake of God, for the sake of any person who meets us and challenges us to be compassionate, to be loving, to be understanding.[26]

Lent is an invitation to follow our coach from here to eternity.

---

[26] Bloom, Anthony - *http://www.mitras.ru/eng/eng_155.htm*

Simplicity Isn't So Simple

The more you act with simplicity in regard to what is to be observed,
the more the practice of it will become easy for you.

- St. John Baptist de La Salle [28]

For those of you who have been to Disneyland – and not just for a quickie visit, but for that multiday, multipass, parkhopper sort of visit – you will relate to my recent experience of its focused frenetic fabrication of fun. It reminded me of an insight from many years ago, when another Brother and I spent some time in Orlando, bird-watching and going to the Disney parks there. One day we quietly watched birds while ambling through Sanibel Island, the next we rushed hither and yon from one nice artificial experience to the next. I have to say that I enjoyed it all. But I also have to admit that what I remember, what took root inside, and what I hold most dear today, are the bird-watching days. There is a depth and richness in the complex simplicity of nature that finally and easily outweighs the simple complexity of theme parks. Chesterton wrote, *"Men rush*

---

[27] Photo by Jacek Dylag on www.unsplash.com

[28] De La Salle, John Baptist, *Meditations by St. John Baptist de La Salle*, trans. Richard Arnandez, and Augustine Loes, eds. Augustine Loes and Francis Huether, (Landover, MD: Christian Brothers Conference, 1994), 262 (Med. 142.3)

toward complexity; but yearn for simplicity." [29]   And for education, "*the chief object of education should be to restore simplicity. If you like to put it so, the chief object of education is not to learn things; nay, the chief object of education is to unlearn things.*" [30]

John Baptist de La Salle and his early followers knew this well. Some things have to be learned and others things have to be unlearned if genuine education is to occur, and this is especially true in the development of new teachers. In the early Lasallian operational handbook, *The Conduct of Christian Schools* (1720), there is an extensive appendix dedicated simply to the training of new teachers. These are the opening lines: "*This section on the training of teachers comprises two parts: (1) making new teachers lose the traits they have but should not have; and (2) making them acquire those traits that they lack, and which are very necessary for them.*" [31] (Notice that unlearning comes first.) Among the fifteen listed traits that must be unlearned are talking too much, impatience, undue familiarity, and partiality. For each, a full description of the trait is followed by how it may be corrected, with specific suggestions. The ten traits that must be acquired include professionalism, prudence, winning manners, and decisiveness. Each one likewise is fully described and includes suggestions as to how to acquire it.

This approach could easily be applied to ourselves. As Lent continues, are there things that we should unlearn, habits that we might uninhabit, thoughts or actions or tendencies that deserve our attention? Likewise – and after starting to dismantle some of those less helpful traits – are there habits we might cultivate, and thoughts or actions or tendencies that deserve to be developed, or at least started? Just thinking about it all reminds me of walking down a crowded Main Street at Disneyland. Where to start? What to pay attention to? Which shop to enter and browse? It doesn't seem to be a simple process.

---

[29] Chesteron, G.K., *The Complete Works* (2014). *Chapter X – The Moral Of Stevenson*

[30] Chesteron, G.K., *All Things Considered* (1908). *https://www.azquotes.com/quote/1253779*

[31] De La Salle, John Baptist. *Conduct of Christian Schools*. Translated by Richard Arnandez and William Mann. Edited by Richard Arnandez and William Mann. Moraga, CA: Buttimer Institute of Lasallian Studies, 1989. Pg. 255, ff.

De La Salle's quote about simplicity may be helpful here. What would it meant to "act with simplicity" when addressing personal areas that deserve our attention? For me, the experience at Sanibel Island is a simplicity touchstone. What brings you simplicity, peace, and a quiet settledness of spirit? Where are important things allowed to have a voice, to poke out of the chaos of daily life and breathe? Such places of simplicity – which today require intentionality and effort – allow the little things to emerge, allow the birds to be heard and seen. A short, daily evening reflection about lessons learned that day has been the practice of religious orders for centuries. Today, even successful CEOs have discovered its benefits,[32] backed up by a Harvard study that those who do so were 23% more successful than those who didn't.[33]

Finally, simplicity requires breadth, and today it is not the practical that deserves our most focused attention. Our souls are like nature, bearing a simplicity that is profoundly complex, and demanding a wider reach. Finally, *"it is a fundamental point of view, a philosophy or religion which is needed, and not any change in habit or social routine. The things we need most for immediate practical purposes are all abstractions. We need a right view of the human lot, a right view of the human society . . . Desire and danger make every one simple. 'Take no thought what ye shall eat or what ye shall drink, or wherewithal ye shall be clothed. . . . But seek first the kingdom of God and His righteousness, and all these things shall be added unto you.' Those amazing words are not only extraordinarily good, practical politics; they are also superlatively good hygiene. The one supreme way of making all those processes go right, the processes of health, and strength, and grace, and beauty . . . is to think about something else."*[34]

As Lent moves towards Holy Week, perhaps it is worthwhile to think about something else, something more like Sanibel Island than like Disneyland. Simplicity does not require a parade.

---

[32] https://tinyurl.com/yya5bggm

[33] https://papers.ssrn.com/sol3/papers.cfm?abstract_id=2414478

[34] Chesteron, G.K., *Heretics.* (1906)

Why Lasallian Education Endures

Be convinced that, provided you are willing, you can do more
with the help of God's grace than you imagine."
- St. John Baptist de La Salle [36]

Why is it that this particular educational vision and approach—what we call Lasallian education—has stood the test of time, going strong 340 years down the line. What is it about this unique educational movement that has allowed it, has driven it, to adapt to so many places and contexts, taking on a variety of education-related works, and persisting through so many challenges and difficulties?

Here are what might be called five transformative operational dimensions of our Lasallian network and charism. Others exist, and you may (and should) highlight your own. But these for me seem to be some of the key aspects that have helped ensure its ongoing vitality.[37]

1) ***De La Salle Himself.*** John Baptist de La Salle's personality and approach shape the DNA of this apostolate, this charism.

---

[35] Photo from New Zealand by George Van Grieken, FSC.

[36] De La Salle, John Baptist. *Reflections on Their State and Employment That the Brothers Should Make from Time to Time, Especially During Retreat,* "Regarding the Use of Time," # 10, in *Collection of Various Short Treatises.*

[37] This reflection is based on a longer talk delivered at APLEC 2019 (Asia Pacific Lasallian Educator's Conference), 2019.

His spirit and story imbue our educational vision, approach, and execution. He was a dedicated, hard worker who persisted in what he set out to do, with a solid faith life, genuine humility, a streak of stubbornness, and natural leadership abilities. He "was content to lead the teachers by the hand, so to speak, to let them see from their own experience and from his exhortations and example what was the best course to follow."[38] He allowed his trust in God's presence in and through others to guide the future of the work that they shared.

2) ***Focus on Education***. We do one thing, and we work very hard to do it well. The focus of those in the Lasallian world is on education, writ large. This is meant both literally and figuratively. Our apostolate is education, education, and education. AND such education is not confined to the classroom, to lessons and tests, or only to knowledge and skills. Education for us is a sacred project, a holy endeavor, a privileged encounter. If it deals with teaching and learning, education, schools and services for kids and families, we want to be part of it. Education is our primary vocation, and we are more than content with that reality. It fills our lives and vocations very well.

3) ***Self-Adjusting, Adaptable, & Relevant***. Lasallian education is essentially experience-driven, using what might be called a "monitor and adjust" process for ensuring success. The early Brothers worked together so that the best methodologies for the time were being used, creating new ones when required. They paid attention to what students really needed in their specific context and worked hard to provide it; e.g., teaching navigation and seamanship courses at the school in Calais; teaching ledgers and invoices to inner-city students and life-skills to those working students attending the Sunday school. The "franchise binder" called *The Conduct of Christian Schools*, was a practical school manual, built over 40 years and constantly revised and updated via a collaborative, experience-driven

---

38 Aroz, Leon, Yves Poutet, and Jean Pungier. Beginnings: De La Salle and his Brothers, trans. by Luke Salm, (Romeoville, IL: Christian Brothers Conference, 1980), Pg. 23.

methodology. It went through 23 editions over 250 years.

4) ***Community & Association***. "The decisive innovation of the Founder is that education is conducted within the context of community."[39] De La Salle came to see that trained, dedicated, faith-led teachers in community were the transformative driver. He insisted that "union in community is a precious gem, [and] if we lose this, we lose everything."[40] This community thing is not just a nice-to-have for us. In defining themselves as brothers to one another and older brothers to the young people confided to them by God, they stated both their identity and their mission. The engine for effective Lasallian education, from the very beginning, was a genuine, living, educational community. Lasallian education revolves around what Lasallian scholar Leon Lauraire calls a "pedagogy of fraternity,"[41] and association is a focused expression of community.

5) ***A Spirit of Faith & Zeal***. De La Salle became involved in the work of educating the young in order "to make the loving and saving presence of Christ a visible and active reality" [42] in the lives of those God confides to our care. He came to see that his teachers were to "preach" an alternative way of life, living the Gospel for and with their students. The addition he made to the Brothers Rule just before he died identified Faith & Zeal as the primary Spirit of the Institute, and "those who do not possess it and those who have lost it, should be looked upon as dead members."[43]

---

[39] Attributed to Br. Robert Schieler, FSC, Superior General.

[40] De La Salle, John Baptist. *Meditations by St. John Baptist de La Salle*. (Landover, MD: Christian Brothers Conference, 1994), Pg. 386. [Med. 91.2]

[41] Lauraire, Leon, FSC. "A Pedagogy of Fraternity." AXIS: Journal of Lasallian Higher Education 7, no. 3 (2016).

[42] Johnson, John. "1998 - Look to the Future," in *The Pastoral Letters (1986-2000)*. (Napa, CA: Lasallian Resource Center, 2016) Pg. 401.

[43] Brothers of the Christian Schools, The Rule of the Brothers of the Christian Schools. (Rome, Italy: Institute of the Brothers of the Christian Schools, 2015), 11-12. This entire short section of the Rule is worth reading and sharing.

What Will You Do This Summer?

I do not like to make the first move in any endeavor. ... I leave it to Divine Providence to make the first move and then I am satisfied. When it is clear that I am acting only under the direction of Providence, I have nothing to reproach myself with. When I make the first move, it is only I myself who am active, so I don't expect to see much good result; neither does God usually give the action his special blessing.

- St. John Baptist de La Salle [45]

De La Salle's life sparkled with a radical adherence to Divine Providence – the conviction that God speaks to us through people, circumstances, events, and requests that arise in the course of our daily affairs; not fate, luck, happenstance, or coincidence, but God's invitations to move in a certain direction, do a certain thing, respond in a certain way. It's like the gaze of a young child towards its parent, acutely conscious of the many ways concern, direction, interest, and care are communicated non-verbally. It is the language of loving attention, of contemplation.

---

[44] Photo by Cristina Cerda on www.unsplash.com

[45] De La Salle, John Baptist. *The Letters*. Translated by Colman Molloy, FSC. Edited by Colman Molloy and Augustine Loes. Romeoville, IL: Lasallian Publications, 1988. Pg. 75

Yet there is another piece that might be easily overlooked; i.e., he knew that you actually have to do something in order to learn something; you actually have to act in order to move forward. One of the striking things about De La Salle is that he acted, he responded. He did not just think "Oh, boy. I better do something about this sometime." Instead, he listened carefully, prayed deeply, thought fervently, consulted widely, concluded courageously, and acted confidently.

This combination of radical trust and conscious action—of faith and zeal if you will—is worth paying attention to vis-à-vis our contemporary engagement with the Christian tradition. A few years ago, *America* magazine had a book review that disagreed with the book's substance but also admitted that the thing the author got right was "… his steady insistence that in order to be Christians today—to bear the name of Christ in truth as well as in title—we must relearn two things: practices and disciplines. … [W]hen it comes to the question of how we build Christian persons, how we become Christians in habit as well as in mind, 'what we think does not matter as much as what we do—and how faithfully we do it.' [46] The shivering importance of this emphasis on practices can be better seen when we notice that we are, all of us, being formed by the things we do every day. As the philosopher Will Durant put it in his one-line-synthesis of Aristotle: 'We are what we repeatedly do.' And what do we do every day? We check our phones; we watch our televisions; we drive our cars. We perform these 'cultural liturgies,' as James K.A. Smith names them, by rote. They sink so deeply into us that they become muscle memory. It is these repeated actions that shape our habits, our habits that shape our character, our characters that shape our tastes, and our tastes that shape ourselves."[47]

It is a long quotation, but every word speaks to our capacity to be aware of God's Providence. Can the language of mutual loving attention with God survive amidst the habits that are our second nature? Do we have *any* habits that resonate with God or God's life

---

[46] Dreher, Rod. *The Benedict Option: a Strategy for Christians in a Post-Christian Nation.* Sentinel, an Imprint of Penguin Random House LLC, 2018. Pg. 52.

[47] Gilger, Patrick. *America Magazine.* April 17, 2017. "Navigating the Benedict Option" Pg. 20.

in our midst? God's providential care warrants a cultivated capacity to habitually engage that presence. But this is not very easy today. According to another author, "the convergence of two major trends in our own time calls for a new assessment of the barriers of faith. … These two major trends are (1) the practice of continuous engagement in immediately gratifying activities that resist reflection and meditation, and (2) the growth of secularism, defined as a state in which theism is seen as one of the many visible choices for human fullness and satisfaction, and in which the transcendent feels less and less plausible." [48] His proposed solution is the title of his book.

De La Salle's combination of praying and doing, trusting and acting, faith and zeal, was just as difficult in his own time as it is today. Unfortunately, you can't just think your way to salvation. If we live in a time where our attention is structured by largely unconscious habits introduced and shaped by popular culture, then it makes sense to 1) be aware of that dynamic in our lives, 2) find opportunities to step behind and beyond such habits, and 3) include at least a few practices and disciplines that resonate with our faith-informed convictions. Without such plain and simple measures, Thoreau's "lives of quiet desperation" remain society's default norm.

So what will you do this summer?

---

[48] Noble, Alan. *Disruptive Witness: Speaking Truth in a Distracted Age.* InterVarsity Press, 2018. Pg. 2

Remaining in God's Presence

All you need and all God wants of you is that you remain in his presence.

- St. John Baptist de La Salle[50]

The quotation above is from one of the few letters that we have from the thousands that De La Salle wrote. While it is only one sentence out of a long letter – and the letter's tone is definitely 17th century French spirituality – it represents an invitation to dwell in the presence of God that pervades all aspects of Lasallian life. This is an ongoing, recurring theme in De La Salle's writings and a deep current of his personal spiritual life. His enduring desire was to deepen the spiritual lives of his followers and of the students who attended his schools, so that they might come to realize God's intimate involvement in their lives, as the one who "guides all things

---

[49] Photo by Joshua Sortino on www.unsplash.com

[50] De La Salle, John Baptist, *The Letters*, Translation, introduction, and commentary by Colman Molloy, FSC. Edited with additional commentary by Augustine Loes, FSC, (Landover, MD: Christian Brothers Conference, 1988), 233 (Letter 111).

with wisdom and serenity . . . in an imperceptible way and over a long period of time."[51]

Remembering the presence of God was one of the "interior supports of the Institute," showing up throughout his writings: "Are you attentive to the holy presence of God?" (*List of Topics for Self-Examination*)[52], "What is meant by keeping our attention fixed on God? It is to think of the presence of God." (*Explanation of the Spirit of Our Institute*)[53], "When you recite the Divine Office … apply yourself as much as you can to the meaning of the words … or simply to the presence of God." (*The Divine Office*)[54], "They will be inspired to enter the classroom with profound respect, out of consideration for the presence of God." (*The Conduct of Schools*)[55], "At each hour of the day, some short prayers will be said. These will help the teachers to recollect themselves and recall the presence of God; it will serve to accustom the students to think of God from time to time …" (*The Conduct of Schools*)[56], "When they [parents and teachers] wish to train children in practices pertaining to bodily care and simple modesty, they should carefully lead them to be motivated by the presence of God. … Children should do these things out of respect for God in whose presence they are." (*Rules of Christian Decorum and Civility*).[57]

Okay. So how might we go about this "presence of God" business intentionally? One answer De La Salle gives is *interior prayer*. In his

---

[51] Blain, Jean-Baptiste. *The Life of John Baptist de La Salle.* Translated by Richard Arnandez, FSC. (Romeoville, IL: Christian Brothers Conference, 1983). Vol. 1, Bk. 1, 60–61.

[52] De La Salle, John Baptist. *Collection of Various Short Treatises.* Translated by W.J. Battersby, FSC. Edited by Daniel Burke, FSC. (Romeoville, IL: Christian Brothers Conference, 1993), 16.

[53] Ibid., 34.

[54] Ibid., 56.

[55] De La Salle, John Baptist. *Conduct of Christian Schools.* Translated by F. de La Fontainerie and Richard Arnandez, FSC. Edited by William Mann, FSC. (Landover, MD: Lasallian Publications, 1996). 49.

[56] Ibid. 92.

[57] De La Salle, John Baptist. The Rules of Christian Decorum and Civility. Translated by Richard Arnandez, FSC. Edited by Gregory Wright, FSC. (Romeoville, IL: Lasallian Publications, 1990), 3–4.

book *Explanation of the Method of Interior Prayer*, he "defines exactly what he means by 'interior'—the whole person in the depths of our being, the 'heart' in the biblical sense, where vital decisions are made and where there is real dialogue with God."[58] It is that place of quiet depth and attention where room is made for the small still voice to be heard. It is where serenity and consciousness converge in silence. It is a mindfulness that is focused on the Spirit of Faith, "which should lead … [us] to look upon nothing except with the eyes of faith, to do nothing except in view of God, and to attribute all to God."[59]

And why should this be something worthy of our attention today? One of the best answers came from Gery Short, a lay Lasallian partner for over thirty years and head of the SF/SFNO office of education for over twenty years – so his experience has been long, wide, and deep. When he accepted the John Johnston Award at the 2018 Huether Conference, he said:

 "We must commit ourselves to firmly establish the spirit of faith as a foundational and effective reality in each and every one of our works. We must ask, how do we make prayer and spirituality, the spirit of faith, the core of who we are and what we are about? How do we make prayer and spirituality real for ourselves as educators and our students in an authentic, understandable, and deeply significant way?"

This squarely hits the mark. How do we, can we, should we remain in God's presence today? God's presence shines out from countless undiscovered places in our lives and in the lives of others. We don't have to put him there. We just have to figure out how to roll the stone away.

---

[58] See the article by Maurice-August Hermans, FSC, and Michael Sauvage, FSC, in *Spirituality in the Time of John Baptist de La Salle*, edited by Robert Berger, FSC. (Landover, MD: Lasallian Publications, 1999), 207.

[59] De La Salle, John Baptist. *The Rule of 1705: An English Translation.* Translated by O'Gara, Eugene. (Moraga, CA: Buttimer Institute, 1989), 1.

Our Encounters (*choose a verb*) *Your Vocation*

60

*The remembrance of God's presence will be a great advantage
in helping you and in inspiring you to do all your actions well.*

- St. John Baptist de La Salle[61]

Like De La Salle himself, we keep coming back to that central,
shimmering, pregnant insight about remembering God's presence
in all that we see, do, and pursue. Christ dwells in the midst of the
daily tasks, encounters, decisions, and experiences that make up our
day. Where else find the resurrected Christ, the Holy Spirit alive?[62]
You can't think your way to salvation.

This struck me most powerfully recently when I was reading a com-
mencement address by Fred Buechner at a (non-Catholic) seminary.
"Again and again Christ is present not where, as priests, you would

---

[60] Lewis University Installation – "The Encounter" – Photo by George Van
Grieken, FSC.

[61] De La Salle, John Baptist, *The Letters*, Translation, intro., and commentary by
Colman Molloy, FSC. Edited with additional commentary by Augustine Loes,
FSC, (Landover, MD: Christian Brothers Conference, 1988), 20 (Letter 2).

[62] "Earnestly ask Jesus that all your work be energized by his Spirit and draw all
its power from him." (Med 195.3)

be apt to look for him but precisely where you wouldn't have thought to look for him in a thousand years. The great preacher, the sunset, the Mozart Requiem can leave you cold, but the child in the doorway, the rain on the roof, the half-remembered dream, can speak of him and for him with an eloquence that turns your knees to water."[63] Nicely put! How many of us haven't noticed, heard, said, or did something that, small though it was, made our world spin? De La Salle's generous response during the brief encounter with Adrian Nyel at the door of the Sister of the Infant Jesus convent was such a pivotal moment, although even this wouldn't have happened if a whole chain of other events hadn't brought them both there at precisely that time, with precisely their personalities and interests, and with precisely their priorities and religious sensibilities. It was this unlikely providential mash-up, if you will, that resulted in an educational movement that was started by a lay man, established and shaped by a priest, and that is now carried out by Brothers and Partners from all backgrounds, vocations, and cultures. You just can't make this stuff up! It brings to mind parallels to the overwhelming providential circumstances that led to our own blue planet's physical existence.

"Astronomers disagree on just how rare life is in the universe, but Earth nonetheless boasts several features that make it 'just right' for life as we know it. *The right ingredients*: A planet needs liquid water, an energy source, and chemical building blocks like carbon, oxygen, hydrogen and nitrogen for the life forms we're familiar with to thrive. *The right crust*: Gas giants and molten worlds need not apply. Luckily, Earth possesses the suitable distribution of elements to ensure a hot metallic core and a rocky mantle. *The right temperature*: The necessity for liquid water also means that planetary temperatures must permit the substance to retain its liquid form in some regions. *The right moon*: Our large moon ensures climate stability by minimizing changes in planetary tilt. If our planet didn't have a tilt, it wouldn't have seasons. Likewise, a severe tilt would result in extreme seasons. *The right star*: The sun provides Earth with the energy for life and is thankfully rather stable. [Earth lies in a habitable zone that allows water to remain a liquid – The Goldilocks Zone – and have

---

[63] Buechner, Frederick. *Buechner 101: Essays, Excerpts, Sermons and Friends*, Kindle Edition, Location 309.

a stable orbit because of the moon's distance and size.] ... *The right core*: Earth's solid inner core and liquid outer core play crucial roles in protecting life from deadly solar radiation. Differences in temperature and composition in the two core regions drive this powerful dynamo, emitting Earth's protective electromagnetic field. *The right neighbors*: Jupiter shields Earth from constant stellar bombardment. Without the gas giant in the neighborhood, scientists predict that Earth would endure 10,000 times as many asteroid and comet strikes."[64] And this list doesn't even include things like breathable air, the variety of species, and our human brain.[65]

What does all that mean for us, as educators who value the complexity of God's presence? Buechner says it best and echoes De La Salle. "God speaks into or out of the thick of our days. He speaks not just through the sounds we hear, of course, but through events in all their complexity and variety, though the harmonies and disharmonies and counterpoint of all that happens. As to the meaning of what he says, there are times that we are apt to think we know. ... To try to express in even the most insightful and theologically sophisticated terms the meaning of what God speaks through the events of our lives is as precarious a business as to try to express the meaning of the sound of rain on the roof or the spectacle of the setting sun. But I choose to believe that he speaks nonetheless, and the reason that his words are impossible to capture in human language is of course that they are ultimately always incarnate words. They are words fleshed out in the everydayness not less than in the crises of our experience."[66]

May we each discover the active verb that ties our daily encounters to our life's vocation.

---

[64] https://science.howstuffworks.com/life/evolution/earth-just-right-for-life.htm (Retrieved August 1, 2019)

[65] For a really interesting overview of all this, see "One Strange Rock" (National Geographic). Available on Netflix.

[66] Buechner, Frederick. *Buechner 101: Essays, Excerpts, Sermons and Friends*, Kindle Edition, Location 354

The Dance of Grace and Faith

*Applying ourselves to the presence of God
is a most useful practice; be faithful to it.*
                                    - St. John Baptist de La Salle[68]

There has been a lot of press over David Brook's new book, *The Second Mountain*. In one section, he talks about how "grace" is, or becomes, a part of our lives. Grace, he says, is not the result of a rational process, but instead can only be a totally free gift from God. You can't make grace happen. This is why: "We have this amazing ability to care about each other and to love each other and love God in ways that are beyond any normal requirement. So we're just made that way. And it is a gracious universe that gave us this capacity, and it seems to me it didn't have to be that way." That's well put. The next bit reminded me of a positive notion from the 17th century that emerged with Jansenism. He writes, "Faith and grace are not about losing agency. They are about strengthening and empowering agency while transforming it. When grace floods in, it gives us better things to desire and more power to desire them."[69]

In an article by Louis *Dupré* about Jansenism — a controversial movement during the time of St. John Baptist de La Salle — a surprisingly similar perspective is expressed. Beyond Jansenism's

---

[67] Photo by Andrew Seaman on www.unsplash.com

[68] De La Salle, John Baptist, *Interior Prayer*. Translated by Richard Arnandez & Donald Mouton. Edited by Donald Mouton. (Landover, ML: Christian Brothers Conference) Pg. 51.

[69] Brooks, David. *The Second Mountain*. (Random House Publishing Group, 2019) Pg. 255.

general impact of conveying an "unqualified pessimism about human nature," figures like Blaise Pascal also highlighted a "humble awareness of an unmerited union with God." And this deep awareness is not, and cannot be, something that comes from reason alone. "Only from God himself (in faith) can one learn about a total, intrinsic redemption that sanctifies one's attitudes and grants merit to one's works. Yes the object of faith itself, the 'mystery of Jesus,' is such that it blinds some while enlightening others. Only with 'eyes of faith' … can we see the true reality of this mystery."[70] Jansenism highlighted that it is only the grace of faith that provides the capacity to learn about God's presence in Scripture, in nature, and in others. Pascal writes, "Those to whom God has given religious faith by moving their hearts are very fortunate, and feel quite legitimately convinced, but to those who do not have it we can only give such faith through reason, until God gives it by moving their heart, without which faith is only human and useless for salvation."[71] In other words, faith and grace empower agency while transforming it.

And what engages that dynamic in the lives of ordinary people? Do we just wait around until God decides to shower us with this grace? De La Salle provides a related insight in one of his meditations: "God gives two kinds of reward in this world to those who commit themselves untiringly to the work of the salvation of souls. First, he gives them an abundance of grace; second, he gives them a more extended ministry and a greater ability to procure the conversion of souls."[72] In others words, it is in the pursuit of one's vocation, in the doing of good and faithful things, that God's dynamic is engaged and that the seeds of faith, however conceived, are watered. Like any relationship, one's relationship with God is also cumulative, multi-layered, built up through activity and attention. There are no shortcuts in the spiritual journey.

---

[70] Dupré, Louis. *Jansenism and Quietism* article in *Christian Spirituality: Post-Reformation and Modern.* (New York: Crossroad, 1989) Pg. 127.

[71] Pascal, Blaise, *Pensees.* # 110.

[72] De La Salle, John Baptist, *Meditations by St. John Baptist de La Salle,* trans. Richard Arnandez, and Augustine Loes, eds. Augustine Loes and Francis Huether, (Landover, MD: Christian Brothers Conference, 1994), Pg. 467 (M207.1)

One of the best illustrations of this is provided in the novel *Brothers Karamazov*, when the Elder monk answers a genuine plea for guidance. "What will give me back my faith? … How can it be proved, how can one be convinced?" … [The elder answers] "By the experience of active love. Try to love your neighbors actively and tirelessly. The more you succeed in loving , the more you'll be convinced of the existence of God and the immortality of the soul. And if you reach complete selflessness in the love of your neighbor, then undoubtedly you will believe, and no doubt will even be able to enter your soul. This has been tested. It is certain."[73] However, if it is pursued for the sake of honor or the admiration of others, it goes nowhere. Active love is tied to active faith when they are aligned with genuine humility and pursued with pure desire. This careful integration needs at least as much care and attention as whipping up a hollandaise.

If grace, from God or from anywhere or anyone, is "unmerited love" lived out in daily life, then we are indeed inundated with invitations to jump into the deep ends of things. Thomas Merton: "For the world and time are the dance of the Lord in emptiness. The silence of the spheres is the music of a wedding feast. The more we persist in misunderstanding the phenomena of life, the more we analyze them out into strange finalities and complex purposes of our own, the more we involve ourselves in sadness, absurdity and despair. But it does not matter much, because no despair of ours can alter the reality of things, or stain the joy of the cosmic dance which is always there. Indeed, we are in the midst of it, and it is in the midst of us, for it beats in our very blood, whether we want it to or not. Yet, the fact remains that we are invited to forget ourselves on purpose, cast our awful solemnity to the winds and join in the general dance."[74]

---

[73] Dostoevskly, Fyodor, *Brothers Karamazov*, Part 1, Book 2, Ch.4 - "A Lady of Little Faith
 (Cf. https://bloggingsbetter.wordpress.com/2009/02/11/1702)
[74] Merton, Thomas. *New Seeds of Contemplation*. (New Directions Publishing, 2007) Pg. 296.

Gratitude's Abundance

To whom ought we to give ourselves if not to the One from whom we have received everything. … This thought and the gratitude we owe him for all his goodness to us ought to have frequently occupied our minds and touched our hearts during this year.

- St. John Baptist de La Salle[76]

Have you ever noticed that the most grateful people we know are those with little apparent reason for being so? Those who give, give, and give – like Mother Teresa, Jean Vanier, and many silently busy unknown saints – have few material things. They do have great gratitude. Compared to those admired in popular culture – sports and movie stars, famous musicians and authors, online personalities, etc. – those with the least obvious advantages possess the greatest ones. Philip Yancey, who has interviewed a wide host of people, divides them into stars and servants. The stars, by and large, he found to be "as miserable a group of people as I have ever met …" But more significantly, "I was prepared to honor and admire the servants, to hold them up as inspiring examples. I was not, however, prepared to envy them. But as I now reflect on the two groups side by side, stars and servants, the servants clearly emerge as the favored ones, the graced ones. They work for low pay, long hours,

---

[75] Photo by Randy Faith on www.unsplash.com

[76] De La Salle, John Baptist, *Meditations by St. John Baptist de La Salle*, trans. Richard Arnandez, and Augustine Loes, eds. Augustine Loes and Francis Huether, (Landover, MD: Christian Brothers Conference, 1994), 384 (Med. 90.2).

and no applause, 'wasting' their talents and skills among the poor and uneducated. But somehow in the process of losing their lives they have found them. They have received the 'peace that is not of this world.'"

His experienced conclusion is aligned to what the Gospel proclaims: "The way up is down."[77]

Teachers are such servants, educating by word, example, and personality. Gospel seeds appear gently but directly, filtered by life experience, reflection, intentionality, and a genuine care for students. How, then, might gratitude be revealed within the focused, organized chaos of daily school life? What are the deeper challenges in education today to developing a real sense of gratitude? Where should we turn our attention in order to "teach" Gospel priorities?

Young people are often energetic, curious, and given to spontaneous outbursts of well-intentioned leaps of purpose-filled activity, and popular expectations, whether in society or personal relationships, are not conducive to lengthy reflection or deep filters, especially when it comes to today's economic drivers. "Successive echelons of youth mean a perpetual supply of unspoilt 'virgin land' ready for cultivation, without which even the simple reproduction of the capitalist economy, not to mention economic growth, would be all but unconceivable. Young people are thought of and paid attention to as 'yet another market' to be commodified and exploited."[78] An economic juggernaut that is powered by personalized Facebook ads, clever social media and gaming advertising strategies, easily becomes a society where early Black Friday deals trump [intentional use] the genuine benefits of a convivial Thanksgiving meal with family and friends. While one might say with genuine gratitude that there are plenty of examples of young people who resist these and similar well-hidden societal forces, there is "a gathering volume of evidence casting 'the problem of youth' fairly and squarely as an issue of 'drilling them into consumers', and leaving all other youth-

---

[77] Yancey, Philip, *I Was Just Wondering*, (B. Eerdmans Publishing Company, 1989), Pg. 91.

[78] Bauman, Zygmunt, *On Education-Conversations with Riccardo Mazzeo,* (Polity Press, Cambridge, UK) Pg. 55.

related issues on a side shelf, or effacing them altogether from the political, social and cultural agenda."[79]

This is a large part of the landscape of education today. It is the one within which the gratitude called for by the Gospel is much needed. How? "Isn't it true that gratitude springs up in our hearts more powerfully, more gloriously when what we receive is undeserved, when it is a miracle of divine and human love?" Turning the eyes of youth toward the miracle of divine and human love – in retreats, in personal encounters, in undeserved forgiveness, in just saying "hello" – is an immediate, real, and powerful agent for change. It is grounded in the conviction that God trusts us to be the love that created us. "How wonderful it would be if out of gratitude we lived in such a way as to give God joy, the joy of knowing that He has not created us in vain, that He does not believe in us in vain, that He has not put His trust in us in vain, that His love has been received, is now incarnate, not only in emotion, but in action!"[80]

At the end of the magical video, *Gratitude Revealed*,[81] Br. David Steind-Rast, OSB, invites us to notice the blessings that we encounter each day: "I wish that you will open your heart to all these blessings, and let them flow through you, that everyone whom you will meet on this day will be blessed by you, just by your eyes, by your smile, by your touch, just by your presence. Let the gratefulness overflow into blessing all around you."

Allow me to suggest that the capacity for gratitude itself is one of those blessings, and the more we notice its presence and exercise its agency for grace, the more we and others will find that God's presence isn't all that far away. In fact, we yet dwell within its silent, rich abundance.

---

[79] Ibid., Pg. 56.

[80] Bloom, Anthony, Sermon on Gratitude, www.mitras.ru/eng/eng_96.htm

[81] https://vimeo.com/282760088

No Boxing Gloves Permitted

Do you instruct those for whom you are responsible with the attention and the zeal God asks of you in so holy a work? By your good conduct, be worthy of this distinguished role. Act in such a way that your life may begin today to be holy and edifying and continue to be such in the future.

- St. John Baptist de La Salle[83]

One of the reasons that humanity has been able to thrive on the earth, according to those who study human progress, is our shared sense of curiosity, our interest in the new and the different, our exploratory dispositions. It is what caused early migratory movements across land masses, the constant pursuit of better ways of life – such as farming instead of hunting -- and the development of comprehensive ways of making sense of the world through meaning-filled activities like folklore, rituals (religious and otherwise), and the arts. This sense of curiosity, this drive for knowledge and creativity, is what today causes us to enjoy wrapped packages, pick up a new book, scroll down beyond the screen, listen to gossip, and even simply get up in the morning to see what the day will bring. It all comes from an inborn, essential, and ever-living capacity for plumbing the deeper wells of the possible. It's the motor for *joie de vivre*. It's the poet's instinct, the explorer's drive, the lover's

---

[82] Photo by Matt Popovich on www.unsplash.com

[83] De La Salle, John Baptist, *Meditations by St. John Baptist de La Salle*, trans. Richard Arnandez, and Augustine Loes, eds. Augustine Loes and Francis Huether, (Landover, MD: Christian Brothers Conference, 1994), 174 (Med. 93.2).

persistence, and from a depth awareness / engagement perspective, it is the mystic's contentment, exemplified in how John Baptist de La Salle came to gradually embrace his life's journey and living in God's loving presence, decision by decision over a long period of time.

The beginning of any new calendar year is now celebrated worldwide with parties, count-downs to midnight, fireworks, confetti, and jubilation. Isn't this yet another expression of the possibilities for the future, to hope perhaps previously deferred and now extended once again? We revive our motivations in mutual support of yet another chance, yet another set of days to do what we know we want to do. The new year's celebration invests the wisdom of the old into the hope of the young; the old man of 2019 stands next to the bright-eyed baby of 2020 . . . every single year. It is an annual ritual that, again and again, attests to the deeply-rooted human dynamic of hope, of curiosity, of what is possible, of an innate hunger for the "something more" in our universe.

David Brooks concisely describes our pursuit of this "more" in life as the second mountain, "...the one people begin climbing once the goals of the first mountain—the goals of success, personal fulfillment and happiness—have been met and found wanting. 'If the first mountain is about building up the ego and defining the self," he writes, "the second mountain is about shedding the ego and losing the self.'"[84] All the new year's resolutions in the world won't equal that insight.

Such topsy-turvy insights into the less obvious aspects of the universe are regularly conveyed within most of the major religious traditions, most viscerally and profoundly by Jesus Christ in the New Testament.[85] With the best of intentions, we ignore or explain them away as hopelessly (!) idealistic and unachievable. And society's popular voice is as myopic as it is ubiquitous. What's been problematic ". . . has been what he [David Brooks] believes is the secular news media's tin ear on issues of faith. 'They treat it like you have

---

[84] Bill McGarvey, "The Confessions of David Brooks," *America Magazine* 221, no. 6 (September 16, 2019): 47.

[85] "The one who finds his life will lose it, and the one who loses his life because of me will find it." (Matthew 10:39)

changed from being Republican to a Democrat,' he says. "As if it's that kind of choice. 'I used to like French fries; now I like sweet potatoes.' You feel like there's something sacred and mysterious that is being handled with boxing gloves."[86]

What, then, of our students and staff, our Lasallian educational communities? When De La Salle and two Brothers went to the school in the parish of St. Sulpice in Paris in 1688, the place was a bit of a mess. De La Salle told the Brothers to concentrate on their own classrooms, on the things that they could do within their own area of responsibility. That strategy led to the transformation of the entire school in less than a year. By focusing on the possible, the impossible gradually recedes.

T.S. Elliot famously wrote, "We shall not cease from exploration, and the end of all our exploring will be to arrive where we started and know the place for the first time."[87] The most worthwhile knowledge, the greatest journey, lies within. The more we can help our students and educational communities look deeper, beyond the obvious – in literature, science, history, sports, religion, etc. – the more they will be disposed (and trained) to do so in the future, to engage in their own exploring. "It is apostolic to awaken in students a serious attitude towards life and the conviction of the greatness of human destiny; it is apostolic to make it possible for them, with intellectual honesty and responsibility, to experience the autonomy of personal thought; it is apostolic to help the students to use their liberty to overcome their own prejudices, preconceived ideas, social pressures, as well as the pressures that come from disintegration within the human person; it is apostolic to dispose students to use their intelligence and their training in the service of others, to open them to others: to teach them how to listen and to try to under-stand, to trust and love; it is apostolic to instill in students a sense of trustworthiness, brotherhood, and justice."[88]

---

[86] McGarvey, "Confessions," 47.

[87] T.S. Elliot. *Little Gidding.* (http://www.columbia.edu/itc/history/win-ter/w3206/edit/tseliotlittlegidding.html)

[88] Brothers of the Christian Schools. *The Brother of the Christian Schools in the World Today: A Declaration.* Rome: 1967. (Section 41) *Slightly edited for inclusive language.*

Teaching indeed is a holy work: the cultivation of curiosity, of hope, of the poet's instinct, the explorer's drive, the lover's persistence, and the mystic's contentment. Something sacred and mysterious is at work here.

A sign in every classroom should read "No boxing gloves permitted."

Giver-Taken & Talker-Doer

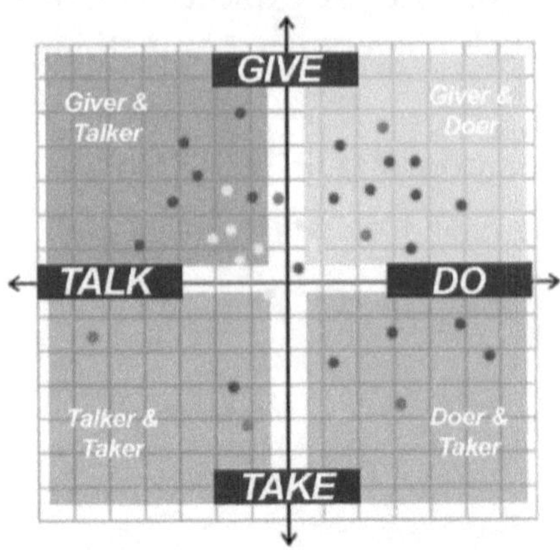

Jesus Christ compares those who have charge of souls to a good shepherd who has great care for the sheep. One quality he must possess, according to our Savior, is to know each one of them individually. This ought also to be one of the main concerns of those who instruct others: to be able to understand their students and to discern the right way to guide them.

– St. John Baptist de La Salle[89]

The personal quality of Lasallian education has often been highlighted by both students, teachers, and parents. It is a quality that is part of being an "older brother / sister" to those "entrusted to our care." We well know – or quickly come to know – that those we encounter in the classroom and around the school are eminently unique and different, sacred drops of God's manifest presence in our daily lives. Teachers with long experience know that the strangers in their classrooms at the beginning of the school year will by the end of the year be perceived by them as highly individual characters, richly textured and nuanced – some good, some not so good, but more and more fully alive and revealed. Their personality traits, strengths, and weaknesses will have settled into the teachers' minds in cumulative layers of awareness. Time and experience thus become privileged means for gaining occasional glimpses into the souls of our students.

---

[89] De La Salle, John Baptist, *Meditations by St. John Baptist de La Salle*, trans. Richard Arnandez, and Augustine Loes, eds. Augustine Loes and Francis Huether, (Landover, MD: Christian Brothers Conference, 1994), 91 (Med. 33.1).

This is why the quote from De La Salle at the top of this reflection is so important. Not only is the connection made with how Jesus treated his disciples and others during his ministry, but there is a direct responsible parallel to "one of the main concerns of those who instruct others." And that main concern is not how well the student does in class, how smart or helpful or responsive the student is to the teacher's directions. In fact, all those other things depend on this "main concern." The focus is rather on "to understand" and "to discern" how to guide them. It is deep listening.

Ever practical, this concern that De La Salle advocated is not left in midair, with a hope that others will address it responsibly. There is also a practical side to it; a way to actually do it. That is seen in the 1720 school handbook, the franchise's three-ring binder. In the description of the Admissions Register, which contains all the relevant information about each student, there is this sentence: *"After all of this information has been recorded, some blank space should be left to contain what may need to be added later. Examples of what might be added are: what is the child's character and disposition …?"* [90] This is the part that the next teacher of the same student would want to see. Wouldn't you, if you were teaching the same student? It's a help to being able to "understand" and "discern" the student, although it certainly is not a substitute for it. Merely helpful advice.

An example of such a record was this one: "*Francis Delevieux; 8 1/2, two years at school, in 3rd section of Writing since July 1st. Somewhat turbulent; little piety at church or prayers unless supervised. Lacks reserve. Conduct satisfactory; needs encouragement to effort; punishment of no avail; light-headed. Rarely absent except when with bad companions; often late. Application moderate but he learns with ease. Twice nearly expelled for negligence. Submissive to a strong hand. Not a difficult character. Must be won over. Spoiled at home. Parents resent his being punished.*"[91] With that kind of description, I think most of us might have a running start at understanding a

---

[90] De La Salle, John Baptist, *The Conduct of Schools*, Translated by F. de La Fontainerie and Richard Arnandez, FSC, Edited with notes by William Mann, FSC (Landover, MD: Christian Brothers Conference, 1996), 240.
[91] De La Salle, Jean-Baptiste. *Œuvres Complètes.* (Rome: Frères des Ecoles Chrétiennes, 1993), 657.

student and determining how we might guide his/her character and disposition.

In more recent times, we've been provided with all sorts of systems for understanding and discerning the character of ourselves or others – Enneagram, Meyers-Briggs, Strength Finder etc. And more methods appear with each new book season. But one of the ones that I've found both simple and elegant was shared by a friend of mine many years ago. I don't know if she found it or if she came up with it herself. I just find it generally helpful; not to pigeon-hole but to provide some sort of framework for understanding where a person's dispositional inclinations are leaning.

The quadrant chart at the top of this reflection is a crude representation of this schema. She said, "Generally, there are two characteristics that you can pick up about people. There are the Givers or the Takers, and there are the Doers or the Talkers. The best sort are the Givers and the Doers, and the worst ones are the Takers and the Talkers." In the other quadrants are those who have a mix of different characteristics, and it's interesting to think about professions that might fit each of the quadrants. I don't know, for example, where I'd generally put politicians or poets. Most of us are a mix, of course, depending on "with whom" and "for what" and the like. But the cluster of what we do, like the cluster of blue dots, show a general preference for one area of the chart.

The point of sharing this chart is to highlight the fact that each of us has their own way of understanding and discerning the students they encounter. (And this GT-TD chart seems more appropriate to adults than to developing students.) However, De La Salle's insight is that we should have something, some intentionality, some method, by which we engage this most potentially transformative dimension of our educational ministry. His advice? *"This guidance requires understanding and discernment of spirits, qualities you should frequently and earnestly ask of God, for they are most necessary for you in the guidance of those placed in your care."*[92]

BTW. I think that De La Salle was a Giver and a Doer big-time!

---

[92] De La Salle, John Baptist, *The Meditations*, Op. Cit.

The Threads That Remain

Take care not to let yourself be discouraged by anxieties and ailments; life is full of them. Leave aside all your worry about the present and all your anxiety about the future; occupy yourselves with what you have to do at each moment as it is given to you, and do not burden the day which is passing with doubts about the day to follow. God gives us not only the will to do what is right, but also the grace to accomplish it.

- St. John Baptist de La Salle[93]

There is no lack in opinion surrounding the current world COVID-119 pandemic. The most honest assessments – such as those by Anthony Fauci or Andrew Cuomo – appear to be the most successful in providing reliable, fact-based, and personable perspectives. They remind me of how De La Salle himself dealt with the legal, ecclesiastical, inter-personal, and administrative challenges that confronted him on a regular basis and all throughout his 40-year relationship with the Brothers and with many others in France. His approach was invariably decisive, consultative, honest, and generous, fueled by his deep life of faith and powered by his tremendous zeal to respond to the needs that regularly reached his ears or desk.

---

[93] This is a combination of two quotations from De La Salle – first sentence and last sentence – and a section from the biography of De La Salle by Jean-Baptiste Blain where he quotes his speech to the Brothers on the topic of Providence.

In one of his letters, he had good advice about this: "Do not let the opportunities you might find slip away, but do not hurry things."[94]

We tend to forget that there were a number of active wars that France was engaged in during De La Salle's lifetime: Franco-Spanish War (1635-59), Catalan Revolt (1640-59), Beaver Wars in the U.S. (1640-1701), Cretan War (1645-69), Fronde (1648-49, 1650-53), Anglo-Dutch War (1665-67) Second Anglo-Spanish War (1657-59), War of Devolution (1667-68), Franco-Dutch War (1672-78), Scanian War (1675-79), War of Reunions (1683-84), Nine Years' War (1688-87), King William's War (1689-97), War of Spanish Succession (1701-14), Rákóczi's War of Independence (1703-11), War of the Quadruple Alliance (1718-1720), and the various revolts that happened inside of France.[95] These ongoing wars and social upheavals must certainly have strongly impacted many people of the time, especially in Reims in the case of wars with the Dutch, and not only when it came to the obligation to house soldiers, but also with the various taxes imposed to support these wars, not to mention the series of famines that occurred during the same time period.

When you combine all this with the political situation in different parts of France – plus Jansenism, Gallicanism, & Quietism – along with the intrigues of social position, wealth, and power in society and the Church, it's a wonder that he was able to do so much good with so little for so many.

As all of us continue to face the direct challenges in maintaining our Lasallian institutions and relationships during these pandemic times, it is well to remember that we are not the first people that have circumstances thrust upon us, ones where we must figure out how to deal with immediate and long-term needs both personally, professionally and societally. Recalling what others have faced – and faced successfully – should give us some comfort and convince us that by drawing on our best and deepest connections, we will most directly benefit those near and far.

---

[94] De La Salle, John Baptist. *The Letters.* Translated by Colman Molloy, FSC. Edited by Colman Molloy and Augustine Loes. Romeoville, IL: Lasallian Publications, 1988. Pg. 75.
[95] https://en.wikipedia.org/wiki/List_of_wars:_1500%E2%80%931799

Over the last few days, some general thoughts have come to mind. They may be of help to you. Here they are either in verse (below) or by way of a very simple musical setting (bit.ly/Threads-GVG).

Every choice, every gesture, every action that we take;
They are all part of the fabric of the shared lives that we make.
Woven close to one another by the frail threads we contain.
Let us care for and deliver on the best threads that remain.

As the breeze in the forest reaches every smallest place,
As the bright sun in the heavens touches gently every face,
Let the warm love that we harbor be released in every case,
So that all that makes us human may each silent need embrace.

We are all tied together in a world that is our home.
In the silence of the night stars, we are bright stars of our own.
If the small drops in an ocean move as one and move alone,
So the things we do for others are both shared and still our own.

With the grace of our nature, with the deep love that we bear,
With the strength that lies within us, with unbroken power to care,
Nothing truly can destroy us, whether found both here and there.
What's within is what has made us. Let it shine out everywhere.